TEXT BOOK OF PHARMACOGNOSY AND PHYTOCHEMISTRY – I

[According to latest syllabus of B Pharm – IV semester of Pharmacy Council of India]

Dr. Brijesh Shivhare

Assistant Professor

Department of Botany

Faculty of Sciences

Baba Mastnath University

Rohtak (Haryana)

Dr. Rakesh Singh

Associate professor

Faculty of Pharmaceutical Sciences

RKDF university

Bhopal (M. P.}

Dr. Reetesh Yadav

Principal

Shri Ram Institute of Pharmacy

near ITI Madhotal

Jabalpur (M. P.)

Dr. Ravindra Goswami

Assistant Professor

Department of Botany

Seth G. B. Podar College

Nawalgarh (Rajasthan)

Dr. Seema Agrawal

Professor

Shri Ram Institute of Pharmacy

near ITI Madhotal

Jabalpur (M. P.)

TEXT BOOK OF

PHARMACOGNOSY AND PHYTOCHEMISTRY – I

First Edition 2024

Published by:

NOTION PRESS

Publisher and distributor

Head office: Notion press Media Pvt. Ltd.

7, Red cross Road,

Egmore, Chennai, Tamil Nadu 60008

Website: www.notionpress.com

TEXT BOOK OF PHARMACOGNOSY AND PHYTOCHEMISTRY – I

ABOUT THE BOOK

The field of pharmacognosy delves into the vast and fascinating world of natural drugs, exploring their sources, classification, and utilization. This discipline studies the identification, cultivation, and preservation of drugs derived from plants, animals, marine life, and tissue culture. One of the oldest branches of pharmaceutical science, pharmacognosy plays a vital role in both traditional and modern medicine. It encompasses the study of organized and unorganized drugs, ranging from dried extracts to complex resins.

The evaluation of crude drugs involves organoleptic, microscopic, physical, chemical, and biological methods, ensuring that the natural origin drugs maintain their quality and efficacy. Cultivation, collection, and storage of medicinal plants are essential aspects, influenced by various factors such as plant hormones, polyploidy, mutations, and hybridization.

The importance of pharmacognosy is evident in its application across various medical systems, including Ayurveda, Unani, Siddha, Homeopathy, and traditional Chinese medicine. Plant tissue culture has also found its place in this field, offering advanced methods for growth, maintenance, and the production of edible vaccines.

The study of secondary metabolites such as alkaloids, glycosides, flavonoids, tannins, volatile oils, and resins further enriches pharmacognosy, while fibers like cotton, jute, and hemp have been studied for their biological source, chemical nature, and uses.

The exploration of hallucinogens, teratogens, and natural allergens, as well as primary metabolites like carbohydrates, proteins, enzymes, and lipids, underscores the depth of pharmacognosy. Additionally, marine drugs introduce a novel dimension to the search for medicinal agents, providing a glimpse into the ocean's potential as a source of healing.

TEXT BOOK OF PHARMACOGNOSY AND PHYTOCHEMISTRY – I
NOTION PRESS
PREFACE

The authors feel great pleasure in presenting the first edition of the book **"Text Book of Pharmacognosy and Phytochemistry – I"** for graduate and post graduate students. The present book on **Text Book of Pharmacognosy and Phytochemistry – I** has been written according to the syllabus of B. Pharm – IV semester of Pharmacy Council of India and covers full course of the subject.

THE SALIENT FEATURES OF THE BOOK ARE: -

- *Easy to understand style of writing* which makes the book a self-study material.
- *Each new concept has been introduced through day-today problem of interest* to the students which makes the subject matter interesting.
- *The language of the book, on the whole, is lucid and easy to understand.*
- Wherever needed *neatly labeled figures have been drawn.*

The authors hope that the students, teachers and other readers will find the book interesting and to the point covering the course. We hope that the students will receive the book warmly.

I express a sincere thank you to the Management of Department of Botany, Faculty of Sciences, Baba Mastnath University, Faculty of Pharmaceutical Sciences, RKDF University, Shri Ram Institute of Pharmacy and Department of Botany, Seth G.B. Podar College for their support during the writing of this book.

Every effort is made to keep the book error free. The author will gratefully acknowledge the suggestions to improve the book to make it more useful.

Wishing our readers success in examination and life ahead. The authors feel that their efforts will be fully rewarded if the book serves the purpose for which it is written.

TEXT BOOK OF PHARMACOGNOSY AND PHYTOCHEMISTRY – I
CONTENTS

CHAPTER – 1

INTRODUCTION TO PHARMACOGNOSY

INTRODUCTION:

Pharmacognosy is the branch of pharmaceutical sciences that deals with the study of natural products, particularly those obtained from plants, animals, microbes, and minerals. It encompasses the identification, extraction, analysis, and therapeutic application of biologically active substances found in natural sources. Pharmacognosy is one of the oldest disciplines in pharmacy and plays a crucial role in drug discovery and development.

Historical Background

Pharmacognosy has its roots in ancient civilizations, where people relied on natural substances for healing and medicinal purposes. Early records of herbal medicine date back to ancient Egypt, China, India, and Greece. For instance, the ancient Egyptian text, Ebers Papyrus (circa 1550 BCE), contains a wealth of information on medicinal plants. Similarly, the Indian Ayurveda and Chinese Materia Medica are rich sources of traditional medicine knowledge.

The term "pharmacognosy" was coined in 1815 by Johann Adam Schmidt, a German scientist. It is derived from the Greek words "pharmakon," meaning drug, and "gnosis," meaning knowledge. The discipline evolved from the study of medicinal plants to include all natural sources of drugs.

Scope of Pharmacognosy

1. **Identification and Classification of Medicinal Plants:**
    a. Pharmacognosy involves the classification of medicinal plants based on their botanical characteristics and therapeutic properties. It helps in the correct identification and classification of plants used in traditional and modern medicine.

2. **Extraction and Isolation of Natural Products:**

a. The extraction and isolation of bioactive compounds from natural sources are central to pharmacognosy. Techniques such as solvent extraction, distillation, and chromatography are used to obtain pure compounds from plants, animals, or microbes.

3. **Phytochemistry:**

   a. Phytochemistry is a sub-discipline of pharmacognosy that focuses on the chemical composition of plants. It involves the study of the structure, biosynthesis, and function of plant-derived chemicals, including alkaloids, flavonoids, terpenoids, glycosides, and polyphenols.

4. **Ethnopharmacology:**

   a. Ethnopharmacology is the study of traditional medicines used by indigenous peoples and communities. It bridges the gap between traditional knowledge and modern drug discovery by exploring the therapeutic potential of traditional remedies.

5. **Pharmacological and Toxicological Evaluation:**

   a. Pharmacognosy also involves the evaluation of the pharmacological activity and safety of natural products. This includes in vitro and in vivo studies to determine the efficacy and toxicity of plant extracts and isolated compounds.

6. **Standardization and Quality Control:**

   a. Standardization and quality control are essential aspects of pharmacognosy. This ensures that herbal medicines and natural products meet specific standards of purity, potency, and safety. Techniques such as High-Performance Liquid Chromatography (HPLC) and Thin Layer Chromatography (TLC) are commonly used in quality control.

7. **Role in Drug Discovery and Development:**

   a. Natural products have historically been a significant source of new drugs. Pharmacognosy plays a crucial role in the early stages of drug discovery by identifying and isolating potential lead compounds from natural sources. Many modern drugs, such as paclitaxel (from the Pacific yew tree) and artemisinin (from Artemisia annua), are derived from natural products.

8. **Economic Importance:**

   a. The commercial production of herbal medicines, nutraceuticals, and dietary supplements contributes significantly to the global economy. Pharmacognosy helps in the development of standardized and effective herbal products that meet consumer demands.

Modern Pharmacognosy

With advancements in technology, pharmacognosy has expanded beyond traditional methods. Modern pharmacognosy incorporates molecular biology, biotechnology, and bioinformatics to explore natural products. Techniques such as genomics, proteomics, and metabolomics are used to understand the molecular mechanisms of action of natural compounds and to discover new drugs.

Definition of Pharmacognosy

Pharmacognosy is the branch of pharmaceutical sciences that focuses on the study of natural products derived from plants, animals, microbes, and minerals for their medicinal properties. It involves the identification, analysis, extraction, and application of biologically active compounds found in nature for therapeutic purposes. Pharmacognosy combines aspects of botany, chemistry, and pharmacology to explore natural substances and their potential uses in medicine.

History of Pharmacognosy

The history of pharmacognosy is deeply intertwined with the history of medicine itself. The use of natural substances for healing dates back thousands of years, with early civilizations relying heavily on plants, animals, and minerals for medicinal purposes.

1. **Ancient Civilizations**:
    a. **Egypt**: One of the earliest records of medicinal plants is the Ebers Papyrus (circa 1550 BCE), an ancient Egyptian document containing a comprehensive list of medicinal plants and their uses.
    b. **China**: Traditional Chinese Medicine (TCM) has a rich history, with texts like the **Shennong Bencao Jing** (The Divine Farmer's Materia Medica), which dates back to around 2000 BCE, documenting the use of herbs in medicine.
    c. **India**: The **Ayurveda** system of medicine, with texts such as the **Charaka Samhita** and **Sushruta Samhita**, provides extensive information on the use of plants and other natural products in health and disease management.
    d. **Greece**: The ancient Greeks, particularly Hippocrates (460-377 BCE) and Dioscorides (40-90 CE), made significant contributions to the understanding of medicinal plants. Dioscorides' work, **De Materia Medica**, served as a reference for centuries in both Europe and the Middle East.
2. **Middle Ages**:
    a. During the Middle Ages, the knowledge of medicinal plants was preserved and expanded by Islamic scholars. **Avicenna's** (980-1037 CE) **Canon of Medicine** is one of the most famous works of this period, blending Greek, Roman, and Islamic knowledge.

3. **Renaissance and the Age of Exploration**:
   a. The Renaissance era (14th-17th centuries) saw a resurgence of interest in natural sciences, including pharmacognosy. The discovery of the New World introduced many new medicinal plants to Europe, such as quinine (from the bark of the Cinchona tree) used for treating malaria.
4. **Modern Era**:
   a. The term **"pharmacognosy"** was coined in 1815 by Johann Adam Schmidt, a German scientist. The discipline became more formalized in the 19th and 20th centuries with the development of pharmacopoeias and the establishment of pharmaceutical sciences as a distinct field. The advent of organic chemistry and pharmacology further advanced the study of natural products, leading to the isolation and synthesis of many active compounds from natural sources.

Scope of Pharmacognosy

Pharmacognosy is a multidisciplinary field with a broad scope, encompassing various aspects of natural product research:

1. **Botanical Classification and Identification**:
   a. Pharmacognosy involves the accurate identification and classification of medicinal plants based on their botanical characteristics. This ensures the correct sourcing of plants for medicinal use.
2. **Phytochemistry**:
   a. The study of the chemical constituents of plants, known as phytochemistry, is a key aspect of pharmacognosy. Phytochemists analyze the structure, function, and biosynthesis of plant secondary metabolites like alkaloids, flavonoids, terpenoids, glycosides, and tannins.

3. **Extraction and Isolation**:

   a. Pharmacognosy involves the extraction and isolation of bioactive compounds from natural sources using various techniques like solvent extraction, distillation, and chromatography. The isolated compounds can then be tested for their therapeutic properties.

4. **Ethnopharmacology**:

   a. Ethnopharmacology studies traditional medicines and the use of natural products by indigenous cultures. It seeks to understand the cultural context of medicinal plant use and to identify potential new drugs based on traditional knowledge.

5. **Pharmacological and Toxicological Evaluation**:

   a. Once bioactive compounds are isolated, they are subjected to pharmacological testing to determine their efficacy, mechanism of action, and therapeutic potential. Toxicological studies ensure the safety of these compounds for human use.

6. **Standardization and Quality Control**:

   a. Ensuring the quality and consistency of herbal medicines is critical. Pharmacognosy plays a role in the standardization of natural products, developing protocols for their quality control, and ensuring they meet regulatory standards.

7. **Role in Drug Discovery and Development**:

   a. Many modern drugs have been derived from natural products, and pharmacognosy continues to play a crucial role in the discovery of new drugs. For example, drugs like morphine, aspirin, and paclitaxel have their origins in natural sources.

8. **Nutraceuticals and Dietary Supplements**:

   a. The growing interest in health and wellness has led to the expansion of pharmacognosy into the development of nutraceuticals and dietary supplements, which are derived from natural products and have health benefits.

Development of Pharmacognosy

The development of pharmacognosy as a distinct scientific discipline has been shaped by advancements in various fields:

1. **Botany and Taxonomy**:
   a. The systematization of plant classification and the development of taxonomic principles have been fundamental to pharmacognosy. The work of botanists like Carl Linnaeus, who developed the binomial nomenclature system, laid the groundwork for the scientific study of medicinal plants.

2. **Chemistry**:
   a. The development of organic chemistry in the 19th century revolutionized pharmacognosy. It enabled scientists to isolate and characterize the active constituents of plants, leading to the discovery of many important drugs.

3. **Pharmacology**:
   a. The field of pharmacology, which studies the effects of drugs on biological systems, has greatly influenced pharmacognosy. The integration of pharmacological principles has allowed for a better understanding of how natural products exert their effects.

4. **Technology and Instrumentation**:
   a. Advances in technology, such as High-Performance Liquid Chromatography (HPLC), Mass Spectrometry (MS), and Nuclear Magnetic Resonance (NMR) spectroscopy, have enhanced the ability to analyze and characterize natural products with precision.

5. **Biotechnology and Molecular Biology**:
   a. The application of biotechnology in pharmacognosy has opened new avenues for drug discovery. Techniques such as genetic

engineering, tissue culture, and recombinant DNA technology are used to produce and study natural compounds on a molecular level.

6. **Regulatory Science**:

   a. The establishment of regulatory frameworks for the approval and standardization of herbal medicines and natural products has contributed to the development of pharmacognosy. Organizations like the World Health Organization (WHO) and the U.S. Food and Drug Administration (FDA) have set guidelines for the safe and effective use of natural products.

SOURCES OF DRUGS

Pharmacognosy focuses on the study of natural sources of drugs, which include plants, animals, marine organisms, and tissue culture. These sources have been integral to the development of traditional and modern medicines. Each source provides unique compounds that have therapeutic potential, and pharmacognosy plays a crucial role in identifying, extracting, and characterizing these bioactive substances.

1. Plant Sources

Plants are one of the most significant sources of drugs in pharmacognosy. Historically, medicinal plants have been used in various traditional medicine systems across the world, such as Ayurveda, Traditional Chinese Medicine (TCM), and Western herbal medicine. Plants continue to be a rich source of bioactive compounds used in modern pharmaceuticals.

   a. **Types of Plant-Derived Drugs**:

      i. **Alkaloids**: These are nitrogen-containing compounds with potent biological activity. Examples include morphine (from the opium poppy), quinine (from Cinchona bark), and atropine (from belladonna).

ii.   **Glycosides**: These are compounds that consist of a sugar part and a non-sugar part (aglycone). Cardiac glycosides like digoxin (from Digitalis purpurea) are used to treat heart conditions.

iii. **Terpenoids**: A large and diverse class of organic chemicals, terpenoids include compounds like taxol (from the Pacific yew tree), which is used in cancer treatment.

iv.   **Flavonoids**: These polyphenolic compounds have antioxidant properties and are found in a wide variety of plants. Examples include quercetin and rutin.

v.   **Tannins**: These are polyphenolic compounds with astringent properties, often used for their anti-inflammatory and antimicrobial effects.

vi.   **Volatile Oils**: Essential oils from plants like peppermint, eucalyptus, and lavender are used for their therapeutic properties, including antimicrobial, anti-inflammatory, and calming effects.

b. **Plant Parts Used**:
   i.   **Roots** (e.g., ginseng, licorice)
   ii.   **Leaves** (e.g., digitalis, tea)
   iii. **Barks** (e.g., cinchona, willow)
   iv.   **Flowers** (e.g., chamomile, saffron)
   v.   **Fruits** (e.g., belladonna, senna)
   vi.   **Seeds** (e.g., castor, nux vomica)
   vii. **Gums and Resins** (e.g., myrrh, frankincense)

2. Animal Sources

Animals have been a traditional source of drugs and therapeutic agents, providing unique bioactive compounds that are often difficult to obtain from other sources.

a. **Types of Animal-Derived Drugs**:

i.   **Hormones**: Many hormones used in therapy, such as insulin (originally derived from pig and cow pancreases) and thyroid hormones (from porcine thyroid glands), have animal origins.

ii. **Enzymes**: Enzymes like pepsin (from pig stomachs) and pancreatin (from porcine pancreas) are used in digestive aids.

iii. **Antitoxins and Antivenoms**: These are prepared from the blood serum of animals that have been immunized with specific toxins or venoms. For example, horse serum is used to produce antivenoms for snake bites.

iv. **Vaccines**: Some vaccines are derived from animals, such as the rabies vaccine, which was originally developed using neural tissue from infected rabbits.

v.   **Heparin**: A widely used anticoagulant, heparin is traditionally extracted from the mucosal tissues of animals like pigs and cows.

vi. **Immunoglobulins**: These are derived from animal plasma and used for passive immunization.

3. Marine Sources

Marine organisms have emerged as a promising source of novel bioactive compounds with unique chemical structures and potent biological activities. The vast biodiversity of the oceans offers a largely untapped reservoir for drug discovery.

a. **Types of Marine-Derived Drugs**:

   i.   **Marine Algae**: Seaweeds and other marine algae produce polysaccharides like carrageenan and alginates, which are used as stabilizers in the food and pharmaceutical industries. Algae also produce bioactive compounds with antiviral, anticancer, and anti-inflammatory properties.

ii. **Sponges**: Marine sponges are a rich source of novel compounds, such as **Ara-A** (a nucleoside analog used in antiviral therapy) and **Halichondrin B** (a precursor to the anticancer drug eribulin).

iii. **Marine Mollusks**: Some mollusks produce toxins with potent pharmacological effects, such as **conotoxins** from cone snails, which are being studied for their potential as pain relievers.

iv. **Marine Bacteria and Fungi**: Marine microorganisms produce a wide range of secondary metabolites with antibiotic, antifungal, and anticancer properties. For example, **salinosporamide A** from the marine bacterium *Salinispora tropica* is being developed as an anticancer drug.

v. **Marine Vertebrates**: Compounds like **squalamine** (from dogfish sharks) have shown promise in treating various conditions, including cancer and viral infections.

4. Tissue Culture

Tissue culture involves the cultivation of plant, animal, or microbial cells in a controlled environment outside of their natural habitat. This technique allows for the production of specific bioactive compounds and offers a sustainable alternative to harvesting natural resources.

a. **Plant Tissue Culture:**

i. Plant tissue culture enables the production of secondary metabolites under controlled conditions, independent of seasonal and environmental variations. This technique is used to produce high-value compounds like **paclitaxel** (from the yew tree) and **shikonin** (from *Lithospermum erythrorhizon*).

ii. **Callus culture**, **suspension culture**, and **hairy root culture** are some of the methods used in plant tissue culture to produce specific compounds. For example, the production of **vinblastine** and

vincristine (anticancer alkaloids) from *Catharanthus roseus* can be optimized using tissue culture techniques.

b. **Animal Tissue Culture**:
   i. Animal cell culture is used to produce monoclonal antibodies, vaccines, and other therapeutic proteins. For example, **recombinant insulin** and **erythropoietin** are produced using genetically engineered cells in culture.
   ii. **Stem cell culture** is another area of interest, with potential applications in regenerative medicine and drug development.

c. **Microbial Culture**:
   i. Microbial cultures, including bacteria, fungi, and yeast, are used to produce antibiotics, enzymes, and other bioactive compounds. For instance, the antibiotic **penicillin** is produced by culturing the fungus *Penicillium notatum*.
   ii. Microbial fermentation processes are also used to produce **vitamins** (like vitamin B12), **amino acids** (like glutamic acid), and **bioactive peptides**.

ORGANIZED DRUGS, UNORGANIZED DRUGS

In pharmacognosy, drugs derived from natural sources are categorized into two main types: **organized drugs** and **unorganized drugs**. This classification is based on the structural characteristics of the natural product, specifically whether the drug retains its original cellular structure or not.

1. Organized Drugs

Organized drugs are those that retain their cellular structure, typically derived from plant or animal tissues. These drugs are often recognized by their specific morphological features, which can include roots, stems, leaves, flowers, seeds, or entire organisms. The cellular integrity of these drugs is maintained, making it possible to identify the specific tissue or organ from which they were derived.

a. **Examples of Organized Drugs**:

i. **Leaves**: Digitalis, Senna

ii. **Roots**: Rauwolfia, Ginseng

iii. **Barks**: Cinchona, Cascara

iv. **Flowers**: Chamomile, Clove

v. **Fruits**: Fennel, Cardamom

vi. **Seeds**: Nux vomica, Fenugreek

vii. **Woods**: Sandalwood, Quassia

Morphological Identification:

a. Organized drugs can often be identified based on their external morphology (shape, color, size) and internal histology (cell structure, arrangement). For example:

   i. **Digitalis Leaves**: Known for their lanceolate shape and serrated margins.

   ii. **Cinchona Bark**: Identified by its brown color, bitter taste, and microscopic features like stone cells and fibers.

Uses:

a. These drugs are typically used directly in traditional medicine or processed to extract active constituents. For example, Digitalis leaves are used to extract cardiac glycosides, which are employed in treating heart conditions.

2. Unorganized Drugs

Unorganized drugs are natural products that do not retain any specific cellular structure, often resulting from a process such as extraction, drying, or exudation. These drugs are usually amorphous or semi-solid substances, making it difficult to identify the original tissue from which they were derived. They are generally obtained from plant exudates or other natural processes.

a. **Types of Unorganized Drugs**:

   i. Dried Latex

   ii. Dried Juices

iii.   Dried Extracts

iv.   Gums and Mucilages

v.   Oleoresins

vi.   Oleo-gum-resins

a. Dried Latex

Latex is a milky fluid secreted by certain plants, primarily from the family Euphorbiaceae and Papaveraceae. When latex is collected and dried, it solidifies into a rubbery or resinous mass.

1. **Example**:

    i.   **Opium**: Derived from the dried latex of *Papaver somniferum* (opium poppy). It contains alkaloids like morphine and codeine, used for pain relief and as cough suppressants.

2. **Uses**:

    i.   Dried latex is a source of important bioactive compounds like alkaloids, which are extracted and used in pharmaceuticals.

b. Dried Juices

Dried juices are the concentrated and dried form of the sap or juice obtained from plants. The process involves evaporating the moisture content from the juice to obtain a solid or semi-solid mass.

1. **Example**:

    i.   **Aloe**: Derived from the dried juice of *Aloe vera*. It is used as a laxative and in skincare products for its soothing and healing properties.

2. **Uses**:

    i.   Dried juices are often used in traditional and modern medicine for their therapeutic properties, such as in wound healing or as a natural laxative.

c. Dried Extracts

Dried extracts are concentrated forms of plant or animal material obtained by evaporating the solvent used during the extraction process. The resulting product is a powder or solid that contains the active constituents of the original material.

1. **Example:**
    i. **Belladonna Extract**: A dried extract from the leaves of *Atropa belladonna*, containing alkaloids like atropine, used in ophthalmology and as an antispasmodic.
2. **Uses:**
    i. Dried extracts are used in pharmaceutical formulations to provide a consistent and concentrated dose of active ingredients.

d. Gums and Mucilages

Gums are natural plant exudates that form when the plant is injured, while **mucilages** are polysaccharides produced by the plant that swell in water to form a gel-like substance. Both are unorganized in nature and have a variety of applications in medicine and industry.

1. **Examples:**
    i. **Gum Acacia**: A gum obtained from *Acacia senegal*, used as a demulcent and emulsifying agent in pharmaceuticals.
    ii. **Tragacanth**: A mucilage from *Astragalus* species, used as a thickening agent and emulsifier.
2. **Uses:**
    i. Gums and mucilages are widely used in the pharmaceutical industry as stabilizers, emulsifiers, and thickening agents. They also have therapeutic uses, such as in soothing inflamed tissues.

e. Oleoresins

Oleoresins are a natural mixture of an essential oil and a resin, obtained from plants through the process of solvent extraction or distillation. They are highly concentrated and retain the aroma and flavor of the original plant.

1. **Example**:
    i. **Capsicum Oleoresin**: Extracted from chili peppers (*Capsicum annuum*), used in topical pain relief formulations and as a flavoring agent in foods.
2. **Uses**:
    i. Oleoresins are used in the food and pharmaceutical industries for their flavoring, aromatic, and therapeutic properties.

f. Oleo-gum-resins

Oleo-gum-resins are a combination of essential oils, gums, and resins. These substances exude naturally from certain plants or are extracted through incision and collection methods.

1. **Example**:
    i. **Myrrh**: An oleo-gum-resin obtained from *Commiphora myrrha*, used in traditional medicine for its antiseptic and anti-inflammatory properties.
2. **Uses**:
    i. Oleo-gum-resins are used in traditional medicine, perfumery, and in the preparation of certain pharmaceutical products due to their aromatic and therapeutic properties.

Key Features of Unorganized Crude Drugs:

- **No definite structure**: Unlike organized crude drugs, these substances are not whole plant parts or animal organs but rather products like gums, resins, or oils.
- **Amorphous nature**: They often exist as powders, liquids, or semi-solids.
- **Usage**: Many unorganized crude drugs are used as excipients (binders, emulsifiers, stabilizers) or as active ingredients in various medicinal preparations.

Multiple Choice Questions (MCQs)

1. What is the primary focus of pharmacognosy?

    A) Study of synthetic drugs

    B) Study of natural products derived from plants, animals, microbes, and minerals

    C) Study of pharmaceutical marketing

    D) Study of drug manufacturing processes

2. Who coined the term "pharmacognosy" in 1815?

    A) Hippocrates

    B) Carl Linnaeus

    C) Johann Adam Schmidt

    D) Avicenna

3. Which ancient text from India is a rich source of traditional medicine knowledge?

    A) Ebers Papyrus

    B) Shennong Bencao Jing

    C) Charaka Samhita

    D) De Materia Medica

4. What is the primary therapeutic use of Aloe Vera latex?

    A) Laxative

    B) Antifungal

    C) Antiviral

    D) Immunosuppressant

5. Which of the following is an example of an organized drug?

    A) Opium

    B) Digitalis leaves

    C) Aloe Vera gel

    D) Senna extract

6. What is the primary active compound in Cinchona bark used for treating malaria?

    A) Quinine

    B) Morphine

    C) Digoxin

    D) Atropine

7. Which type of marine organism is a source of the polysaccharide carrageenan?

    A) Marine bacteria

    B) Marine algae

    C) Marine sponges

    D) Marine mollusks

8. What is the main pharmacological action of penicillin?

    A) Inhibiting bacterial cell wall synthesis

    B) Reducing inflammation

    C) Stimulating immune response

    D) Enhancing protein synthesis

9. Which part of the Senna plant is primarily used for its laxative effect?

    A) Roots

    B) Leaves

    C) Flowers

    D) Seeds

10. What is the primary use of kaolin in medicine?

    A) Antibacterial agent

    B) Laxative

    C) Adsorbent in treating diarrhea

    D) Pain reliever

11. Which compound in Chamomile is responsible for its anxiolytic and sedative effects?

A) Apigenin

B) Bisabolol

C) Chamazulene

D) Flavonoids

12. What is the primary pharmacological action of Heparin?

A) Anticoagulant

B) Analgesic

C) Antipyretic

D) Antiemetic

13. Which of the following is a side effect of long-term use of Senna?

A) Melanosis Coli

B) Hyperglycemia

C) Cardiotoxicity

D) Osteoporosis

14. What is the source of Agar used in microbiological culture media?

A) Green algae

B) Red algae

C) Brown algae

D) Blue-green algae

15. Which active compound in Peppermint Oil provides a cooling sensation and is used to relieve headaches?

A) Menthol

B) Limonene

C) Menthyl acetate

D) Pulegone

16. What is the primary role of insulin in the body?

A) Regulate fat metabolism

B) Regulate glucose metabolism

C) Inhibit protein synthesis

D) Increase cholesterol levels

17. Which of the following drugs is derived from animal sources?

A) Penicillin

B) Quinine

C) Insulin

D) Taxol

18. Which marine organism is a source of the anticancer compound salinosporamide A?

A) Marine sponges

B) Marine mollusks

C) Marine bacteria

D) Marine algae

19. What is the therapeutic use of Chamomile in gastrointestinal health?

A) Reducing acid secretion

B) Relieving spasms and soothing the digestive tract

C) Promoting bowel movements

D) Increasing bile production

20. What is a potential side effect of excessive use of iodine tincture on the skin?

A) Hyperpigmentation

B) Skin irritation and dermatitis

C) Enhanced wound healing

D) Increased hair growth

Short Answer Type Questions (Subjective)

1. Define pharmacognosy and its significance in pharmaceutical sciences.

2. Explain the historical significance of the Ebers Papyrus in pharmacognosy.

3. What are the main chemical constituents of Aloe Vera, and what are their pharmacological actions?

4. Describe the difference between organized and unorganized drugs with examples.

5. How is penicillin produced, and what is its mechanism of action?

6. Discuss the therapeutic uses and side effects of Senna leaves.

7. What are the primary active compounds found in Cinchona bark, and what are their uses?

8. Explain the role of marine algae in pharmacognosy and their potential therapeutic applications.

9. What are the pharmacological actions of chamomile, and how is it used in traditional medicine?

10. Describe the mechanism of action of heparin and its therapeutic applications.

11. What is the role of insulin in glucose metabolism, and how is it used in the treatment of diabetes?

12. Explain the extraction process and medicinal uses of agar from marine algae.

13. Discuss the therapeutic applications and potential side effects of peppermint oil.

14. What are the chemical constituents of kaolin, and how is it used in medicine?

15. Describe the historical and modern significance of quinine in treating malaria.

16. Explain the use of marine sponges in drug discovery, particularly for anticancer drugs.

17. Discuss the safety considerations and side effects associated with the use of iodine tincture.

18. What are the pharmacological properties of aloe-emodin found in Aloe Vera?

19. How do marine bacteria contribute to the discovery of new antibiotics?

20. Describe the role of bisabolol in chamomile's anti-inflammatory effects.

Long Answer Type Questions (Subjective)

1. Discuss the evolution of pharmacognosy from ancient times to the modern era, highlighting key developments and their impact on drug discovery.

2. Explain the process of extracting and isolating bioactive compounds from natural sources, using examples from plant and marine organisms.

3. Analyze the role of pharmacognosy in the development of traditional medicines and how it contributes to modern drug discovery.

4. Describe the pharmacological properties, therapeutic uses, and potential side effects of Aloe Vera, with a focus on its role in dermatology and gastrointestinal health.

5. Discuss the chemical structure, pharmacological actions, and therapeutic applications of quinine, including its historical significance in treating malaria.

6. Explain the role of marine algae in pharmacognosy, focusing on their chemical constituents and potential therapeutic applications, including antioxidant and anticancer properties.

7. Discuss the pharmacology of heparin, including its mechanism of action, therapeutic uses, and potential side effects.

8. Analyze the importance of chamomile in herbal medicine, including its chemical composition, pharmacological actions, and therapeutic applications.

9. Describe the production, pharmacological actions, and therapeutic uses of insulin, and discuss the challenges associated with its use in diabetes management.

10. Evaluate the role of marine organisms in pharmacognosy, with a focus on the discovery of new drugs from marine sponges, mollusks, and bacteria.

Answer Key for MCQs

1. (B) Study of natural products derived from plants, animals, microbes, and minerals:

2. (C) Johann Adam Schmidt

3. (C) Charaka Samhita

4. (A) Laxative

5. (B) Digitalis leaves

6. (A) Quinine

7. (B) Marine algae

8. (A) Inhibiting bacterial cell wall synthesis

9. (B) Leaves

10. (C) Adsorbent in treating diarrhe

11. (A) Apigenin

12. (A) Anticoagulant

13. (A) Melanosis Coli

14. (B) Red algae

15. (A) Menthol

16. (B) Regulate glucose metabolism

17. (C) Insulin

18. (C) Marine bacteria

19. (B) Relieving spasms and soothing the digestive tract

20. (B) Skin irritation and dermatitis

CHAPTER – 2

CLASSIFICATION OF DRUGS

INTRODUCTION:

Crude drugs can be classified in several ways based on different criteria, such as their origin, the part of the plant or animal used, the chemical constituents they contain, or their therapeutic uses. Below are some common methods of classification of crude drugs

Alphabetical Classification of Crude Drugs

Alphabetical classification is a simple and straightforward method of organizing crude drugs based on the first letter of their name. This method is often used in pharmacopoeias, reference books, and drug indexes. The drugs are listed in alphabetical order, making it easy to locate and reference them. This classification does not consider the origin, chemical composition, or therapeutic use of the drugs but simply arranges them alphabetically by their common or botanical name.

Key Features of Alphabetical Classification:

1. **Simplicity**: Easy to understand and use.
2. **Quick Reference**: Helps in quickly locating a particular drug in large compilations.
3. **No Scientific Basis**: Does not consider pharmacological or chemical properties.

Examples of Alphabetical Classification of Crude Drugs:

1. **A:**
   - **Acacia**: Derived from the Acacia tree, used as a binder and emulsifier in pharmaceuticals.

- o **Aconite**: Derived from *Aconitum napellus*, used for its analgesic and anti-inflammatory properties.
- o **Aloe**: Extracted from *Aloe vera*, used for its soothing and healing properties in skin care and digestive aids.

2. **B**:

- o **Belladonna**: Obtained from *Atropa belladonna*, used for its anticholinergic properties.
- o **Benzoin**: A resin obtained from *Styrax benzoin*, used in topical antiseptics and incense.
- o **Buchu**: Derived from the leaves of *Barosma betulina*, used as a diuretic.

3. **C**:

- o **Cinchona**: Derived from *Cinchona officinalis*, a source of quinine used to treat malaria.
- o **Clove**: Obtained from the flower buds of *Syzygium aromaticum*, used for its analgesic and antiseptic properties.
- o **Cascara**: Sourced from the bark of *Rhamnus purshiana*, used as a laxative.

4. **D**:

- o **Digitalis**: Obtained from *Digitalis purpurea*, used as a cardiotonic for heart conditions.
- o **Datura**: Derived from *Datura stramonium*, used for its anticholinergic and sedative effects.
- o **Dandelion**: Obtained from *Taraxacum officinale*, used as a diuretic and liver tonic.

5. **E**:

- o **Ephedra**: Sourced from *Ephedra sinica*, used for its bronchodilator properties in asthma and colds.

- o **Eucalyptus**: Derived from *Eucalyptus globulus*, used for its antiseptic and decongestant properties.
- o **Ergot**: Obtained from *Claviceps purpurea*, used in treating migraines and inducing labor.

6. **F**:

- o **Fennel**: Derived from *Foeniculum vulgare*, used as a digestive aid and carminative.
- o **Foxglove**: Common name for *Digitalis purpurea*, used for its cardiac glycosides.
- o **Feverfew**: Obtained from *Tanacetum parthenium*, used for migraines and inflammation.

7. **G**:

- o **Ginger**: Derived from *Zingiber officinale*, used for its anti-nausea and anti-inflammatory properties.
- o **Ginseng**: Obtained from *Panax ginseng*, used as an adaptogen and to boost energy.
- o **Guarana**: Sourced from *Paullinia cupana*, used as a stimulant and for weight loss.

8. **H**:

- o **Hyoscyamus**: Derived from *Hyoscyamus niger*, used for its sedative and anticholinergic properties.
- o **Hops**: Obtained from *Humulus lupulus*, used for its calming effects in treating anxiety and insomnia.
- o **Hibiscus**: Sourced from *Hibiscus sabdariffa*, used for its diuretic and antioxidant properties.

9. **I**:

- o **Ipecac**: Derived from *Cephaelis ipecacuanha*, used as an emetic and in the treatment of amoebic dysentery.

- o **Indian Gooseberry (Amla)**: Obtained from *Phyllanthus emblica,* used for its high vitamin C content and antioxidant properties.
- o **Isabgol (Psyllium husk)**: Sourced from *Plantago ovata,* used as a laxative and dietary fiber supplement.

10.**J**:

- o **Jalap**: Derived from the roots of *Ipomoea purga,* used as a purgative.
- o **Jasmine**: Obtained from *Jasminum officinale,* used in aromatherapy and for its soothing properties.
- o **Juniper**: Sourced from *Juniperus communis,* used as a diuretic and in the treatment of urinary tract infections.

11.**K**:

- o **Kava**: Derived from *Piper methysticum,* used for its anxiolytic and sedative properties.
- o **Kino**: Obtained from *Pterocarpus marsupium,* used as an astringent and in treating diarrhea.
- o **Kola**: Sourced from *Cola acuminata,* used as a stimulant due to its caffeine content.

12.**L**:

- o **Liquorice**: Derived from *Glycyrrhiza glabra,* used for its soothing effects on the throat and as an anti-inflammatory.
- o **Lemon Balm**: Obtained from *Melissa officinalis,* used for its calming and antiviral properties.
- o **Lavender**: Sourced from *Lavandula angustifolia,* used in aromatherapy and for its relaxing effects.

13.**M**:

- o **Mentha (Peppermint)**: Derived from *Mentha piperita,* used as a digestive aid and for its cooling effect.

- o **Myrrh**: Obtained from the resin of *Commiphora myrrha*, used as an antiseptic and in oral care.
- o **Milk Thistle**: Sourced from *Silybum marianum*, used for liver protection and detoxification.

14.**N**:

- o **Nutmeg**: Derived from *Myristica fragrans*, used as a spice and for its digestive properties.
- o **Nux Vomica**: Obtained from *Strychnos nux-vomica*, used in small doses for its stimulant effects.
- o **Neem**: Sourced from *Azadirachta indica*, used for its antibacterial and antifungal properties.

15.**O**:

- o **Opium**: Derived from the latex of *Papaver somniferum*, used as a powerful analgesic.
- o **Olive Leaf**: Obtained from *Olea europaea*, used for its antioxidant and cardiovascular benefits.
- o **Orris Root**: Sourced from *Iris germanica*, used in perfumes and for its anti-inflammatory properties.

16.**P**:

- o **Peppermint**: Derived from *Mentha piperita*, used for digestive issues and as a flavoring agent.
- o **Poppy (Opium)**: Obtained from *Papaver somniferum*, used for its analgesic alkaloids.
- o **Psyllium**: Sourced from *Plantago ovata*, used as a bulk-forming laxative.

17.**Q**:

- o **Quassia**: Derived from *Quassia amara*, used as a bitter tonic and in treating digestive issues.

- o **Quinine**: Obtained from *Cinchona officinalis*, used to treat malaria.
- o **Quillaja**: Sourced from *Quillaja saponaria*, used as a foaming agent and in traditional medicine for cough.

18.**R**:

- o **Rhubarb**: Derived from *Rheum officinale*, used as a laxative and for digestive disorders.
- o **Rosemary**: Obtained from *Rosmarinus officinalis*, used for its antioxidant and anti-inflammatory properties.
- o **Rauwolfia**: Sourced from *Rauvolfia serpentina*, used for hypertension and mental disorders.

19.**S**:

- o **Senna**: Derived from *Cassia angustifolia*, used as a laxative.
- o **Strophanthus**: Obtained from *Strophanthus kombe*, used for its cardiotonic effects.
- o **Sandalwood**: Sourced from *Santalum album*, used for its fragrance and in traditional medicine.

20.**T**:

- o **Turmeric**: Derived from *Curcuma longa*, used for its anti-inflammatory and antioxidant properties.
- o **Tea Tree**: Obtained from *Melaleuca alternifolia*, used as an antiseptic and for skin conditions.
- o **Thyme**: Sourced from *Thymus vulgaris*, used for respiratory issues and as a culinary herb.

21.**U**:

- o **Uva-Ursi**: Derived from *Arctostaphylos uva-ursi*, used for urinary tract infections.
- o **Ulex (Gorse)**: Obtained from *Ulex europaeus*, used traditionally for respiratory ailments.

o **Ulmus (Slippery Elm)**: Sourced from *Ulmus rubra*, used for its soothing effect on the digestive tract.

22.**V**:

o **Valerian**: Derived from *Valeriana officinalis*, used for anxiety and insomnia.

o **Vitex (Chaste Tree)**: Obtained from *Vitex agnus-castus*, used for menstrual disorders.

o **Vanilla**: Sourced from *Vanilla planifolia*, used for its flavoring properties.

23.**W**:

o **Willow Bark**: Derived from *Salix alba*, used for its salicylic acid content to relieve pain and inflammation.

o **Witch Hazel**: Obtained from *Hamamelis virginiana*, used as an astringent in skin care.

o **Wild Cherry**: Sourced from *Prunus serotina*, used as a cough suppressant.

24.**Y**:

o **Yohimbine**: Derived from *Pausinystalia johimbe*, used for its stimulant and aphrodisiac effects.

o **Yarrow**: Obtained from *Achillea millefolium*, used for its anti-inflammatory and wound-healing properties.

o **Yucca**: Sourced from *Yucca schidigera*, used in traditional medicine for arthritis and inflammation.

25.**Z**:

o **Zedoary**: Derived from *Curcuma zedoaria*, used for digestive

Morphological Classification of Crude Drugs

Morphological classification categorizes crude drugs based on the part of the plant or animal from which they are derived. This system is useful because many medicinal drugs are obtained from specific plant parts like roots, leaves, seeds, flowers, and bark. Each of these parts may contain different chemical compounds with various therapeutic effects. The classification makes it easy to identify and study crude drugs based on their external appearance or morphology.

1. Drugs Derived from Roots and Rhizomes

Roots are underground plant organs that absorb water and nutrients, while **rhizomes** are underground stems that store food and help plants survive during unfavorable conditions.

- **Examples:**
    - **Liquorice (Glycyrrhiza glabra)**: The root is used for its demulcent and expectorant properties, commonly in treating cough and sore throat.
    - **Ginger (Zingiber officinale)**: The rhizome is used as an anti-inflammatory, digestive aid, and anti-nausea remedy.
    - **Rauwolfia (Rauvolfia serpentina)**: The root is used for its antihypertensive properties.

2. Drugs Derived from Barks

Barks are the outer protective layer of stems and branches in woody plants. Barks are rich in secondary metabolites like alkaloids, glycosides, and tannins, which often have therapeutic properties.

- **Examples:**
    - **Cinchona (Cinchona officinalis)**: The bark is the source of quinine, an antimalarial alkaloid.
    - **Cinnamon (Cinnamomum zeylanicum)**: The inner bark is used as a spice and for its carminative and antibacterial properties.
    - **Cascara Sagrada (Rhamnus purshiana)**: The bark is used as a laxative.

3. Drugs Derived from Leaves

Leaves are the primary photosynthetic organs of plants and are often rich in volatile oils, glycosides, alkaloids, and other bioactive compounds.

- **Examples**:
    - **Senna (Cassia angustifolia)**: The leaves contain anthraquinone glycosides used as a laxative.
    - **Belladonna (Atropa belladonna)**: The leaves contain alkaloids like atropine, used for their anticholinergic effects.
    - **Eucalyptus (Eucalyptus globulus)**: The leaves are rich in volatile oils, especially eucalyptol, used as an expectorant and antiseptic.

4. Drugs Derived from Flowers

Flowers are the reproductive parts of plants, often containing volatile oils, glycosides, and flavonoids with therapeutic effects.

- **Examples**:
    - **Clove (Syzygium aromaticum)**: The dried flower buds are used for their analgesic and antiseptic properties, especially in dental care.
    - **Chamomile (Matricaria chamomilla)**: The flowers contain flavonoids and volatile oils, used for their calming, anti-inflammatory, and digestive properties.
    - **Saffron (Crocus sativus)**: The stigmas of the flowers are used as a spice and for their antioxidant, anti-inflammatory, and antidepressant effects.

5. Drugs Derived from Fruits

Fruits are the mature ovaries of flowering plants and often contain essential oils, glycosides, and other active compounds. They are commonly used for their nutritional value as well as medicinal purposes.

- **Examples**:
    - **Fennel (Foeniculum vulgare)**: The fruits contain volatile oils and are used as a digestive aid and carminative.

- o **Coriander (Coriandrum sativum)**: The dried fruits are used as a spice and for their digestive and carminative properties.
  - o **Amla (Phyllanthus emblica)**: The fruit is rich in vitamin C and is used for its antioxidant, immunomodulatory, and rejuvenating effects.

6. Drugs Derived from Seeds

Seeds are the embryonic plants enclosed in a protective outer covering and contain a high concentration of oils, proteins, and other compounds with medicinal benefits.

- **Examples**:
  - o **Nux Vomica (Strychnos nux-vomica)**: The seeds contain alkaloids like strychnine and brucine, used as a stimulant in controlled doses.
  - o **Castor Seed (Ricinus communis)**: The seeds are used to extract castor oil, which is used as a laxative and in skin care.
  - o **Isabgol (Plantago ovata)**: The seeds' husks are used as a bulk-forming laxative and dietary fiber supplement.

7. Drugs Derived from Woods

Woods are the hard, dense parts of tree stems and roots that contain compounds such as lignans, tannins, and essential oils.

- **Examples**:
  - o **Sandalwood (Santalum album)**: The heartwood contains essential oils, used for its fragrance and anti-inflammatory, antimicrobial properties.
  - o **Quassia (Quassia amara)**: The wood is used for its bitter tonic properties, improving digestion and acting as an insecticide.
  - o **Pterocarpus (Pterocarpus marsupium)**: The wood is used in traditional medicine for managing diabetes.

8. Drugs Derived from Herbs and Whole Plants

In some cases, the **whole plant** or the **herb** (above-ground parts of the plant) is used as a crude drug. These plants are rich in bioactive compounds like alkaloids, glycosides, and flavonoids.

- **Examples**:
    - **Ephedra (Ephedra sinica)**: The whole plant contains alkaloids like ephedrine, used as a bronchodilator in treating asthma and colds.
    - **Belladonna (Atropa belladonna)**: Both leaves and roots of the whole plant are used for their alkaloids in treating various conditions.
    - **Mentha (Mentha piperita)**: The whole herb is used for its essential oils, which have carminative and antiseptic properties.

9. Drugs Derived from Gums and Resins

Gums are plant exudates rich in polysaccharides, and **resins** are plant secretions that are solid or semi-solid, often used for their medicinal and adhesive properties.

- **Examples**:
    - **Acacia (Acacia senegal)**: A gum used as a binder in pharmaceuticals and as a soothing agent in sore throats.
    - **Tragacanth (Astragalus gummifer)**: A gum used as an emulsifier and thickener in medications.
    - **Myrrh (Commiphora myrrha)**: A resin used as an antiseptic and anti-inflammatory agent in dental care and wound healing.

10. Drugs Derived from Latex

Latex is a milky fluid secreted by some plants and used for its bioactive properties, including alkaloids and glycosides.

- **Examples**:
    - **Opium (Papaver somniferum)**: The dried latex contains alkaloids like morphine, used as a powerful analgesic.

- o **Rubber (Hevea brasiliensis)**: The latex is used in making medical gloves and other materials.
- o **Euphorbia latex**: Used in traditional medicine for its irritant and purgative properties.

11. Drugs Derived from Animal Products

Although less common, some crude drugs are derived from **animal parts or products** like secretions, hormones, or enzymes.

- **Examples**:
  - o **Cod Liver Oil (Gadus morhua)**: Derived from fish liver, rich in vitamin A and D, used for bone health and immune function.
  - o **Lanolin (Ovis aries)**: A secretion from sheep's wool, used as an emollient in skin care products.
  - o **Honey (Apis mellifera)**: Used for its antimicrobial and soothing properties in wound healing and cough treatments.

Summary of Morphological Classification of Crude Drugs:

Part of the Plant/Animal	Examples
Roots and Rhizomes	Liquorice, Ginger, Rauwolfia
Barks	Cinchona, Cinnamon, Cascara Sagrada
Leaves	Senna, Belladonna, Eucalyptus
Flowers	Clove, Chamomile, Saffron
Fruits	Fennel, Coriander, Amla
Seeds	Nux Vomica, Castor Seed, Isabgol
Woods	Sandalwood, Quassia, Pterocarpus
Whole Plants/Herbs	Ephedra, Belladonna, Mentha
Gums and Resins	Acacia, Tragacanth, Myrrh
Latex	Opium, Rubber, Euphorbia

Part of the Plant/Animal	Examples
Animal Products	Cod Liver Oil, Lanolin, Honey

Chemical Classification of Crude Drugs

Chemical classification categorizes crude drugs based on the presence of specific chemical constituents responsible for their pharmacological actions. These bioactive compounds are often classified into broad chemical groups like alkaloids, glycosides, tannins, volatile oils, resins, and more. Understanding the chemical composition of a drug helps in predicting its therapeutic effects, toxicity, and possible drug interactions.

1. Alkaloids

Alkaloids are nitrogen-containing organic compounds found mainly in plants. They often have potent physiological effects on the human body and are used in medicine for their diverse actions, such as analgesic, antimalarial, and stimulant properties.

- **Examples:**
    - **Morphine** (from *Papaver somniferum*, the opium poppy): Used as a potent analgesic for severe pain.
    - **Quinine** (from *Cinchona officinalis*): Used to treat malaria.
    - **Atropine** (from *Atropa belladonna*): Used as an anticholinergic to treat bradycardia and as an antidote for organophosphate poisoning.
    - **Strychnine** (from *Strychnos nux-vomica*): Used as a stimulant in controlled doses, but highly toxic in large quantities.

2. Glycosides

Glycosides are compounds where a sugar molecule (glycone) is attached to a non-sugar molecule (aglycone or genin). They are often used for their cardiac, laxative, and other therapeutic effects.

- **Examples:**

- o **Digoxin** (from *Digitalis purpurea*): A cardiac glycoside used to treat heart failure and atrial fibrillation.
- o **Sennosides** (from *Cassia angustifolia*, Senna): Anthraquinone glycosides used as a stimulant laxative.
- o **Aloe-emodin** (from *Aloe vera*): An anthraquinone glycoside used as a laxative.
- o **Salicin** (from *Salix alba*, willow bark): A glycoside used for its anti-inflammatory and analgesic properties.

3. Volatile Oils (Essential Oils)

Volatile oils are aromatic, volatile substances that evaporate easily. They are found in various parts of plants and have a wide range of therapeutic applications, such as antiseptic, carminative, and expectorant.

- **Examples**:
  - o **Eucalyptus oil** (from *Eucalyptus globulus*): Used as an expectorant and antiseptic.
  - o **Peppermint oil** (from *Mentha piperita*): Used as a carminative, digestive aid, and for its cooling effect.
  - o **Clove oil** (from *Syzygium aromaticum*): Used for its analgesic properties, especially in dental care.
  - o **Lavender oil** (from *Lavandula angustifolia*): Used in aromatherapy for its calming and soothing effects.

4. Tannins

Tannins are polyphenolic compounds that have astringent properties. They are used in treating wounds, burns, and diarrhea due to their ability to precipitate proteins and protect tissues.

- **Examples**:
  - o **Catechu** (from *Acacia catechu*): Used as an astringent and in the treatment of diarrhea.

- o **Hamamelis (Witch hazel)**: Tannins from witch hazel are used in skin care for their astringent and anti-inflammatory properties.
- o **Myrobalan** (from *Terminalia chebula*): Used in traditional medicine for its antioxidant and astringent properties.
- o **Oak bark** (from *Quercus robur*): Rich in tannins, used in treating skin inflammation and diarrhea.

5. Resins

Resins are non-volatile, solid, or semi-solid plant secretions that contain a mixture of hydrocarbons, terpenes, and other organic compounds. They are often used for their antiseptic, expectorant, and protective properties.

- **Examples**:
  - o **Benzoin** (from *Styrax benzoin*): Used in topical antiseptics and for its soothing properties in respiratory conditions.
  - o **Cannabis resin** (from *Cannabis sativa*): Contains cannabinoids like THC and CBD, used for pain relief and anti-inflammatory effects.
  - o **Myrrh** (from *Commiphora myrrha*): Used for its antimicrobial and anti-inflammatory properties, particularly in dental and oral care.
  - o **Rosin** (from *Pinus species*): Used in topical applications for its antiseptic and adhesive properties.

6. Saponins

Saponins are glycosides that form a soap-like foam when shaken with water. They have various therapeutic applications, such as expectorant, anti-inflammatory, and cholesterol-lowering effects.

- **Examples**:
  - o **Ginseng** (from *Panax ginseng*): Contains saponins known as ginsenosides, which are used as adaptogens to reduce stress and improve overall health.

- **Liquorice** (from *Glycyrrhiza glabra*): Contains glycyrrhizin, a saponin used for its anti-inflammatory and expectorant properties.
- **Quillaja** (from *Quillaja saponaria*): Used as an expectorant and in veterinary medicine as a vaccine adjuvant.
- **Dioscorea** (from *Dioscorea species*): Contains steroidal saponins, which are precursors for the synthesis of corticosteroids and hormones.

7. Fixed Oils and Fats

Fixed oils and fats are non-volatile and greasy substances that do not evaporate. They are used in nutrition, as emollients, and as carriers in pharmaceutical preparations.

- **Examples:**
  - **Castor oil** (from *Ricinus communis*): Used as a laxative and in skincare products for its moisturizing properties.
  - **Olive oil** (from *Olea europaea*): Used as a nutritional supplement and for its emollient properties in topical preparations.
  - **Cocoa butter** (from *Theobroma cacao*): Used as a moisturizer in cosmetics and topical preparations.
  - **Coconut oil** (from *Cocos nucifera*): Used for its moisturizing, anti-inflammatory, and antimicrobial effects.

8. Steroids and Steroidal Glycosides

Steroids are a class of organic compounds that play vital roles in various physiological processes. Steroidal glycosides, also called cardenolides, have specific effects on the heart and other systems.

- **Examples:**
  - **Diosgenin** (from *Dioscorea species*): Used as a precursor in the synthesis of corticosteroids and sex hormones.
  - **Cardiac glycosides** (from *Digitalis purpurea*): Used to treat heart failure by increasing the force of heart contractions.

- o **Hecogenin** (from *Agave species*): A steroid sapogenin used in the synthesis of corticosteroids.

9. Flavonoids

Flavonoids are a group of polyphenolic compounds found in various plants. They possess antioxidant, anti-inflammatory, and antiviral properties and are often used to strengthen capillaries and improve circulation.

- **Examples**:
  - o **Rutin** (from *Fagopyrum esculentum*): Used to strengthen blood vessels and treat conditions like varicose veins and hemorrhoids.
  - o **Hesperidin** (from citrus fruits): Used to improve capillary function and treat venous disorders.
  - o **Quercetin** (from *Sophora japonica*): Known for its antioxidant and anti-inflammatory effects, used in allergic conditions and to boost immunity.
  - o **Silymarin** (from *Silybum marianum*, milk thistle): Used for liver protection and detoxification.

10. Proteins and Enzymes

Proteins and enzymes derived from plants and animals are used in various therapeutic applications, such as wound healing, digestion aids, and as anti-inflammatory agents.

- **Examples**:
  - o **Papain** (from *Carica papaya*): A proteolytic enzyme used to aid digestion and as an anti-inflammatory agent in wound care.
  - o **Pepsin** (from the stomach lining of animals): Used as a digestive enzyme in cases of hypochlorhydria (low stomach acid).
  - o **Gelatin** (from animal collagen): Used as a gelling agent in foods and pharmaceuticals and in wound healing applications.

11. Carbohydrates

Carbohydrates are organic compounds consisting of carbon, hydrogen, and oxygen. They are widely used in medicine as demulcents, emollients, and binding agents.

- **Examples**:
    - **Acacia gum** (from *Acacia senegal*): Used as a binder and emulsifier in pharmaceutical preparations.
    - **Tragacanth** (from *Astragalus gummifer*): Used as a thickening agent in emulsions and as a stabilizer in food and pharmaceuticals.
    - **Starch** (from various sources like maize, wheat, and potato): Used as a filler, binder, and disintegrant in tablets.
    - **Honey** (from *Apis mellifera*): Used for its antimicrobial, soothing, and wound-healing properties.

Summary of Chemical Classification:

Chemical Group	Examples	Therapeutic Uses
Alkaloids	Morphine, Quinine, Atropine, Strychnine	Analgesic, antimalarial, anticholinergic
Glycosides	Digoxin, Sennosides, Aloe-emodin, Salicin	Cardiotonic, laxative, anti-inflammatory
Volatile Oils	Eucalyptus oil, Peppermint oil, Clove oil, Lavender oil	Expectorant, carminative, antiseptic, sedative
Tannins	Catechu, Witch hazel, Myrobalan, Oak bark	Astringent, anti-inflammatory, antioxidant
Resins	Benzoin, Cannabis, Myrrh, Rosin	Antiseptic, expectorant, antimicrobial
Saponins	Ginseng, Liquorice, Quillaja, Dioscorea	Expectorant, anti-inflammatory, adaptogen
Fixed Oils and	Castor oil, Olive oil, Cocoa	Laxative, emollient,

Chemical Group	Examples	Therapeutic Uses
Fats	butter, Coconut oil	moisturizing
Steroids	Diosgenin, Cardiac glycosides, Hecogenin	Hormone synthesis, cardiac stimulant
Flavonoids	Rutin, Hesperidin, Quercetin, Silymarin	Antioxidant, anti-inflammatory, venotonic
Proteins/Enzymes	Papain, Pepsin, Gelatin	Digestive aid, wound healing
Carbohydrates	Acacia gum, Tragacanth, Starch, Honey	Binding agent, demulcent, emollient, wound healing

Pharmacological Classification of Crude Drugs

Pharmacological classification categorizes crude drugs based on their physiological effects or therapeutic applications. This method is particularly useful for understanding the clinical and medicinal use of various crude drugs in treating different conditions or diseases. Each pharmacological class contains drugs that exert similar actions on specific body systems or functions.

1. Analgesics

Analgesics are drugs used to relieve pain. They can act on the central or peripheral nervous system to reduce the sensation of pain.

- **Examples**:
    - **Opium (Papaver somniferum)**: Contains morphine and codeine, which are potent pain relievers.
    - **Willow bark (Salix alba)**: Contains salicin, a precursor to aspirin, used to treat pain and inflammation.
    - **Capsicum (Capsicum frutescens)**: The active component capsaicin is used topically for its analgesic properties.

2. Antipyretics

Antipyretics are drugs used to reduce fever by acting on the hypothalamus to regulate body temperature.

- **Examples**:
  - **Willow bark (Salix alba)**: Contains salicin, which is converted to salicylic acid in the body and acts as an antipyretic.
  - **Feverfew (Tanacetum parthenium)**: Used to treat fevers and migraines due to its anti-inflammatory and fever-reducing effects.
  - **Quinine (Cinchona officinalis)**: Historically used to treat malaria-induced fever.

3. Anti-inflammatory Drugs

Anti-inflammatory drugs reduce inflammation by inhibiting the production of inflammatory mediators like prostaglandins.

- **Examples**:
  - **Turmeric (Curcuma longa)**: Contains curcumin, which has potent anti-inflammatory properties.
  - **Ginger (Zingiber officinale)**: Known for its anti-inflammatory effects, often used in the treatment of arthritis and other inflammatory conditions.
  - **Boswellia (Boswellia serrata)**: Used for its anti-inflammatory effects, particularly in treating arthritis and inflammatory bowel disease.

4. Antimalarial Drugs

Antimalarial drugs are used to prevent or treat malaria, a disease caused by *Plasmodium* parasites transmitted through mosquito bites.

- **Examples**:
  - **Quinine (Cinchona officinalis)**: One of the earliest antimalarial drugs, derived from the bark of the Cinchona tree.
  - **Artemisinin (Artemisia annua)**: A potent antimalarial agent used in combination therapies to treat malaria.
  - **Picrorhiza (Picrorhiza kurroa)**: Used traditionally in Ayurveda to treat malaria and other fevers.

5. Cardiotonics

Cardiotonics are drugs that strengthen heart contractions and are commonly used to treat heart failure and other heart-related conditions.

- **Examples:**
    - **Digitalis (Digitalis purpurea):** Contains cardiac glycosides such as digoxin and digitoxin, which are used to increase the force of heart contractions and treat heart failure.
    - **Strophanthus (Strophanthus kombe):** Contains cardiac glycosides used as a cardiotonic in treating heart conditions.
    - **Convallaria (Convallaria majalis):** Known as lily of the valley, it contains cardiac glycosides used to strengthen heart contractions.

6. Laxatives

Laxatives are substances that stimulate bowel movements and are used to treat constipation.

- **Examples:**
    - **Senna (Cassia angustifolia):** Contains anthraquinone glycosides, which act as stimulant laxatives.
    - **Isabgol (Plantago ovata):** The husk of the seeds is used as a bulk-forming laxative.
    - **Aloe (Aloe vera):** The latex contains anthraquinones, which have a stimulant laxative effect.

7. Expectorants

Expectorants are drugs that help in the expulsion of mucus from the respiratory tract by thinning the mucus, making it easier to cough up.

- **Examples:**
    - **Liquorice (Glycyrrhiza glabra):** Used for its expectorant properties to treat cough and respiratory infections.
    - **Vasaka (Adhatoda vasica):** Contains alkaloids like vasicine, which have expectorant and bronchodilator properties.

- o **Eucalyptus oil (Eucalyptus globulus)**: Used for its expectorant and decongestant properties in treating colds and respiratory infections.

8. Diuretics

Diuretics are drugs that promote the excretion of urine and are used to treat conditions like hypertension and fluid retention.

- **Examples:**
  - o **Dandelion (Taraxacum officinale)**: Used as a natural diuretic to reduce water retention and treat urinary disorders.
  - o **Juniper (Juniperus communis)**: Known for its diuretic properties and used in treating urinary tract infections and kidney stones.
  - o **Buchu (Agathosma betulina)**: Used as a diuretic and antiseptic in urinary tract infections.

9. Antiseptics

Antiseptics are substances that inhibit the growth of microorganisms and are used to prevent infections in wounds and on the skin.

- **Examples:**
  - o **Tea Tree oil (Melaleuca alternifolia)**: Known for its antiseptic and antimicrobial properties, widely used in treating skin infections.
  - o **Myrrh (Commiphora myrrha)**: Used as an antiseptic in oral care products and for wound healing.
  - o **Eucalyptus oil (Eucalyptus globulus)**: Contains antiseptic and antimicrobial properties, commonly used for respiratory infections.

10. Sedatives and Hypnotics

Sedatives and hypnotics are drugs that calm the nervous system, reduce anxiety, and induce sleep.

- **Examples:**

- o **Valerian (Valeriana officinalis)**: Used as a mild sedative and sleep aid due to its calming effects.
  - o **Hops (Humulus lupulus)**: Contains sedative properties, often used in combination with valerian to treat insomnia and anxiety.
  - o **Passionflower (Passiflora incarnata)**: Used for its sedative and anxiolytic properties.

11. Bronchodilators

Bronchodilators are drugs that relax the muscles in the airways, expanding the bronchi and improving airflow to the lungs. They are often used to treat asthma and other respiratory conditions.

- **Examples**:
  - o **Ephedra (Ephedra sinica)**: Contains ephedrine, used as a bronchodilator in treating asthma and bronchitis.
  - o **Lobelia (Lobelia inflata)**: Used for its bronchodilator properties to treat respiratory conditions like asthma.
  - o **Vasaka (Adhatoda vasica)**: Used for its bronchodilator and expectorant effects in treating respiratory conditions.

12. Antidiabetic Drugs

Antidiabetic drugs help to lower blood sugar levels in patients with diabetes.

- **Examples**:
  - o **Gymnema (Gymnema sylvestre)**: Known as the "sugar destroyer," it is used to manage diabetes by reducing the absorption of glucose in the intestines.
  - o **Bitter Melon (Momordica charantia)**: Contains compounds that have hypoglycemic effects and are used in managing blood sugar levels in diabetic patients.
  - o **Fenugreek (Trigonella foenum-graecum)**: Used to control blood sugar levels and improve insulin sensitivity.

13. Anthelmintics

Anthelmintics are drugs used to expel parasitic worms from the body, particularly from the intestines.

- **Examples**:
  - **Wormwood (Artemisia absinthium)**: Used for its anthelmintic properties to expel intestinal worms.
  - **Quassia (Quassia amara)**: Contains quassin, which is used as an anthelmintic to treat intestinal parasites.
  - **Pumpkin seeds (Cucurbita pepo)**: Used in traditional medicine as a natural remedy to expel intestinal parasites like tapeworms.

14. Emetics

Emetics are drugs used to induce vomiting, often in cases of poisoning.

- **Examples**:
  - **Ipecac (Cephaelis ipecacuanha)**: Used as an emetic to induce vomiting in cases of poisoning.
  - **Lobelia (Lobelia inflata)**: In large doses, it acts as an emetic and can be used to treat poisoning or to expel toxins.
  - **Senega (Polygala senega)**: Traditionally used as an emetic and expectorant.

15. Astringents

Astringents are substances that cause the contraction of body tissues, often used to reduce bleeding or treat skin conditions.

- **Examples**:
  - **Witch Hazel (Hamamelis virginiana)**: Used as an astringent in skin care products to reduce inflammation and treat minor skin irritations.
  - **Oak Bark (Quercus robur)**: Used for its astringent properties in treating diarrhea and skin inflammations.
  - **Catechu (Acacia catechu)**: Used as an astringent in treating diarrhea and in mouthwashes for oral health.

16. Antispasmodics

Antispasmodics are drugs that relieve muscle spasms, particularly in the digestive or respiratory tract.

- **Examples**:
    - **Belladonna (Atropa belladonna)**: Contains alkaloids like atropine, used as an antispasmodic in treating gastrointestinal and respiratory spasms.
    - **Hyoscyamus (Hyoscyamus niger)**: Used for its antispasmodic effects in treating gastrointestinal and urinary tract disorders.
    - **Peppermint (Mentha piperita)**: The oil is used as an antispasmodic in treating irritable bowel syndrome (IBS) and digestive spasms.

17. Antidiarrheals

Antidiarrheal drugs are used to treat diarrhea by reducing intestinal motility or absorbing excess fluid in the intestines.

- **Examples**:
    - **Bael (Aegle marmelos)**: Used for its antidiarrheal properties, especially in chronic diarrhea and dysentery.
    - **Pomegranate (Punica granatum)**: The fruit rind is used for its astringent and antidiarrheal effects.
    - **Catechu (Acacia catechu)**: Used as an antidiarrheal due to its astringent properties.

Summary of Pharmacological Classification:

Pharmacological Class	Examples	Therapeutic Uses
Analgesics	Opium, Willow bark, Capsicum	Pain relief
Antipyretics	Willow bark, Feverfew,	Fever reduction

Pharmacological Class	Examples	Therapeutic Uses
	Quinine	
Anti-inflammatory	Turmeric, Ginger, Boswellia	Reducing inflammation
Antimalarials	Quinine, Artemisinin, Picrorhiza	Treating malaria
Cardiotonics	Digitalis, Strophanthus, Convallaria	Strengthening heart contractions
Laxatives	Senna, Isabgol, Aloe	Treating constipation
Expectorants	Liquorice, Vasaka, Eucalyptus oil	Expelling mucus
Diuretics	Dandelion, Juniper, Buchu	Promoting urine excretion
Antiseptics	Tea Tree oil, Myrrh, Eucalyptus oil	Inhibiting the growth of microorganisms
Sedatives/Hypnotics	Valerian, Hops, Passionflower	Calming the nervous system, inducing sleep
Bronchodilators	Ephedra, Lobelia, Vasaka	Expanding airways, improving breathing
Antidiabetics	Gymnema, Bitter melon, Fenugreek	Managing diabetes, lowering blood sugar levels
Anthelmintics	Wormwood, Quassia, Pumpkin seeds	Expelling parasitic worms
Emetics	Ipecac, Lobelia, Senega	Inducing vomiting
Astringents	Witch Hazel, Oak Bark,	Reducing bleeding, tightening

Pharmacological Class	Examples	Therapeutic Uses
	Catechu	tissues
Antispasmodics	Belladonna, Hyoscyamus, Peppermint	Relieving muscle spasms
Antidiarrheals	Bael, Pomegranate, Catechu	Treating diarrhea

Chemo-taxonomical and Sero-taxonomical Classification of Crude Drugs

1. Chemo-taxonomical Classification of Crude Drugs

Chemo-taxonomy, also known as chemical taxonomy, classifies plants and other organisms based on their chemical constituents, particularly the secondary metabolites they produce. It combines principles of taxonomy (classification of organisms based on characteristics) with chemistry, focusing on the types and concentrations of biochemical compounds (such as alkaloids, glycosides, flavonoids, terpenes, and tannins) in plants.

This classification system helps in understanding the evolutionary relationships between different plant species, as chemical compounds are often conserved within plant families or genera. It also assists in drug identification and authentication based on chemical profiles.

Key Features of Chemo-taxonomy:

- **Chemical Constituents**: Crude drugs are classified based on their major chemical constituents like alkaloids, terpenoids, flavonoids, tannins, glycosides, etc.
- **Evolutionary Relationships**: Chemo-taxonomy is often used to understand the evolutionary relationships between plant species by analyzing their chemical profiles.

- **Medicinal Applications**: Plants with similar chemical compounds may have similar therapeutic applications.

Examples of Chemo-taxonomical Classification:

1. **Alkaloid-producing Plants**:
   - **Papaveraceae family (Poppy family)**:
     - **Opium (Papaver somniferum)**: Contains alkaloids like morphine and codeine, which are used as analgesics.
     - **Fumaria officinalis**: Contains isoquinoline alkaloids, used as a mild diuretic and to treat liver disorders.
   - **Solanaceae family (Nightshade family)**:
     - **Belladonna (Atropa belladonna)**: Contains tropane alkaloids like atropine, used as an anticholinergic.
     - **Tobacco (Nicotiana tabacum)**: Contains nicotine, a stimulant and addictive compound.

2. **Cardiac Glycoside-producing Plants**:
   - **Apocynaceae family (Dogbane family)**:
     - **Digitalis (Digitalis purpurea)**: Contains cardiac glycosides like digoxin and digitoxin, used in treating heart failure.
     - **Strophanthus (Strophanthus kombe)**: Contains strophanthin, a cardiac glycoside used to treat heart conditions.
   - **Scrophulariaceae family (Figwort family)**:
     - **Foxglove (Digitalis lanata)**: Another source of cardiac glycosides, used similarly to *Digitalis purpurea*.

3. **Flavonoid-producing Plants**:
   - **Rutaceae family (Citrus family)**:
     - **Citrus species (Citrus sinensis, Citrus aurantium)**: Contain flavonoids like hesperidin and naringin, which have antioxidant and vascular protective effects.

- o **Leguminosae family (Pea family)**:
  - ▪ **Glycyrrhiza glabra (Liquorice)**: Contains flavonoids and saponins with anti-inflammatory and expectorant properties.

4. **Terpenoid-producing Plants**:
   - o **Lamiaceae family (Mint family)**:
     - ▪ **Peppermint (Mentha piperita)**: Contains menthol, a terpenoid with carminative and cooling properties.
     - ▪ **Lavender (Lavandula angustifolia)**: Contains linalool and other terpenoids used for their calming and antimicrobial effects.
   - o **Apiaceae family (Carrot family)**:
     - ▪ **Fennel (Foeniculum vulgare)**: Contains anethole, a terpenoid with carminative and estrogenic properties.

Advantages of Chemo-taxonomy:

- **Identification**: Helps in the identification and authentication of crude drugs based on their chemical profile.
- **Evolutionary Insight**: Provides insights into the evolutionary relationships between plant species.
- **Drug Development**: Assists in the discovery of new drugs by targeting families or genera known to produce specific secondary metabolites.

2. Sero-taxonomical Classification of Crude Drugs

Sero-taxonomy, or serological taxonomy, is the classification of organisms (including crude drugs) based on the antigenic properties of proteins, usually by studying their reactions with specific antibodies. It relies on immunological techniques to classify plants, animals, or microbes based on their protein profiles.

Sero-taxonomy is less commonly used in the direct classification of crude drugs but is significant in distinguishing plant species or strains based on their protein or antigen profiles. It helps in identifying specific plant or animal sources for medicinal drugs by using antigen-antibody interactions.

Key Features of Sero-taxonomy:

- **Antigen-Antibody Reactions**: Sero-taxonomy uses serological methods to identify proteins in plants and animals by their reaction with specific antibodies.
- **Protein Analysis**: Plants or crude drugs are classified based on their protein or peptide content rather than their chemical constituents.
- **Specific Identification**: It helps differentiate closely related species or strains, especially when morphological or chemical distinctions are minimal.

Examples of Sero-taxonomical Classification:

1. **Distinction of Closely Related Species**:
   - **Digitalis species**: Sero-taxonomical methods can help differentiate between *Digitalis purpurea* and *Digitalis lanata*, which produce similar cardiac glycosides but differ slightly in protein content.
2. **Protein-based Differentiation**:
   - **Solanaceae family**: Sero-taxonomy can be used to differentiate between species of the Solanaceae family, such as *Atropa belladonna* (used for its tropane alkaloids) and *Datura stramonium*, even though they share similar chemical profiles.
3. **Authentication of Crude Drugs**:
   - **Ginseng Species**: Different species of ginseng (*Panax ginseng*, *Panax quinquefolius*) can be distinguished based on their protein and peptide profiles using serological methods.

Advantages of Sero-taxonomy:

- **Species Identification**: Sero-taxonomy can precisely identify and differentiate closely related species or varieties of medicinal plants.

- **Protein-based Classification**: It classifies plants or crude drugs based on their protein profiles, which may be distinct even in chemically similar species.
- **Quality Control**: Sero-taxonomy is useful in quality control, ensuring the correct species or strain of a plant or animal is used in drug preparation.

Summary of Chemo-taxonomical and Sero-taxonomical Classification:

Classification Type	Basis of Classification	Examples	Key Features
Chemo-taxonomy	Based on chemical constituents like alkaloids, glycosides, etc.	Alkaloid-producing plants: *Papaver somniferum* (morphine), *Atropa belladonna* (atropine)	Focuses on secondary metabolites (e.g., alkaloids, flavonoids) and provides insights into evolutionary relationships.
Sero-taxonomy	Based on antigen-antibody reactions to proteins or peptides	Differentiation of *Digitalis* species, *Atropa belladonna* vs. *Datura stramonium*, identification of ginseng species	Focuses on protein/peptide profiles using immunological techniques, useful for species identification and quality control of crude drugs.

CHAPTER – 3

ADULTERATION OF DRUGS OF NATURAL ORIGIN

INTRODUCTION:

Adulteration of drugs of natural origin refers to the practice of adding or substituting inferior or debased substances to natural drugs, thereby compromising their quality, purity, and efficacy. This is a significant issue in the pharmaceutical industry, especially for drugs derived from natural sources like plants, animals, or minerals.

Key Aspects of Adulteration:

1. **Types of Adulteration:**
   a. **Substitution:** Replacing the genuine drug with a similar-looking but less effective or entirely different substance. This could be intentional or accidental.
   b. **Spoilage:** Involves the degradation of the drug due to improper storage, leading to the presence of mold, bacteria, or other contaminants.
   c. **Inferior Quality:** Mixing the original drug with substances of lower quality or potency, thereby diluting its effectiveness.
   d. **Synthetic Additives:** Adding synthetic substances to increase the weight or volume of the drug, which can alter its intended medicinal effects.
   e. **False Claims:** Mislabeling or misrepresenting the drug in terms of its origin, quality, or potency.

2. **Reasons for Adulteration:**
   a. **Economic Gain:** The primary motive behind adulteration is often to increase profit margins by reducing the cost of production.

b. **Lack of Regulation:** In regions with poor regulatory oversight, the chances of adulteration increase as there are fewer checks on the quality of natural drugs.

c. **Scarcity of Resources:** When a particular natural drug is scarce, there is a higher likelihood of adulteration to meet demand.

3. **Consequences of Adulteration:**

a. **Health Risks:** Adulterated drugs can lead to adverse health effects, ranging from mild allergic reactions to severe poisoning or death.

b. **Loss of Efficacy:** Adulterated drugs may not provide the intended therapeutic effects, leading to treatment failures.

c. **Economic Impact:** The presence of adulterated drugs in the market can lead to a loss of consumer trust and financial losses for manufacturers who produce genuine products.

d. **Legal Implications:** Adulteration is illegal in most countries, and those found guilty may face significant penalties, including fines and imprisonment.

4. **Detection and Prevention:**

a. **Quality Control:** Rigorous testing of raw materials and finished products can help in detecting adulteration. Techniques like chromatography, spectroscopy, and microscopy are commonly used.

b. **Good Manufacturing Practices (GMP):** Adhering to GMP can minimize the risk of adulteration by ensuring the quality and purity of drugs throughout the production process.

c. **Regulatory Oversight:** Strong regulatory frameworks and regular inspections can deter the adulteration of natural drugs.

d. **Education and Awareness:** Educating consumers and healthcare professionals about the risks of adulterated drugs can help in early detection and prevention.

Examples of Adulteration in Natural Drugs:

1. **Substitution of Atropa belladonna (Deadly Nightshade) with Solanum nigrum (Black Nightshade):** Both plants look similar but have different pharmacological effects, leading to potential harm.

2. **Mixing of Cassia senna (True Senna) with Cassia angustifolia (Indian Senna):** The latter may have weaker laxative properties, leading to reduced efficacy.

DEFINITION OF ADULTERATION OF CRUDE DRUGS

Adulteration of crude drugs in the context of drugs of natural origin refers to the deliberate or unintentional process by which the quality and purity of these drugs are compromised. Crude drugs, which are unrefined substances obtained from natural sources like plants, animals, or minerals, may be adulterated through various methods, leading to a reduction in their therapeutic efficacy and safety.

Detailed Definition:

Adulteration of crude drugs involves the incorporation of foreign or inferior substances that are either completely different from the original drug or are of lower quality. This practice may occur at different stages of the supply chain, including during collection, processing, or storage. The primary aim of adulteration is often to increase profits, though it can also result from poor knowledge, lack of proper identification techniques, or inadequate regulatory oversight.

Key Elements of Adulteration in Crude Drugs:

1. **Substitution with Similar-Looking Substances:**
   a. Replacing the genuine crude drug with a cheaper, similar-looking material that lacks the desired therapeutic properties.
   b. For example, substituting **Digitalis purpurea** with **Digitalis lanata,** where the latter may contain different glycosides affecting its potency.

2. **Mixing with Inferior Quality Material:**
   a. Adding substances that are of lower quality or potency, thereby diluting the effectiveness of the drug.
   b. For instance, mixing high-quality **Cinchona bark** with an inferior species of **Cinchona.**

3. **Spoilage and Contamination:**
   a. The presence of foreign matter such as dirt, mold, or other contaminants that can arise due to improper storage conditions.
   b. Example: Storing **ginger** in a damp environment, leading to mold growth and a decline in its medicinal properties.

4. **Use of Synthetic Chemicals:**
   a. Adding synthetic chemicals or artificial substances to mimic the appearance or increase the weight of the crude drug.
   b. For example, adding artificial colorants to turmeric to enhance its yellow color.

5. **Partial Substitution:**
   a. A part of the genuine drug is replaced with a different, often cheaper, substance while still retaining some of the original material.
   b. An example would be mixing powdered bark of a valuable tree with that of a cheaper, non-medicinal tree.

6. **Intentional Mislabeling:**
   a. Labeling and selling a crude drug under a false name, which can mislead consumers and healthcare providers.
   b. For example, selling **Valeriana officinalis** (Valerian) under the name of **Withania somnifera** (Ashwagandha).

Reasons for Adulteration:

1. **Economic Gain:** Manufacturers or suppliers may adulterate crude drugs to increase their profits by reducing production costs.

2. **Scarcity of Resources:** When the authentic drug is scarce or difficult to obtain, adulteration may be used to meet market demand.

3. **Lack of Regulatory Enforcement:** In areas with weak regulations, adulteration can occur more frequently due to the absence of stringent checks and balances.

4. **Inadequate Identification Skills:** Collectors and processors may unintentionally adulterate crude drugs due to the misidentification of plant or animal species.

Impact of Adulteration on Crude Drugs:

1. **Loss of Therapeutic Efficacy:** The presence of adulterants can diminish the intended medicinal effects of the drug.

2. **Health Risks:** Consumers may experience adverse reactions or toxicity due to the presence of harmful substances.

3. **Decreased Consumer Trust:** The reputation of natural medicines can be tarnished, leading to a loss of trust among consumers.

4. **Legal Consequences:** Adulteration is illegal and can lead to severe penalties, including fines and imprisonment.

CLASSIFICATION WITH EXAMPLES OF CRUDE DRUGS

Adulteration of crude drugs can be classified based on the methods or practices used to adulterate them. Understanding these classifications helps in identifying and preventing the adulteration of drugs of natural origin.

Classification of Adulteration of Crude Drugs:

1. **Substitution Adulteration:**

   a. **Deliberate Substitution:** The genuine crude drug is intentionally replaced with another substance that may or may not resemble the original drug. This is often done to reduce costs or due to the scarcity of the authentic drug.

      i. **Example: Atropa belladonna** (Deadly Nightshade) being substituted with **Solanum nigrum** (Black Nightshade).

While both plants look similar, they have different alkaloid profiles and therapeutic effects.

b. **Accidental Substitution:** Occurs when the collector or supplier unintentionally substitutes the drug due to misidentification or lack of knowledge.

  i. **Example: Curcuma longa** (Turmeric) being confused with **Curcuma zedoaria** (White Turmeric), which has different medicinal properties.

2. **Inferior Quality Adulteration:**

a. In this type of adulteration, the drug is mixed with materials of inferior quality, resulting in a reduction in its potency and effectiveness.

b. **Example:** Mixing high-quality **Cinchona bark** with inferior bark from a different **Cinchona** species that contains lower amounts of quinine.

3. **Exhausted Drug Adulteration:**

a. **Exhausted drugs** are those from which the active constituents have been partially or wholly removed by previous extraction processes. These exhausted drugs are then mixed with fresh drugs to increase bulk.

b. **Example: Clove** buds that have had their volatile oil removed are mixed with fresh clove buds to increase weight and volume, thus adulterating the product.

4. **Adulteration with Artificially Manufactured Substances:**

a. This involves adding synthetic or artificial substances that mimic the physical appearance or increase the weight of the crude drug.

b. **Example:** Adding artificial colorants to **saffron** (Crocus sativus) to enhance its appearance, or adding starch or chalk to **morphine** powder to increase its weight.

5. **Adulteration with Non-Drug Components:**

   a. In this type of adulteration, the drug is mixed with foreign matter, such as dust, sand, stones, or other non-drug substances, to increase its weight or volume.

   b. **Example: Senna** leaves mixed with foreign leaves, dirt, and sand to increase the bulk, reducing the overall quality and efficacy of the product.

6. **Substitution with Superficially Similar Drugs:**

   a. This occurs when a drug is replaced with another substance that closely resembles the original in appearance but differs in chemical composition and therapeutic properties.

   b. **Example: Rhizome of Curcuma longa** (Turmeric) substituted with **Curcuma aromatica** (Wild Turmeric), which has different therapeutic properties.

7. **Chemical Adulteration:**

   a. In this type, the crude drug is adulterated by the addition of chemicals that alter its appearance, smell, or weight.

   b. **Example:** Adding lead salts to **black pepper** to increase its weight, which can be toxic and hazardous to health.

8. **Adulteration by Addition of Harmful Substances:**

   a. Sometimes, harmful substances are added to crude drugs, either intentionally or accidentally, that can pose serious health risks.

   b. **Example: Poppy capsules** (Papaver somniferum) mixed with **opium** adulterated with materials like talc or sand to increase weight, posing health risks to users.

Specific Examples of Adulterated Crude Drugs:

1. **Powdered Drugs:**

   a. **Example: Powdered ginger** mixed with flour or chalk to increase bulk.

b. **Example: Powdered opium** adulterated with clay or brick powder.

2. **Gums and Resins:**
   a. **Example: Gum Arabic** adulterated with inferior quality gums like **Gum Ghatti.**
   b. **Example: Myrrh** adulterated with similar-looking but less effective resins.

3. **Leaves:**
   a. **Example: Senna** leaves adulterated with non-medicinal leaves that resemble the original.
   b. **Example: Datura** leaves substituted with **Ailanthus** leaves, which can be toxic.

4. **Barks:**
   a. **Example: Cinchona** bark adulterated with bark from non-medicinal trees.
   b. **Example: Cinnamon** bark adulterated with inferior quality **Cassia** bark.

5. **Roots and Rhizomes:**
   a. **Example: Ginseng** root adulterated with cheaper roots like **Siberian Ginseng** (Eleutherococcus senticosus), which is not true ginseng.
   b. **Example: Turmeric** rhizome adulterated with colored powders or other rhizomes like **Zedoary.**

Adulteration Concerns:

1. **Substitution with Inferior or Non-Medicinal Materials:**
   a. **Risk:** Powdered opium may be adulterated with other plant materials, soil, or synthetic substances to increase weight and volume.

b. **Effect:** This reduces the concentration of active alkaloids, leading to decreased analgesic and therapeutic effects, which can be dangerous in pain management.

2. **Adulteration with Synthetic Opioids:**
   a. **Risk:** In some cases, synthetic opioids may be added to opium to enhance its potency or mimic its effects.
   b. **Effect:** The use of synthetic opioids increases the risk of overdose, dependence, and other serious adverse effects.

3. **Dilution with Inert Substances:**
   a. **Risk:** Powdered opium may be mixed with inert substances like talc, flour, or other powders to increase bulk.
   b. **Effect:** This dilution significantly reduces the efficacy of opium, particularly in pain management, where accurate dosing is critical.

Multiple Choice Questions (MCQs) - Objective

1. Which of the following is a primary active constituent of Atropa belladonna?
   A) Curcumin
   B) Atropine
   C) Quinine
   D) Ginsenoside

2. What is the primary pharmacological action of sennosides found in Senna leaves?
   A) Anti-inflammatory
   B) Antioxidant
   C) Stimulant laxative
   D) Antimicrobial

3. Which substance is commonly used to adulterate powdered ginger?
   A) Flour

B) Quinine

C) Curcumin

D) Cinnamaldehyde

4. Which drug of natural origin is often adulterated with Solanum nigrum?

A) Turmeric

B) Atropa belladonna

C) Senna

D) Myrrh

5. Which is the primary active compound responsible for the therapeutic effects of Curcuma longa (Turmeric)?

A) Atropine

B) Quinine

C) Curcumin

D) Ginsenoside

6. What is the main reason for adulterating drugs of natural origin?

A) To improve therapeutic efficacy

B) Economic gain

C) To increase purity

D) To reduce toxicity

7. Which method is commonly used to detect adulteration in natural drugs?

A) Chromatography

B) Surgery

C) Radiation therapy

D) Ultrasonography

8. Which active compound is primarily responsible for the antimicrobial properties of Myrrh?

A) Cinnamaldehyde

B) Curcumin

C) Furanosesquiterpenes

D) Atropine

9. What is the main therapeutic use of quinine derived from Cinchona bark?

A) Laxative

B) Antimalarial

C) Analgesic

D) Anti-inflammatory

10. Which of the following is an example of chemical adulteration in natural drugs?

A) Substitution with non-medicinal parts

B) Addition of synthetic chemicals

C) Substitution with lower-quality materials

D) Mislabeling of products

11. What is the key active component in Gum Arabic that contributes to its emulsifying properties?

A) Ginsenoside

B) Crocin

C) Arabinogalactan

D) Eugenol

12. Which natural drug is most commonly associated with the adulteration of lead salts to increase its weight?

A) Black Pepper

B) Ginger

C) Opium

D) Saffron

13. Which pharmacological action is associated with Datura due to its tropane alkaloid content?

A) Anticholinergic

B) Antiviral

C) Antioxidant

D) Antihistamine

14. Which of the following is an example of adulteration by substitution with a superficially similar drug?

    A) Rhizome of Curcuma longa substituted with Curcuma aromatica

    B) Adding lead salts to black pepper

    C) Mixing cassia bark with cinnamon

    D) Adulterating ginseng with fillers

15. What is the primary use of atropine found in Atropa belladonna?

    A) Antipyretic

    B) Antispasmodic

    C) Antidiabetic

    D) Antihypertensive

16. Which of the following is a common adulterant used in powdered opium?

    A) Synthetic dyes

    B) Flour

    C) Talc or clay

    D) Turmeric

17. What is the therapeutic effect of ginsenosides found in Ginseng?

    A) Adaptogenic

    B) Antiviral

    C) Antipyretic

    D) Antihistaminic

18. What type of adulteration is common with Cinchona bark?

    A) Substitution with other barks

    B) Addition of artificial flavors

    C) Substitution with non-drug components

    D) Use of synthetic curcumin

19. Which active compound in saffron contributes to its antioxidant properties?

    A) Crocin

B) Atropine

C) Sennosides

D) Cinnamaldehyde

20. What is the effect of adding synthetic dyes to turmeric?

A) Enhances therapeutic effects

B) Increases bulk and weight

C) Improves color appearance

D) Reduces toxicity

Short Answer Type Questions (Subjective)

1. Explain the primary reason for adulteration of drugs of natural origin.
2. Describe the pharmacological actions of quinine derived from Cinchona bark.
3. What are the potential health risks associated with the adulteration of natural drugs?
4. How does curcumin contribute to the pharmacological effects of turmeric?
5. Discuss the impact of adulteration on the efficacy and safety of natural drugs.
6. What are the methods used to detect adulteration in natural drugs?
7. Explain the therapeutic uses of atropine found in Atropa belladonna.
8. Describe the consequences of adulterating Senna leaves with non-medicinal leaves.
9. What is the role of ginsenosides in the adaptogenic effects of Ginseng?
10. How does gum arabic function as an emulsifying agent?
11. Explain the impact of adulteration with synthetic chemicals on the therapeutic efficacy of natural drugs.
12. What are the primary active constituents of Datura and their pharmacological actions?
13. Discuss the potential dangers of adulteration in powdered opium.

14. How does substitution with Curcuma aromatica affect the therapeutic efficacy of Curcuma longa?

15. What are the pharmacological actions of cinnamaldehyde found in cinnamon?

16. Describe the risks associated with adulteration of saffron with synthetic dyes.

17. What is the therapeutic significance of the anti-inflammatory effects of ginger?

18. How can regulatory oversight help prevent the adulteration of natural drugs?

19. Discuss the consequences of adulteration with synthetic ginsenosides in Ginseng products.

20. What is the pharmacological importance of furanosesquiterpenes found in Myrrh?

Long Answer Type Questions (Subjective)

1. Discuss in detail the various types of adulteration in drugs of natural origin, providing examples for each type.

2. Explain the pharmacological actions, therapeutic uses, and potential adulteration concerns related to Atropa belladonna.

3. Describe the pharmacological properties and therapeutic applications of Ginseng, and discuss the impact of adulteration on its efficacy.

4. Analyze the consequences of adulteration in turmeric, focusing on its pharmacological effects, therapeutic uses, and common adulterants.

5. Discuss the role of Cinchona bark in the treatment of malaria and the potential risks associated with its adulteration.

6. Describe the pharmacological effects of sennosides in Senna leaves and the impact of adulteration on their therapeutic efficacy.

7. Explain the therapeutic applications of Myrrh and the potential consequences of its adulteration on its pharmacological properties.

8. Discuss the challenges and methods involved in detecting adulteration in natural drugs, with a focus on chromatography and other techniques.

9. Analyze the pharmacological importance of curcumin in turmeric and discuss the risks associated with its adulteration.

10. Discuss the significance of quality control and regulatory oversight in preventing the adulteration of drugs of natural origin.

Answer Key for MCQs

1. (B) Atropine
2. (C) Stimulant laxative
3. (A) Flour
4. (B) Atropa belladonn
5. (C) Curcumin
6. (B) Economic gain
7. (A) Chromatography
8. (C) Furanosesquiterpenes
9. (B) Antimalarial
10. (B) Addition of synthetic chemicals
11. (C) Arabinogalactan
12. (A) Black Pepper
13. (A) Anticholinergic
14. (A) Rhizome of Curcuma longa substituted with Curcuma aromatica
15. (B) Antispasmodic
16. (C) Talc or clay
17. (A) Adaptogenic
18. (A) Substitution with other barks
19. (A) Crocin
20. (C) Improves color appearance

CHAPTER – 4

EVALUATION OF CRUDE DRUG

INTRODUCTION:

Evaluating crude drugs is a crucial step in ensuring their quality, efficacy, and safety. This process involves various stages and techniques to assess the physical, chemical, and biological characteristics of plant and animal-derived substances used in medicine. Here's a detailed introduction to the evaluation of crude drugs:

1. Definition and Importance

Crude drugs are natural substances derived from plants, animals, or minerals used in traditional and modern medicine. Evaluating these drugs is essential to confirm their identity, potency, and purity, which directly impacts their therapeutic effectiveness and safety.

2. Types of Evaluation

a. Macroscopic Examination

   i.   **Appearance**: Color, size, shape, and texture.

  ii.   **Odor and Taste**: These can provide initial clues about the drug's identity and quality.

b. Microscopic Examination

   i.   **Histological Features**: Identification of characteristic tissue structures and cell types.

  ii.   **Qualitative Analysis**: Identifying specific types of cells or tissues, such as trichomes in plant drugs.

c. Chemical Evaluation

   i.   **Chemical Tests**: Reactions that confirm the presence of specific compounds.

ii. **Chromatographic Techniques**: Thin-layer chromatography (TLC), high-performance liquid chromatography (HPLC), and gas chromatography (GC) are used to separate and identify compounds.

iii. **Spectroscopic Methods**: UV-Visible, IR, NMR, and mass spectrometry to analyze chemical constituents.

d. Physical Evaluation

i. **Moisture Content**: Determines if the drug has been properly dried and preserved.

ii. **Ash Values**: Total ash and acid-insoluble ash help assess purity and the presence of contaminants.

iii. **Extractive Values**: The amount of extractable material with different solvents can indicate the drug's quality.

e. Biological Evaluation

i. **Pharmacological Testing**: Assessing the biological activity of the drug to ensure it has the desired effects.

ii. **Toxicity Studies**: Evaluating the safety profile of the drug.

3. Standards and Guidelines

a. **Pharmacopoeias**: Such as the USP, BP, or EP, provide standardized methods for evaluating crude drugs.

b. **Regulatory Guidelines**: Ensure compliance with safety, efficacy, and quality standards set by health authorities.

4. Challenges in Evaluation

a. **Variability**: Natural drugs can vary in composition due to factors like geography, climate, and cultivation practices.

b. **Contamination**: Crude drugs may be contaminated with pesticides, heavy metals, or adulterants.

5. Documentation and Reporting

a. **Record-Keeping**: Detailed documentation of all evaluations and tests conducted.

b. **Reporting**: Clear and comprehensive reports on the findings and any deviations from standard quality.

6. Applications

a. **Quality Control**: Ensuring that crude drugs meet the required standards before use in pharmaceutical formulations.

b. **Research and Development**: Identifying new drugs and improving existing ones.

DEFINITION OF EVALUATION OF CRUDE DRUGS

Evaluation of crude drugs refers to the systematic process of assessing the quality, identity, purity, and potency of raw plant, animal, or mineral substances used in medicinal preparations. This process is essential to ensure that these natural substances meet the required standards for efficacy, safety, and consistency before they are utilized in pharmaceutical formulations or therapeutic applications.

Key Aspects of Evaluation:

1. **Identity**: Confirming that the crude drug is what it claims to be. This involves verifying the botanical or zoological origin and ensuring the drug has not been substituted with a different substance.

2. **Quality**: Assessing the overall characteristics and attributes of the crude drug, including its physical, chemical, and biological properties. Quality evaluation ensures that the drug is consistent with its standard specifications and free from contaminants.

3. **Purity**: Determining the absence of adulterants, contaminants, or foreign substances. Purity assessment includes identifying and quantifying any impurities or extraneous materials that may affect the drug's safety and efficacy.

4. **Potency**: Evaluating the drug's effectiveness by measuring its active constituent levels or pharmacological activity. This helps ensure that the drug delivers the intended therapeutic effects.

5. **Consistency**: Ensuring uniformity in the drug's characteristics across different batches. Consistency is critical for maintaining the reliability and reproducibility of the drug's performance.

Methods of Evaluation:

a. **Macroscopic and Microscopic Examination**: Observing physical characteristics and cellular structures.

b. **Chemical Analysis**: Using techniques like chromatography and spectroscopy to identify and quantify chemical constituents.

c. **Physical Testing**: Measuring parameters such as moisture content, ash values, and extractive values.

d. **Biological Testing**: Assessing pharmacological and toxicological effects to confirm the drug's efficacy and safety.

TYPES OF EVALUATION OF CRUDE DRUGS

Evaluating crude drugs involves several methods to assess their quality, purity, identity, and potency. These methods can be broadly categorized into macroscopic, microscopic, chemical, physical, and biological evaluations. Each type of evaluation provides crucial information about the crude drug and ensures its suitability for medicinal use.

1. Macroscopic Evaluation

a. **Appearance**: Examining the drug's physical attributes such as color, size, shape, and texture. This helps in initial identification and comparison with standard descriptions.

b. **Odor and Taste**: Assessing the characteristic smell and taste of the drug, which can aid in confirming its identity and detecting any potential adulteration.

2. Microscopic Evaluation

a. **Histological Features**: Analyzing the drug under a microscope to identify specific tissue structures, cell types, and other microscopic characteristics unique to the drug.

b. **Qualitative Analysis**: Identifying particular cells, tissues, or structures that are characteristic of the crude drug. This can include trichomes, starch grains, or oil cells.

3. Chemical Evaluation

a. **Chemical Tests**: Performing specific reactions to confirm the presence of key chemical constituents. These tests can be qualitative or quantitative and may involve color reactions, precipitation, or solubility tests.

b. **Chromatographic Techniques**:

    i. **Thin-Layer Chromatography (TLC)**: Separates compounds based on their affinity to a stationary phase and a mobile phase, allowing for the identification of individual constituents.

    ii. **High-Performance Liquid Chromatography (HPLC)**: Provides precise separation and quantification of chemical compounds in a liquid sample.

    iii. **Gas Chromatography (GC)**: Used for volatile compounds, separating them based on their interaction with a stationary phase and a carrier gas.

c. **Spectroscopic Methods**:

    i. **UV-Visible Spectroscopy**: Analyzes compounds based on their absorption of ultraviolet or visible light.

    ii. **Infrared (IR) Spectroscopy**: Identifies functional groups based on the absorption of infrared light.

    iii. **Nuclear Magnetic Resonance (NMR) Spectroscopy**: Provides detailed information on the molecular structure of compounds.

    iv. **Mass Spectrometry (MS)**: Determines the molecular weight and structure of compounds by analyzing their mass-to-charge ratio.

4. Physical Evaluation

a. **Moisture Content**: Measures the amount of water present in the crude drug, which affects its stability and shelf life.

b. **Ash Values**:

    i. **Total Ash**: Measures the inorganic residue remaining after combustion, indicating the presence of non-volatile inorganic substances.

    ii. **Acid-Insoluble Ash**: Measures the residue after treatment with acid, helping to assess the presence of silica or other impurities.

c. **Extractive Values**: Quantifies the amount of material extracted using different solvents, which can provide information about the drug's composition and quality.

5. Biological Evaluation

a. **Pharmacological Testing**: Evaluates the biological activity of the crude drug by testing its effects on living organisms or cells. This includes assessing therapeutic efficacy and action mechanisms.

b. **Toxicity Studies**: Determines the safety profile of the crude drug by identifying any potential toxic effects or adverse reactions.

ORGANOLEPTIC METHODS AND PROPERTIES

Organoleptic evaluation involves assessing the sensory attributes of crude drugs, including their appearance, odor, taste, and texture. This method provides preliminary information about the identity and quality of a crude drug and helps in its initial characterization. Here's a detailed look at how organoleptic methods and properties are used in evaluating crude drugs:

1. Appearance

a. **Color**: The color of the crude drug can be an important identifying feature. For example, the yellowish color of turmeric or the greenish hue of certain leaves can be used to confirm the drug's identity.

b. **Size and Shape**: The dimensions and form of the drug, such as the size of plant parts or the shape of seeds, can help differentiate between similar substances.

c. **Texture**: The texture of the drug, such as whether it is smooth, rough, or fibrous, can provide clues about its type and quality.

2. Odor

a. **Characteristic Smell**: Each crude drug has a distinctive odor that can be used for identification. For instance, ginger has a pungent aroma, while cinnamon has a warm, spicy scent.

b. **Consistency**: Evaluating whether the odor is consistent with what is expected from the drug can help detect possible adulteration or degradation.

3. Taste

a. **Flavor Profile**: The taste of the drug can be used to identify it and assess its quality. For example, the bitter taste of certain medicinal herbs like quinine can be indicative of its authenticity.

b. **Taste Consistency**: Changes in taste may suggest that the drug has been adulterated or improperly stored.

4. Texture and Consistency

a. **Surface Texture**: The feel of the drug, whether it is gritty, smooth, or sticky, can help in its identification. For example, powdered drugs should have a fine, consistent texture.

b. **Consistency**: For semi-solid drugs or extracts, evaluating the consistency (e.g., thick, pasty, or liquid) can indicate proper preparation and quality.

Applications of Organoleptic Evaluation

a. **Preliminary Identification**: Organoleptic properties provide initial clues about the crude drug's identity, which can be useful before more sophisticated analytical methods are applied.

b. **Quality Assessment**: Changes in organoleptic properties can signal issues with the drug's quality, such as degradation, contamination, or adulteration.

c. **Consistency Check**: Comparing the sensory attributes of different batches of the same drug ensures consistency and reliability in the drug's characteristics.

Limitations

a. **Subjectivity**: Organoleptic evaluation is subjective and can vary between individuals. It relies on personal perception and experience.

b. **Sensitivity**: This method may not detect subtle adulterations or changes in quality that are not perceptible through sensory evaluation alone.

MICROSCOPIC METHODS AND PROPERTIES

Microscopic evaluation involves examining crude drugs under a microscope to identify and analyze their internal structures and cellular components. This method provides detailed information about the drug's botanical or zoological origin, which is crucial for confirming its identity and ensuring its quality. Here's a detailed overview of how microscopic methods are used in the evaluation of crude drugs:

1. Types of Microscopic Examination

a. Light Microscopy

i. **General Microscopy**: Uses visible light and optical lenses to view the drug's structure. It helps in identifying key features such as cell types, tissue structures, and the overall organization of plant or animal tissues.

ii. **Histological Examination**: Involves the study of tissue samples to identify specific anatomical features. For example, the presence of certain types of cells or structures, such as trichomes or oil cells in plant drugs.

b. Scanning Electron Microscopy (SEM)

i. **Surface Analysis**: Provides high-resolution images of the drug's surface, revealing details about texture and morphology. SEM is useful for examining the surface features of powders or extracts.

ii. **Structural Details**: Offers insights into the surface structure and arrangement of particles, which can help in detecting adulteration or processing errors.

c. Transmission Electron Microscopy (TEM)

i. **Ultrastructural Analysis**: Allows for the visualization of internal structures at the cellular and subcellular levels. TEM is used for detailed examination of cellular components and organelles in plant or animal tissues.

2. Microscopic Properties of Crude Drugs

a. Cellular Structures

i. **Cell Walls**: Observing the thickness and composition of cell walls can help identify plant tissues. For example, the presence of lignified cell walls in certain plant parts.

ii. **Starch Granules**: Identifying the shape, size, and arrangement of starch granules can be important for confirming the identity of starch-containing drugs.

b. Specific Structures

i. **Trichomes**: Hair-like structures on plants that can be glandular or non-glandular. They may be important for identifying specific plant species or detecting adulteration.

ii. **Oil Cells**: Specialized cells containing essential oils or resins, important for confirming the identity and quality of aromatic or medicinal plants.

c. Tissue Types

i. **Xylem and Phloem**: Vascular tissues in plants that transport water and nutrients. Their presence and arrangement can help in identifying plant drugs.

ii. **Epidermal Cells**: The outer layer of cells in plants that provides protection. Changes or abnormalities in these cells can indicate adulteration or quality issues.

3. Applications of Microscopic Evaluation

a. Identification

    i. **Botanical Identification**: Helps confirm the plant species or part used, ensuring the drug is genuine and not substituted with a similar-looking but different substance.

    ii. **Quality Control**: Detects adulteration, contamination, or processing defects by comparing observed structures with standard references.

b. Authentication

    i. **Standardization**: Ensures that the crude drug matches the characteristics described in pharmacopoeias or monographs, which include detailed microscopic descriptions.

c. Detection of Adulterants

    i. **Foreign Materials**: Identifies unwanted substances or contaminants that may be present in the crude drug, such as extraneous plant parts or synthetic materials.

PHYSICAL METHODS AND PROPERTIES

Physical evaluation of crude drugs involves assessing their physical attributes and characteristics to ensure quality, consistency, and suitability for use. These methods provide important information about the drug's purity, stability, and overall quality. Here's a detailed overview of physical methods and properties used in the evaluation of crude drugs:

1. Moisture Content

    a. **Importance**: Moisture content affects the drug's stability, shelf life, and susceptibility to microbial growth.

    b. **Methods**:

        i. **Gravimetric Method**: Weighing the drug before and after drying to determine the moisture content.

        ii. **Karl Fischer Titration**: A precise method for measuring moisture content using a chemical reaction.

2. Ash Values

    a. **Total Ash**:

        i. **Importance**: Indicates the amount of inorganic residue remaining after combustion. It provides insight into the amount of non-volatile inorganic matter.

        ii. **Method**: Burning the drug at high temperatures and measuring the residual ash.

    b. **Acid-Insoluble Ash**:

        i. **Importance**: Measures the portion of ash that is insoluble in acid, which can help in identifying the presence of silica or other impurities.

        ii. **Method**: Treating the ash with dilute acid and measuring the residue left behind.

    c. **Water-Soluble Ash**:

        i. **Importance**: Determines the amount of ash that dissolves in water, which can indicate the presence of water-soluble inorganic salts.

        ii. **Method**: Dissolving the ash in water and measuring the soluble residue.

3. Extractive Values

    a. **Purpose**: Provides information about the quantity of extractable substances in the crude drug using different solvents. It helps in assessing the drug's composition and quality.

    b. **Methods**:

        i. **Cold Extraction**: Soaking the drug in solvents at room temperature and measuring the extracted material.

        ii. **Hot Extraction**: Boiling the drug in solvents and measuring the extracted material. Common solvents include ethanol, water, and chloroform.

4. Particle Size and Distribution

   a. **Importance**: Affects the drug's solubility, dissolution rate, and bioavailability.

   b. **Methods**:

   i. **Sieve Analysis**: Using a series of sieves with different mesh sizes to determine the size distribution of particles.

   ii. **Laser Diffraction**: Analyzing particle size based on the scattering of laser light by the particles.

5. Bulk Density and Tapped Density

   a. **Bulk Density**:

   i. **Importance**: Measures the mass of the drug per unit volume, including the void spaces between particles. It provides information about the drug's packing characteristics.

   ii. **Method**: Weighing a known volume of the drug.

   b. **Tapped Density**:

   i. **Importance**: Measures the maximum packing density of the drug after tapping to remove air gaps.

   ii. **Method**: Tapping a container filled with the drug and measuring the volume change.

6. Solubility

   a. **Importance**: Determines the extent to which the drug dissolves in various solvents, which affects its formulation and therapeutic effectiveness.

   b. **Method**: Testing the drug's solubility in solvents like water, ethanol, or oils under specific conditions (e.g., temperature).

7. Color and Odor

   a. **Color**:

   i. **Importance**: The color of the drug can provide initial information about its identity and quality.

ii. **Method**: Comparing the color with standard references or using colorimeters for quantitative measurement.

b. **Odor**:

i. **Importance**: The characteristic smell of the drug can aid in its identification and quality assessment.

ii. **Method**: Sensory evaluation by trained personnel or using odor-detection equipment.

8. Texture and Consistency

a. **Texture**:

i. **Importance**: Evaluating the feel and consistency of the drug (e.g., gritty, smooth, or fibrous) helps in assessing its quality.

ii. **Method**: Sensory evaluation or using texture analyzers for quantitative measurements.

b. **Consistency**:

i. **Importance**: For semi-solid or liquid drugs, consistency measurements (e.g., viscosity) are important for proper formulation and application.

ii. **Method**: Using viscometers or rheometers to measure the drug's consistency.

Applications of Physical Evaluation

a. **Quality Control**: Ensures that the drug meets the required standards for physical properties.

b. **Standardization**: Helps in establishing consistent specifications for the drug across different batches.

c. **Identification**: Assists in confirming the drug's identity based on its physical characteristics.

CHEMICAL METHODS AND PROPERTIES

Chemical evaluation of crude drugs involves analyzing their chemical composition and properties to confirm their identity, purity, and quality. This evaluation helps ensure that the drug contains the correct active constituents and is free from contaminants or adulterants. Here's a detailed overview of the chemical methods and properties used in evaluating crude drugs:

1. Chemical Tests

a. Preliminary Chemical Tests

    i.   **Purpose**: To quickly identify the presence of specific chemical groups or constituents in the crude drug.

    ii.   **Examples**:

        1. **Color Reactions**: Specific color changes in response to reagents can indicate the presence of certain compounds (e.g., the presence of alkaloids or flavonoids).

        2. **Precipitation Tests**: Formation of precipitates when reagents are added can help identify certain chemical constituents (e.g., tannins forming complexes with iron salts).

b. Confirmatory Tests

    i.   **Purpose**: To provide more specific evidence for the presence of key active constituents.

    ii.   **Examples**:

        1. **Alkaloids**: Dragendorff's reagent or Mayer's reagent to form characteristic color reactions.

        2. **Saponins**: Froth test to detect foam formation in aqueous solutions.

2. Chromatographic Techniques

a. Thin-Layer Chromatography (TLC)

    i.   **Purpose**: To separate and identify compounds based on their affinity to a stationary phase and a mobile phase.

    ii.   **Method**: Applying a sample to a coated plate and developing it in a solvent system. The separated compounds are visualized using UV light or chemical sprays.

b. High-Performance Liquid Chromatography (HPLC)

i. **Purpose**: To separate, quantify, and identify compounds in a liquid sample with high precision.

ii. **Method**: Using a liquid mobile phase to pass the sample through a chromatographic column and measuring the retention time of each component.

c. Gas Chromatography (GC)

i. **Purpose**: To analyze volatile compounds by separating them based on their interaction with a stationary phase and carrier gas.

ii. **Method**: Injecting the sample into a chromatograph, where compounds are separated and detected based on their retention times and peaks.

3. Spectroscopic Methods

a. Ultraviolet-Visible (UV-Vis) Spectroscopy

i. **Purpose**: To identify and quantify compounds based on their absorption of ultraviolet or visible light.

ii. **Method**: Measuring the absorbance of the sample at specific wavelengths to identify characteristic peaks corresponding to different compounds.

b. Infrared (IR) Spectroscopy

i. **Purpose**: To identify functional groups and molecular structures based on their absorption of infrared light.

ii. **Method**: Recording the absorption spectrum of the sample, which provides information about functional groups and molecular bonds.

c. Nuclear Magnetic Resonance (NMR) Spectroscopy

i. **Purpose**: To determine the detailed molecular structure of compounds based on their interaction with a magnetic field.

ii. **Method**: Analyzing the NMR spectrum to identify chemical environments and functional groups within the molecule.

d. Mass Spectrometry (MS)

i. **Purpose**: To determine the molecular weight and structure of compounds by analyzing their mass-to-charge ratio.

ii. **Method**: Ionizing the sample and measuring the resulting ions to identify and quantify different compounds.

4. Chemical Properties

a. pH Value

i. **Purpose**: To measure the acidity or alkalinity of the crude drug, which can affect its stability and activity.

ii. **Method**: Using a pH meter or pH indicator paper to determine the drug's pH.

b. Solubility

i. **Purpose**: To assess the extent to which the drug dissolves in various solvents, which is important for its formulation and activity.

ii. **Method**: Testing the drug's solubility in solvents like water, ethanol, or oils under specific conditions.

c. Chemical Constituents

i. **Purpose**: To identify and quantify specific active or marker compounds in the crude drug.

ii. **Method**: Using analytical techniques like TLC, HPLC, or GC to measure the concentration of key constituents.

5. Applications of Chemical Evaluation

a. **Identity Confirmation**: Ensures that the crude drug matches the specified chemical profile for the intended use.

b. **Purity Assessment**: Detects impurities, contaminants, or adulterants that could affect the drug's quality.

c. **Quality Control**: Establishes standard specifications for the drug's chemical composition to ensure consistency across different batches.

Limitations

a. **Complexity**: Some chemical methods require sophisticated equipment and technical expertise.

b. **Interference**: Other substances in the drug may interfere with the analysis, leading to potential inaccuracies.

BIOLOGICAL METHODS AND PROPERTIES

Biological evaluation of crude drugs involves assessing their biological activity and effects to determine their therapeutic potential, efficacy, and safety. This method helps ensure that the drug has the desired biological effects and is free from harmful side effects. Here's a detailed overview of the biological methods and properties used in evaluating crude drugs:

1. Bioassays

a. Pharmacological Bioassays

i. **Purpose**: To determine the pharmacological activity of the drug and its efficacy in producing specific effects.

ii. **Examples**:

1. **Antimicrobial Assay**: Testing the drug's effectiveness against microorganisms using methods such as the disk diffusion test or broth microdilution.

2. **Antidiabetic Assay**: Evaluating the drug's ability to lower blood glucose levels in diabetic animal models.

b. Toxicological Bioassays

i. **Purpose**: To assess the potential toxicity and safety profile of the drug.

ii. **Examples**:

1. **Acute Toxicity Test**: Determining the lethal dose (LD50) of the drug in animal models to estimate its safety margin.

2. **Chronic Toxicity Test**: Assessing long-term effects and potential side effects over extended periods.

c. Pharmacokinetic Studies

i. **Purpose**: To study the absorption, distribution, metabolism, and excretion (ADME) of the drug.

ii. **Examples**:

1. **Absorption**: Measuring how quickly and to what extent the drug is absorbed into the bloodstream.

2. **Metabolism**: Evaluating how the drug is metabolized in the body and identifying its metabolic products.

d. Pharmacodynamic Studies

i. **Purpose**: To understand the drug's mechanism of action and its physiological effects.

ii. **Examples**:

1. **Receptor Binding Assay**: Assessing the drug's interaction with specific receptors or enzymes to determine its mechanism of action.

2. **Dose-Response Studies**: Evaluating the relationship between the drug dose and its physiological effect.

2. Microbiological Methods

a. Microbial Assays

i. **Purpose**: To evaluate the antimicrobial activity of the drug and its effectiveness in inhibiting or killing microorganisms.

ii. **Examples**:

1. **Agar Diffusion Method**: Applying the drug to an agar plate inoculated with microorganisms and measuring the zone of inhibition.

2. **Broth Dilution Method**: Determining the minimum inhibitory concentration (MIC) of the drug by diluting it in a broth culture and assessing microbial growth.

b. Phytochemical Screening

i. **Purpose**: To identify and confirm the presence of biologically active phytochemicals in the drug.

ii. **Examples**:

1. **Alkaloid Screening**: Testing for the presence of alkaloids using reagents that produce characteristic color changes.

2. **Flavonoid Screening**: Identifying flavonoids using colorimetric tests or chromatography.

3. Cell Culture Studies

a. In Vitro Studies

i. **Purpose**: To assess the drug's effects on cultured cells, providing insights into its mechanism of action and potential therapeutic benefits.

ii. **Examples**:

1. **Cytotoxicity Assay**: Measuring the drug's ability to kill or inhibit the growth of cancer cells using assays such as MTT or Trypan Blue exclusion.

2. **Cell Proliferation Assay**: Evaluating the effect of the drug on cell growth and replication.

b. Cellular Mechanisms

i. **Purpose**: To study how the drug affects cellular processes and signaling pathways.

ii. **Examples**:

1. **Apoptosis Assay**: Assessing the drug's effect on programmed cell death using assays like Annexin V staining.

2. **Signal Transduction Studies**: Investigating how the drug influences cellular signaling pathways and gene expression.

4. Clinical Trials

a. Human Studies

i. **Purpose**: To evaluate the drug's safety and efficacy in humans, confirming its therapeutic potential.

ii. **Examples**:

    1. **Phase I Trials**: Assessing safety, dosage, and side effects in a small group of healthy volunteers.

    2. **Phase II and III Trials**: Evaluating efficacy, optimal dosing, and safety in larger patient populations.

b. Post-Market Surveillance

i. **Purpose**: To monitor the drug's long-term safety and effectiveness after it has been approved for use.

ii. **Examples**:

    1. **Adverse Event Reporting**: Collecting and analyzing reports of adverse effects or complications in patients using the drug.

Applications of Biological Evaluation

a. **Efficacy Assessment**: Determines the therapeutic potential of the drug and its ability to produce the desired biological effects.

b. **Safety Profile**: Identifies potential side effects and toxicity, ensuring that the drug is safe for use.

c. **Mechanism of Action**: Provides insights into how the drug works at the molecular and cellular levels.

Limitations

a. **Ethical Considerations**: Some biological evaluations, especially those involving animal testing, raise ethical concerns.

b. **Complexity**: Biological assays can be complex and require specialized expertise and equipment.

QUANTITATIVE MICROSCOPY OF CRUDE DRUGS INCLUDING

Lycopodium spore method:

The **Lycopodium spore method** is a quantitative microscopy technique used to estimate the number of particles (such as plant fragments or powder) in a given sample of crude drug. This method is particularly valuable for the quantitative evaluation of powdered drugs in pharmacognosy and quality control. Here's a detailed overview:

Principle of the Lycopodium Spore Method

The Lycopodium Spore Method is a quantitative microscopic technique used to determine the amount of active ingredients, particularly in powdered crude drugs. It is based on the principle of counting spores of Lycopodium clavatum (a moss) and comparing their number with the substance being analyzed to estimate the content of a specific active component in a sample.

Principle:

1. **Uniform Particle Distribution:** Lycopodium spores have a consistent shape and size, with a known number of spores per unit weight (usually around 94,000 spores per milligram). This makes them ideal for use as a reference standard.

2. **Comparison:** In the Lycopodium Spore Method, a weighed quantity of the powdered crude drug is mixed with a known amount of Lycopodium spores. The mixture is then examined microscopically to count both the drug particles and Lycopodium spores.

3. **Ratio Calculation:** By comparing the number of Lycopodium spores with the number of active ingredient particles in a fixed volume of the sample, the content of the active ingredient can be calculated. The equation typically used is as follows:

$$\text{Weight of Active Ingredient} = \left(\frac{\text{Number of Drug Particles}}{\text{Number of Lycopodium Spores}} \right) \times \text{Known Weight of Lycopodium Spores}$$

4. **Accuracy and Precision:** The method is highly accurate for drugs where the active components are identifiable under a microscope and can be counted, such as starch grains, calcium oxalate crystals, or glandular trichomes.

Application:

This method is often used in pharmacognosy for the quantitative analysis of powdered herbal drugs, particularly when chemical assays are not feasible. It is useful for determining the concentration of certain crude drugs like ergot, nux vomica, and ginger, where the active constituents are morphologically identifiable.

Advantages

a. **Simplicity**: The method is straightforward and does not require complex equipment.

b. **Accuracy**: Provides a reliable estimate of the quantity of particles in a sample when conducted properly.

c. **Cost-Effective**: Utilizes inexpensive and readily available materials.

6. Limitations

a. **Preparation Sensitivity**: Requires careful preparation and mixing to ensure accurate results.

b. **Microscopic Errors**: Potential for human error in counting particles under the microscope.

c. **Size Variability**: Differences in the size and shape of drug particles can affect the accuracy of the quantification.

Leaf constants:

Leaf constants are specific numerical values or ratios used in the microscopic evaluation of leaves to assist in their identification and standardization. These constants are characteristic features of the leaf structure and help in determining the quality, purity, and authenticity of crude drug samples, especially in powdered form where morphological identification may not be possible. Common leaf constants include stomatal number, stomatal index, vein-islet number, vein termination number, and palisade ratio.

Key Leaf Constants:

1. **Stomatal Number:**

The average number of stomata per unit area of the leaf epidermis. It varies between species and helps in identifying and comparing different leaves.

2. **Stomatal Index**:

The percentage ratio of the number of stomata to the total number of epidermal cells (including stomata) in a given area of the leaf. It is calculated as:

$$\text{Stomatal Index} = \frac{\text{Number of Stomata}}{\text{Number of Stomata} + \text{Number of Epidermal Cells}} \times 100$$

The stomatal index is a constant for a particular species, regardless of environmental conditions.

3. **Vein-Islet Number**:

This is the average number of vein-islets (small areas of the leaf tissue enclosed by veins) per square millimeter of the leaf surface. This number remains constant for a given species and helps differentiate between species.

4. **Vein Termination Number**:

The average number of vein terminations per square millimeter of the leaf surface. Vein terminations are the endings of veins that terminate in the mesophyll without connecting to other veins.

5. **Palisade Ratio**:

The ratio of the number of palisade cells (the elongated cells present below the upper epidermis) to the number of epidermal cells in a given area of the leaf. This ratio helps in identifying different species of leaves.

Importance of Leaf Constants:

- **Identification and Authentication:** Leaf constants help in the identification of powdered or processed leaves where morphological characteristics are not visible.

- **Standardization:** These constants provide a standard reference for the quality control of crude drugs derived from leaves.
- **Detection of Adulteration:** Variations in leaf constants can indicate adulteration or substitution of the authentic leaf material with another species.

Camera lucida and diagrams of microscopic objects to scale with camera lucida:

A **camera lucida** is an optical device used in microscopy to project an image of the specimen being observed onto a surface, such as paper, allowing the observer to trace the image with precision. This technique is widely used for creating accurate diagrams of microscopic objects, ensuring that the details observed under the microscope are accurately reflected in drawings.

Procedure for Using a Camera Lucida:

1. **Setting Up the Microscope:**
   - Focus the microscope on the specimen as usual, ensuring the specimen is clearly visible.
   - Adjust the illumination to provide a sharp and clear image of the specimen.

2. **Attaching the Camera Lucida:**
   - Attach the camera lucida device to the eyepiece of the microscope. Different models may attach differently, so follow the manufacturer's instructions.
   - Some models use a prism or a series of mirrors to project the image from the microscope onto a drawing surface, while others may use digital technology.

3. **Positioning the Drawing Surface:**

- o Place the drawing surface (usually a piece of paper) adjacent to the microscope, at a suitable angle to view both the projected image and the surface.
- o Ensure that the drawing surface is flat and positioned comfortably for tracing.

4. **Adjusting the Field of View:**
- o Look through the camera lucida. You should be able to see both the specimen (as projected by the microscope) and the paper where you will draw.
- o Adjust the mirrors or prisms to ensure the image is centered and clearly visible on the paper.

5. **Focusing the Image:**
- o Fine-tune the focus of the microscope and the position of the drawing surface to ensure that the projected image is sharp and at the correct scale.
- o Some camera lucida devices allow for adjustments in brightness and clarity.

6. **Tracing the Image:**
- o Use a pencil to carefully trace the outlines and details of the specimen projected onto the paper.
- o You may need to adjust the microscope focus slightly as you work to bring different parts of the specimen into sharp detail.

7. **Scaling the Image:**
- o If required, use a scale or ruler to measure the size of the drawing and ensure it accurately reflects the magnification being used.
- o Label the drawing with magnification details, specimen name, and other relevant information.

8. **Final Adjustments:**

o Once the tracing is complete, review the drawing to make sure all necessary details are included.

o Clean the camera lucida and microscope components as needed.

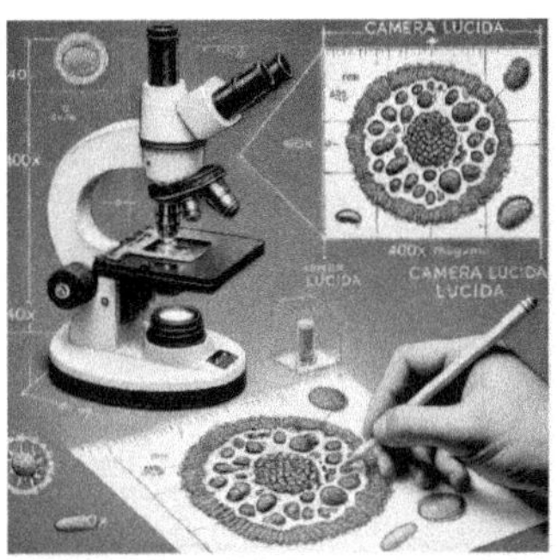

Applications of Camera Lucida:

- **Microscopic Drawings:** Used in biological sciences for drawing microscopic specimens like plant cells, tissues, and microorganisms.
- **Quantitative Microscopy:** Often used in studies where accurate and to-scale drawings of microscopic objects are required, such as in the determination of leaf constants or cellular measurements.
- **Teaching Tool:** Helps students in learning microscopy by allowing them to accurately record their observations.

Applications in Quantitative Microscopy

a. **Accurate Documentation**: Enables precise documentation of the anatomical features of crude drug samples, which is essential for quality control and identification.

b. **Comparison**: Facilitates comparison of microscopic features with reference standards to ensure the authenticity and quality of the drug.

c. **Educational**: Provides a visual reference for educational purposes, helping students and researchers understand the detailed anatomy of plant drugs.

Multiple Choice Questions (MCQs) - Objective

1. What is the primary purpose of evaluating crude drugs?

    A) To enhance flavor

    B) To confirm identity, potency, and purity

    C) To increase moisture content

    D) To decrease production costs

2. Which of the following is a method used in macroscopic evaluation of crude drugs?

    A) Chromatography

    B) Spectroscopy

    C) Appearance and odor

    D) Microscopy

3. What is the significance of total ash in the evaluation of crude drugs?

    A) To measure moisture content

    B) To assess the amount of non-volatile inorganic residue

    C) To determine solubility

    D) To measure pharmacological activity

4. Which technique is used to analyze volatile compounds in crude drugs?

    A) Thin-Layer Chromatography (TLC)

    B) Gas Chromatography (GC)

    C) High-Performance Liquid Chromatography (HPLC)

    D) UV-Visible Spectroscopy

5. What does the Stomatal Index represent in leaf constants?

    A) The total number of stomata in a leaf

    B) The ratio of stomata to epidermal cells

    C) The size of stomata

    D) The thickness of the leaf

6. Which method is used to measure the amount of water present in a crude drug?

   A) Ash value determination

   B) Solubility test

   C) Gravimetric method

   D) Chromatography

7. Which chemical test is used to identify alkaloids in crude drugs?

   A) Froth test

   B) Dragendorff's reagent

   C) Titration

   D) Thin-Layer Chromatography (TLC)

8. What does the Lycopodium spore method estimate in crude drugs?

   A) Moisture content

   B) Particle size

   C) Number of particles in a sample

   D) Color and odor

9. Which type of spectroscopy is used to identify functional groups in crude drugs?

   A) UV-Visible Spectroscopy

   B) Nuclear Magnetic Resonance (NMR) Spectroscopy

   C) Infrared (IR) Spectroscopy

   D) Mass Spectrometry (MS)

10. What is the purpose of pharmacological testing in biological evaluation?

    A) To measure moisture content

    B) To assess the biological activity and efficacy of the drug

    C) To determine particle size

    D) To evaluate color and odor

11. Which leaf constant involves counting the number of trichomes per unit area?

A) Vein pattern

B) Epidermal cell number

C) Stomatal Index

D) Trichome density

12. What does the Ash Value determination help assess in crude drugs?

A) The presence of active constituents

B) The purity and presence of contaminants

C) The solubility of the drug

D) The pharmacological activity

13. Which of the following is a limitation of organoleptic evaluation?

A) Subjectivity

B) High accuracy

C) Requires expensive equipment

D) Provides quantitative data

14. What is the purpose of using a Camera Lucida in microscopy?

A) To magnify images

B) To draw accurate, to-scale diagrams of microscopic objects

C) To measure particle size

D) To analyze chemical composition

15. Which method measures the proportion of ash that is insoluble in acid?

A) Total Ash

B) Water-Soluble Ash

C) Acid-Insoluble Ash

D) Moisture Content

16. What is measured by using sieve analysis in crude drugs?

A) Solubility

B) Particle size distribution

C) Ash values

D) Moisture content

17. What does the term "extractive values" refer to in the evaluation of crude drugs?

    A) The moisture content

    B) The amount of material extracted by different solvents

    C) The solubility of the drug

    D) The pharmacological activity

18. Which microscopic technique is used for ultrastructural analysis of crude drugs?

    A) Light Microscopy

    B) Transmission Electron Microscopy (TEM)

    C) Scanning Electron Microscopy (SEM)

    D) Spectroscopy

19. Which physical property affects the stability and shelf life of crude drugs?

    A) Color

    B) Moisture content

    C) Odor

    D) Texture

20. Which biological method evaluates the drug's interaction with specific receptors?

    A) Microbial Assays

    B) Cytotoxicity Assay

    C) Receptor Binding Assay

    D) Sieve Analysis

Short Answer Type Questions (Subjective)

1. Define the evaluation of crude drugs and explain its importance in the pharmaceutical industry.

2. Describe the role of macroscopic evaluation in the assessment of crude drugs.

3. Explain the significance of moisture content determination in crude drugs.

4. How is thin-layer chromatography (TLC) used in the chemical evaluation of crude drugs?

5. Discuss the importance of ash value determination in ensuring the purity of crude drugs.

6. What are leaf constants, and how are they used in the identification of plant species?

7. Explain the principle behind the Lycopodium spore method in quantitative microscopy.

8. Describe the role of pharmacological testing in the biological evaluation of crude drugs.

9. What are the advantages and limitations of using organoleptic methods for evaluating crude drugs?

10. How is infrared (IR) spectroscopy used to identify functional groups in crude drugs?

11. Discuss the significance of total ash and acid-insoluble ash in evaluating crude drugs.

12. What are the common challenges faced during the evaluation of crude drugs?

13. Explain the purpose of using a camera lucida in microscopy and its applications.

14. How does the determination of extractive values contribute to the quality control of crude drugs?

15. Describe the process and importance of particle size analysis in crude drug evaluation.

16. What is the role of biological evaluation in ensuring the safety and efficacy of crude drugs?

17. How is the stomatal index calculated, and why is it important in leaf analysis?

18. Discuss the procedure for determining the pH value of crude drugs and its significance.

19. Explain the use of gas chromatography (GC) in the evaluation of volatile compounds in crude drugs.

20. Describe the application of scanning electron microscopy (SEM) in the evaluation of crude drugs.

Long Answer Type Questions (Subjective)

1. Discuss the various types of evaluation methods used in assessing the quality of crude drugs, including macroscopic, microscopic, chemical, physical, and biological evaluations.

2. Explain the role of chromatographic and spectroscopic techniques in the chemical evaluation of crude drugs, providing examples of how each method is applied.

3. Describe the concept of leaf constants in detail, and explain how they are used in the identification and standardization of crude drugs.

4. Discuss the importance of moisture content, ash values, and extractive values in the physical evaluation of crude drugs, and explain how these properties are measured.

5. Explain the process and significance of biological evaluation in the assessment of crude drugs, focusing on pharmacological and toxicological bioassays.

6. Describe the procedure and applications of the Lycopodium spore method in the quantitative evaluation of crude drugs, including its advantages and limitations.

7. Discuss the role of microscopic methods, including light microscopy, SEM, and TEM, in the evaluation of crude drugs, and explain the importance of these techniques in quality control.

8. Explain the application and importance of organoleptic methods in the preliminary evaluation of crude drugs, and discuss the limitations of these methods.

9. Discuss the role of Camera Lucida in the documentation and standardization of microscopic features in crude drugs, including its advantages and challenges.

10. Explain the significance of biological methods, such as pharmacokinetic and pharmacodynamic studies, in the evaluation of crude drugs, and discuss how these methods contribute to drug development.

Answer Key for MCQs

1. (B) To confirm identity, potency, and purity

2. (C) Appearance and odor

3. (B) To assess the amount of non-volatile inorganic residue

4. (B) Gas Chromatography (GC)

5. (B) The ratio of stomata to epidermal cells

6. (C) Gravimetric method

7. (B) Dragendorff's reagent

8. (C) Number of particles in a sample

9. (C) Infrared (IR) Spectroscopy

10. (B) To assess the biological activity and efficacy of the drug

11. (D) Trichome density

12. (B) The purity and presence of contaminants

13. (A) Subjectivity

14. (B) To draw accurate, to-scale diagrams of microscopic objects

15. (C) Acid-Insoluble Ash

16. (B) Particle size distribution

17. (B) The amount of material extracted by different solvents

18. (B) Transmission Electron Microscopy (TEM)

19.(B) Moisture content

20.(C) Receptor Binding Assay

CHAPTER – 5

CULTIVATION, COLLECTION, PROCESSING AND STORAGE OF DRUGS OF NATURAL ORIGIN

INTRODUCTION:

Drugs of natural origin, derived from plants, animals, or minerals, play a crucial role in medicine and pharmacology. Their effectiveness and safety depend significantly on how they are cultivated, collected, processed, and stored. This introduction outlines the essential aspects of each stage in ensuring the quality and efficacy of these natural drugs.

1. Cultivation

Cultivation is the first step in the production of drugs from natural sources. It involves growing plants or rearing animals under controlled conditions to obtain the desired medicinal compounds.

a. **Selection of Species:** Choosing the right species with therapeutic potential is crucial. Factors like the plant's environment, soil type, and climatic conditions impact the quality and yield of the drug.

b. **Cultivation Practices:** Includes soil preparation, planting techniques, pest and disease management, irrigation, and fertilization. Sustainable practices are emphasized to maintain the ecological balance and ensure high-quality yield.

c. **Genetic Improvement:** Breeding and genetic modification may be employed to enhance the medicinal properties, yield, and resistance to pests and diseases.

2. Collection

Collection involves harvesting the plant parts or animal products at the optimal time to maximize the medicinal value.

a. **Timing:** Harvesting should occur when the plant parts or animal products contain the highest concentration of active compounds. This timing varies for different species and parts (e.g., roots, leaves, seeds).

b. **Methods:** Techniques include manual harvesting, mechanical harvesting, or a combination, depending on the scale and type of crop.

c. **Ethical Considerations:** Sustainable and ethical collection practices are essential to prevent overexploitation and preserve biodiversity.

3. Processing

Processing transforms raw materials into usable forms for medicinal purposes. This stage includes various steps to extract, purify, and prepare the drug.

a. **Drying:** Proper drying techniques are vital to prevent spoilage and degradation. Methods include air drying, sun drying, and using dehydrators.

b. **Extraction:** Involves obtaining the active constituents from the raw materials using solvents (e.g., alcohol, water). Techniques include maceration, percolation, and distillation.

c. **Purification:** Further purification may be required to remove impurities and isolate the active compounds. Methods include filtration, crystallization, and chromatography.

d. **Formulation:** The processed material is then formulated into medicinal forms such as powders, capsules, tablets, or extracts.

4. Storage

Storage is crucial for maintaining the quality and potency of natural drugs.

a. **Conditions:** Drugs should be stored in suitable conditions to prevent degradation. Factors include temperature, humidity, light, and air exposure.

b. **Packaging:** Proper packaging helps protect the drugs from environmental factors and contamination. Materials should be chosen based on their ability to preserve the drug's integrity.

c. **Shelf Life:** Monitoring and managing the shelf life of natural drugs is essential to ensure their effectiveness and safety.

CULTIVATION OF DRUGS OF NATURAL ORIGIN

The **cultivation** of drugs of natural origin involves growing plants or rearing animals to obtain the raw materials used in medicinal products. Proper cultivation practices are essential to ensure the quality, efficacy, and sustainability of the final product. Here's a detailed look into the various aspects of cultivation:

1. Selection of Species

a. **Medicinal Value:** The chosen species must have proven therapeutic properties. Selection often involves research into traditional medicine or scientific studies to identify plants or animals with desired pharmacological effects.

b. **Adaptability:** The species must be suitable for the local climate, soil, and environmental conditions. This ensures healthy growth and optimal yield.

2. Soil Preparation

a. **Soil Testing:** Conducting soil tests to determine pH, nutrient content, and texture helps in tailoring soil amendments and choosing suitable cultivation methods.

b. **Soil Conditioning:** Adding organic matter (e.g., compost), adjusting pH, and ensuring proper drainage improves soil fertility and structure.

c. **Bed Preparation:** Creating planting beds or rows with appropriate spacing to accommodate plant growth and ensure good air circulation.

3. Planting Techniques

a. **Propagation Methods:** Depending on the species, propagation may be done from seeds, cuttings, or tissue culture. Each method has specific requirements and procedures.

b. **Planting Time:** Timing is crucial and depends on the plant's growing season and climate. Proper planting ensures optimal growth and yield.

c. **Spacing:** Adequate spacing between plants prevents overcrowding, which can lead to poor air circulation, increased disease risk, and reduced yields.

4. Crop Management

a. **Irrigation:** Providing the right amount of water is crucial for plant health. Irrigation methods include drip, sprinkler, or furrow systems, depending on the crop's needs and soil type.

b. **Fertilization:** Nutrient management involves applying fertilizers based on soil tests and plant requirements. Both organic and synthetic fertilizers may be used.

c. **Pest and Disease Control:** Integrated pest management (IPM) strategies are employed to control pests and diseases using biological, chemical, and cultural methods. Regular monitoring and early intervention are key.

d. **Weed Control:** Managing weeds through mechanical, chemical, or manual methods prevents competition for nutrients, water, and light.

5. Harvesting

a. **Optimal Harvest Time:** Timing is critical for harvesting to ensure that the plant or animal product contains the maximum concentration of active compounds. For example, certain plant parts may be harvested at different stages of growth.

b. **Harvesting Methods:** Techniques include manual picking, cutting, or mechanical harvesting, depending on the scale and type of crop. Careful handling during harvest helps prevent damage and contamination.

6. Sustainability

a. **Environmental Impact:** Sustainable cultivation practices aim to minimize environmental impact, such as using eco-friendly pest control, conserving water, and avoiding soil degradation.

b. **Biodiversity:** Cultivating a diverse range of species and maintaining genetic diversity helps preserve ecosystems and ensures a steady supply of high-quality materials.

c. **Ethical Considerations:** Ensuring fair labor practices and respecting indigenous knowledge and rights in the cultivation process.

COLLECTION OF DRUGS OF NATURAL ORIGIN

The **collection** of drugs of natural origin involves harvesting plant parts or animal products to obtain raw materials used in medicinal preparations. This stage is crucial for ensuring that the collected materials are of high quality and suitable for further processing. Here's a detailed look into the various aspects of collection:

1. Timing of Collection

a. **Optimal Harvesting Time:** The timing of collection is critical to ensure that the plant or animal product contains the highest concentration of active compounds. This timing varies based on the type of material:

    i. **Plants:** For example, roots may be harvested in the fall, flowers during bloom, and leaves before flowering.

    ii. **Animal Products:** For instance, certain animal products like honey or milk should be collected during peak production periods.

b. **Environmental Conditions:** Collection should be done under favorable weather conditions to avoid contamination and degradation. For plants, this often means dry weather to prevent excess moisture that could lead to mold growth.

2. Collection Methods

a. **Manual Collection:** Involves hand-picking or cutting, which is often preferred for high-value or delicate materials. It allows for selective harvesting and minimizes damage to the plant or animal.

b. **Mechanical Collection:** For large-scale operations, mechanical methods may be used, such as machines for harvesting grains or fruit. Mechanical collection can increase efficiency but may require careful management to prevent damage to the material.

   c. **Ethical Collection:** Ensuring that the collection methods do not harm the plant or animal populations or disrupt their ecosystems. For instance, only a portion of the plant should be harvested to allow for regrowth.

3. Handling and Transportation

   a. **Minimizing Damage:** During collection, it's essential to handle materials gently to avoid physical damage that could affect their quality. This includes using clean and appropriate tools and avoiding excessive compression.

   b. **Immediate Transport:** Transporting collected materials to processing facilities should be done promptly to prevent deterioration. Materials should be transported in clean, appropriate containers that protect them from contamination and environmental factors.

   c. **Temperature Control:** Depending on the material, temperature control during transportation may be necessary to prevent spoilage. For example, certain animal products may require refrigeration.

4. Quality Control

   a. **Inspection:** Upon collection, materials should be inspected for quality, including checking for signs of disease, pests, or contamination. Only materials meeting quality standards should proceed to processing.

   b. **Documentation:** Proper documentation of the collection process is important for traceability and quality assurance. This includes recording the date, location, and condition of the collected material.

5. Sustainability and Conservation

   a. **Sustainable Practices:** Implementing sustainable collection practices to prevent overharvesting and ensure the long-term availability of resources. This includes following guidelines for the sustainable use of wild plants and animals.

b. **Conservation Efforts:** Engaging in conservation efforts to protect endangered species and habitats from exploitation. For example, cultivating medicinal plants in controlled environments can reduce the need for wild harvesting.

c. **Ethical Considerations:** Respecting the rights of indigenous communities and local populations who may have traditional knowledge or claims related to the collected materials.

FACTORS INFLUENCING CULTIVATION OF MEDICINAL PLANTS

The successful cultivation of medicinal plants depends on a variety of factors that affect the growth, yield, and quality of the plants. Understanding these factors is crucial for optimizing cultivation practices and ensuring the efficacy and safety of the medicinal products. Here's a detailed look at the key factors influencing the cultivation of medicinal plants:

1. Climate and Weather Conditions

a. **Temperature:** Most medicinal plants have specific temperature ranges for optimal growth. Extreme temperatures, whether too hot or too cold, can affect plant health and compound concentration.

b. **Rainfall and Humidity:** Adequate rainfall and humidity levels are necessary for healthy plant growth. However, excessive moisture can lead to fungal diseases, while insufficient moisture can stress plants and reduce yields.

c. **Sunlight:** The amount of sunlight affects photosynthesis and overall plant health. Different plants have varying light requirements, from full sun to partial shade.

2. Soil Conditions

a. **Soil Type:** The type of soil (e.g., sandy, loamy, clay) impacts water drainage, nutrient availability, and root development. Some medicinal plants prefer well-drained soils, while others thrive in more compacted soils.

b. **Soil pH:** The acidity or alkalinity of the soil affects nutrient availability and microbial activity. Most medicinal plants have preferred pH ranges, and soil testing can help adjust pH levels accordingly.

c. **Nutrient Content:** Soil fertility is critical for plant growth. Essential nutrients (nitrogen, phosphorus, potassium, etc.) must be present in appropriate amounts. Soil tests can guide fertilization practices.

3. Propagation Methods

a. **Seed Quality:** High-quality seeds with good germination rates are essential for successful cultivation. Seed selection should be based on factors like purity, viability, and genetic traits.

b. **Propagation Techniques:** Methods such as seed sowing, cuttings, and tissue culture influence plant growth and development. The choice of propagation technique depends on the plant species and desired outcomes.

4. Water Management

a. **Irrigation:** Adequate water supply is crucial for plant growth. Irrigation systems (drip, sprinkler, etc.) should be chosen based on the plant's water requirements and soil type.

b. **Water Quality:** The quality of irrigation water, including its pH and mineral content, can impact plant health. Contaminated water can introduce diseases or toxicities.

5. Pest and Disease Management

a. **Pest Control:** Regular monitoring and control measures are necessary to prevent pest infestations that can damage plants or reduce their medicinal value. Integrated pest management (IPM) strategies are often used.

b. **Disease Management:** Identifying and managing plant diseases through preventive measures and treatments helps maintain plant health and quality.

6. Crop Management Practices

a. **Weed Control:** Weeds compete with medicinal plants for nutrients, water, and light. Effective weed control methods, including manual weeding, herbicides, or mulching, are important for optimal plant growth.

b. **Plant Spacing:** Proper spacing between plants prevents overcrowding, which can lead to poor air circulation, increased disease risk, and reduced yields.

c. **Pruning and Training:** For certain plants, pruning and training can improve yields and quality by promoting better air circulation and light penetration.

7. Environmental Factors

a. **Altitude:** Some medicinal plants thrive at specific altitudes. Altitude affects temperature, atmospheric pressure, and UV radiation, which can influence plant growth and compound concentrations.

b. **Microclimates:** Local microclimates, such as variations in temperature and humidity within a larger climate zone, can impact plant health and yield.

8. Cultural Practices

a. **Traditional Knowledge:** Indigenous and traditional cultivation practices may offer valuable insights into optimizing growth conditions and enhancing medicinal properties.

b. **Modern Techniques:** Advances in agriculture, such as controlled environment agriculture (CEA) and precision farming, can improve the efficiency and sustainability of medicinal plant cultivation.

9. Economic and Legal Considerations

a. **Market Demand:** Understanding market demand and economic viability can influence cultivation decisions. Plants with high market value may receive more attention in cultivation practices.

b. **Regulations:** Compliance with local, national, and international regulations regarding the cultivation of medicinal plants is essential. This includes adhering to standards for organic cultivation and sustainable practices.

PLANT HORMONES AND THEIR APPLICATIONS

Plant hormones, also known as phytohormones, are chemical substances produced by plants that regulate various aspects of growth and development. They play a crucial role in the cultivation, collection, processing, and storage of medicinal plants. Understanding and manipulating plant hormones can enhance the yield, quality, and efficiency of natural drug production. Here's a detailed look at plant hormones and their applications:

1. Auxins

Role:

a. **Cell Elongation:** Auxins promote cell elongation and root development, which is essential for healthy plant growth.

b. **Rooting:** Auxins are crucial for adventitious root formation in cuttings and tissue cultures.

Applications:

a. **Propagation:** Used in rooting hormones to stimulate root development in plant cuttings.

b. **Growth Regulation:** Applied in tissue culture to enhance cell division and development of plantlets.

c. **Crop Management:** Helps in controlling plant growth patterns and improving overall plant health.

2. Gibberellins

Role:

a. **Seed Germination:** Gibberellins promote seed germination and break seed dormancy.

b. **Stem Elongation:** They stimulate stem elongation, which can be useful for optimizing plant height and yield.

Applications:

a. **Seed Treatments:** Used to enhance germination rates and uniformity in medicinal plant seeds.

b. **Growth Promotion:** Applied to increase plant height and improve crop yield.

c. **Flowering and Fruit Development:** Gibberellins can regulate flowering and fruit set, affecting the yield and quality of medicinal plants.

3. Cytokinins

Role:

a. **Cell Division:** Cytokinins stimulate cell division and differentiation, contributing to plant growth and development.

b. **Leaf Senescence:** They delay leaf senescence and promote chlorophyll retention.

Applications:

a. **Tissue Culture:** Used in plant tissue culture media to promote cell division and shoot proliferation.

b. **Growth Enhancement:** Applied to delay aging in plants and improve yield and quality of medicinal parts.

c. **Crop Yield:** Enhances the production of fruits, seeds, and other medicinal plant parts.

4. Abscisic Acid (ABA)

Role:

a. **Stress Response:** ABA regulates plant responses to environmental stress, including drought and salinity.

b. **Seed Dormancy:** It induces seed dormancy and helps in seed desiccation.

Applications:

a. **Stress Management:** Used to enhance plant tolerance to environmental stresses during cultivation.

b. **Seed Storage:** ABA can be used to regulate seed dormancy and improve seed quality during storage.

c. **Water Management:** Helps in developing drought-resistant plant varieties.

5. Ethylene

Role:

a. **Fruit Ripening:** Ethylene regulates fruit ripening and senescence.

b. **Stress Response:** It is involved in plant responses to biotic and abiotic stresses.

Applications:

a. **Harvesting:** Used to synchronize fruit ripening and optimize the timing of harvest for medicinal plants.

b. **Storage:** Controlled application of ethylene can manage the ripening process and prolong shelf life during storage.

c. **Post-Harvest Treatment:** Helps in reducing damage and loss during post-harvest processing.

6. Brassinosteroids

Role:

a. **Growth Regulation:** Brassinosteroids promote cell elongation, division, and overall plant growth.

b. **Stress Tolerance:** They enhance plant resistance to environmental stresses.

Applications:

a. **Growth Enhancement:** Applied to improve plant growth, development, and yield.

b. **Stress Management:** Used to enhance tolerance to environmental stressors, improving plant health and productivity.

7. Jasmonic Acid

Role:

    a. **Defense Mechanism:** Jasmonic acid regulates plant defense responses and secondary metabolite production.

    b. **Flowering:** It influences flowering and fruit development.

Applications:

    a. **Disease and Pest Resistance:** Used to enhance plant defense mechanisms against pests and diseases.

    b. **Secondary Metabolite Production:** Applied to increase the production of secondary metabolites with medicinal value.

Applications in Cultivation, Collection, Processing, and Storage

Cultivation:

    a. **Optimizing Growth:** Hormones like auxins, gibberellins, and cytokinins are used to optimize growth conditions, improve plant health, and increase yields.

    b. **Propagation:** Hormones enhance rooting and growth in tissue culture and cuttings.

Collection:

    a. **Uniform Maturity:** Ethylene and gibberellins help in synchronizing the maturity of plant parts, ensuring uniform quality at harvest.

Processing:

    a. **Quality Control:** Hormones can be used to regulate the production of secondary metabolites and ensure high-quality raw materials for processing.

POLYPLOIDY WITH REFERENCE TO MEDICINAL PLANTS

Polyploidy refers to the condition where a plant has more than two complete sets of chromosomes, unlike the normal diploid state with two sets. This genetic variation can significantly impact plant growth, development, and production of secondary metabolites, including those used in medicinal drugs.

Here's a detailed look at how polyploidy affects medicinal plants across cultivation, collection, processing, and storage stages:

1. Cultivation

Impact on Growth and Yield:

a. **Increased Size:** Polyploid plants often exhibit larger cell sizes, which can lead to larger overall plant size, including bigger leaves, flowers, or fruits. This can be beneficial for medicinal plants where larger parts are desired.

b. **Enhanced Biomass:** Polyploidy can increase the biomass of plants, leading to higher yields of the medicinal parts such as leaves, roots, or seeds.

Impact on Secondary Metabolites:

a. **Increased Production:** Polyploid plants may produce higher quantities of secondary metabolites, such as alkaloids, flavonoids, and essential oils, which are valuable in medicinal applications. This is due to the increased number of gene copies that can enhance the biosynthetic pathways.

b. **Altered Profiles:** The types and ratios of secondary metabolites may change in polyploid plants, which can affect the efficacy and safety of the medicinal products derived from them.

Cultivation Practices:

a. **Selection and Breeding:** Polyploidy can be induced through breeding techniques or chemical treatments. Cultivators may select polyploid varieties for improved yield and quality of medicinal compounds.

b. **Adaptation to Conditions:** Polyploid plants may have different environmental and soil requirements. Understanding these requirements helps in optimizing cultivation practices.

2. Collection

Impact on Harvesting:

a. **Higher Yields:** The increased biomass and size of polyploid plants can lead to greater yields during collection, which is advantageous for obtaining larger quantities of medicinal materials.

b. **Consistency:** Polyploid plants can offer more uniform size and quality of harvested parts, which is beneficial for ensuring consistency in medicinal products.

Collection Techniques:

a. **Careful Handling:** Due to potentially larger plant sizes, collection techniques may need to be adjusted to accommodate the physical characteristics of polyploid plants and prevent damage to the plant parts.

3. Processing

Impact on Quality and Efficiency:

a. **Enhanced Metabolite Extraction:** The higher levels of secondary metabolites in polyploid plants can improve the efficiency and effectiveness of extraction processes used in the production of medicinal products.

b. **Processing Adjustments:** Processing techniques may need to be adapted to handle the larger or more abundant plant material effectively.

Impact on Medicinal Properties:

a. **Consistency in Quality:** The uniformity in metabolite production can lead to more consistent quality in the final medicinal products, which is crucial for therapeutic efficacy.

b. **Potential Variability:** Changes in metabolite profiles due to polyploidy may require adjustments in processing methods to maintain desired product standards.

4. Storage

Impact on Longevity and Stability:

a. **Shelf Life:** Polyploid plants may have different storage requirements due to changes in their biochemical composition. For instance, higher levels of certain metabolites may affect the stability and shelf life of stored materials.

b. **Storage Conditions:** The storage conditions (temperature, humidity, etc.) may need to be optimized based on the altered characteristics of polyploid plants to prevent degradation and maintain quality.

Impact on Storage Practices:

a. **Packaging:** Larger or more abundant plant materials from polyploid plants might require different packaging solutions to ensure proper storage and prevent contamination or damage.

b. **Monitoring:** Regular monitoring for changes in quality and stability during storage is essential, especially if the polyploid plants exhibit altered biochemical properties.

MUTATION WITH REFERENCE TO MEDICINAL PLANTS

Mutation refers to changes in the genetic material of an organism, which can lead to variations in plant traits. In medicinal plants, mutations can impact cultivation, collection, processing, and storage. Understanding and managing mutations can enhance the quality and quantity of medicinal products. Here's a detailed look at how mutations influence various stages in the lifecycle of medicinal plants:

1. Cultivation

Types of Mutations:

a. **Spontaneous Mutations:** Occur naturally without external influence. They may arise from errors in DNA replication or repair.

b. **Induced Mutations:** Result from exposure to mutagens such as chemicals or radiation. These are often used in breeding programs to develop new plant varieties.

Impact on Growth and Yield:

a. **Enhanced Traits:** Mutations can lead to desirable traits such as increased size, improved resistance to pests and diseases, or better growth rates. For example, mutations may produce plants with higher yields of medicinal compounds.

b. **Negative Traits:** Mutations can also cause undesirable traits such as reduced growth, lower yields, or poor quality of medicinal parts. Managing these mutations is crucial to avoid adverse effects.

Cultivation Practices:

a. **Selection and Breeding:** Mutation breeding can be used to develop new plant varieties with improved or novel traits. This involves selecting and propagating plants that exhibit beneficial mutations.

b. **Monitoring:** Regular monitoring of plants for mutation-induced traits helps ensure that only those with desirable characteristics are cultivated.

2. Collection

Impact on Harvesting:

a. **Consistency:** Mutations can result in variations in plant size, shape, or chemical composition. This can affect the uniformity of the harvested medicinal parts.

b. **Enhanced Quality:** Some mutations may improve the concentration of active compounds, leading to higher quality medicinal materials.

Collection Techniques:

a. **Adaptation:** Collection techniques may need to be adapted based on the new traits of mutated plants. For instance, changes in plant size or structure may require different harvesting methods.

b. **Quality Control:** Ensuring the consistency and quality of the collected material from mutated plants is important, particularly if mutations affect the chemical profile.

3. Processing

Impact on Quality and Efficiency:

a. **Altered Metabolite Profiles:** Mutations can affect the production of secondary metabolites, potentially altering the efficacy and safety of the medicinal products. This requires adjustments in processing techniques to accommodate these changes.

b. **Processing Efficiency:** Changes in plant traits due to mutations may impact the efficiency of extraction and processing methods. For example, plants with different cell structures may require different processing conditions.

Processing Adjustments:

a. **Method Optimization:** Processing methods may need to be optimized based on the new biochemical profiles of mutated plants to ensure that the final products meet quality standards.

b. **Standardization:** Ensuring consistent product quality requires careful standardization of processing procedures to handle variability introduced by mutations.

4. Storage

Impact on Longevity and Stability:

a. **Chemical Stability:** Mutations that alter the chemical composition of plant materials may affect their stability and shelf life. This is important for maintaining the quality of stored medicinal products.

b. **Storage Conditions:** Mutated plants may have different storage requirements. For example, changes in moisture content or chemical composition might necessitate adjustments in temperature and humidity control.

HYBRIDIZATION WITH REFERENCE TO MEDICINAL PLANTS

Hybridization involves crossing two different plant varieties or species to produce offspring with a mix of traits from both parents. This technique can significantly influence the cultivation, collection, processing, and storage of medicinal plants. Here's a detailed look at how hybridization impacts these stages:

1. Cultivation

Types of Hybridization:

a. **Interspecific Hybridization:** Crossing between different species within the same genus. For example, hybridizing different species of *Cannabis* for improved medicinal properties.

b. **Intraspecific Hybridization:** Crossing between different varieties or strains within the same species. This is common in crops like *Cannabis sativa* or *Echinacea*.

Impact on Growth and Yield:

a. **Improved Traits:** Hybrids often exhibit enhanced traits such as increased growth rates, higher yields, and better resistance to pests and diseases. This can result in more efficient cultivation and higher productivity of medicinal parts.

b. **Uniformity:** Hybrids can produce more uniform plants with consistent characteristics, which is beneficial for large-scale cultivation.

Cultivation Practices:

a. **Selection and Breeding:** Hybridization is used to develop new plant varieties with desirable traits. This involves selecting parent plants with complementary characteristics and managing the hybridization process to achieve specific goals.

b. **Management:** Cultivating hybrids may require adjustments in management practices to accommodate their specific needs, such as nutrient requirements, water management, or pest control.

2. Collection

Impact on Harvesting:

a. **Consistency:** Hybrids can provide more uniform quality and quantity of harvested material, which is advantageous for ensuring consistent product quality.

b. **Yield:** Improved yield from hybrid plants can increase the amount of medicinal parts collected, enhancing the efficiency of the collection process.

Collection Techniques:

a. **Adaptation:** Collection techniques may need to be adapted based on the characteristics of hybrid plants, such as their size or growth habit.

b. **Quality Control:** Ensuring the quality of the collected material is important, particularly if hybridization affects the chemical profile or physical properties of the plant parts.

3. Processing

Impact on Quality and Efficiency:

a. **Enhanced Metabolite Production:** Hybrids may produce higher levels or different profiles of secondary metabolites, which can improve the efficacy or safety of medicinal products.

b. **Processing Adaptations:** Changes in plant traits due to hybridization may require adjustments in processing techniques to optimize extraction and product formulation.

Processing Adjustments:

a. **Method Optimization:** Processing methods may need to be optimized based on the new biochemical profiles or physical characteristics of hybrid plants.

b. **Standardization:** Ensuring consistent quality in the final product may involve standardizing processing procedures to accommodate variations introduced by hybridization.

4. Storage

CONSERVATION OF MEDICINAL PLANTS

Conservation of medicinal plants is crucial for ensuring the sustainable availability of these valuable resources. Effective conservation practices help protect plant species from extinction, preserve their genetic diversity, and ensure the continued production of high-quality medicinal materials. Here's a detailed look at how conservation impacts cultivation, collection, processing, and storage of medicinal plants:

1. Cultivation

Sustainable Cultivation Practices:

a. **Agroforestry and Permaculture:** Integrating medicinal plants into agroforestry systems and permaculture designs can promote biodiversity, improve soil health, and create more resilient ecosystems.

b. **Organic Farming:** Utilizing organic farming practices reduces the impact of synthetic chemicals on plant health and the environment, supporting the long-term sustainability of medicinal plant cultivation.

c. **Soil and Water Conservation:** Implementing soil conservation techniques (e.g., contour plowing, cover cropping) and efficient water management practices (e.g., drip irrigation) helps maintain healthy plant growth and reduces environmental impact.

Propagation and Breeding:

a. **Seed Banking:** Establishing seed banks to store seeds of medicinal plants ensures the preservation of genetic diversity and availability for future cultivation.

b. **In Situ and Ex Situ Conservation:** In situ conservation involves protecting medicinal plants in their natural habitats, while ex situ conservation includes growing them in botanical gardens or controlled environments.

Cultivation of Endangered Species:

a. **Cultivation Programs:** Developing cultivation programs for endangered medicinal plants can help reduce pressure on wild populations and support species recovery.

2. Collection

Ethical and Sustainable Collection:

a. **Regulated Harvesting:** Implementing regulations and guidelines for the sustainable collection of medicinal plants helps prevent overharvesting and depletion of wild populations.

b. **Harvesting Techniques:** Employing techniques that minimize damage to plant populations and habitats (e.g., selective harvesting, avoiding destruction of root systems) supports long-term sustainability.

Monitoring and Assessment:

a. **Population Monitoring:** Regularly monitoring wild plant populations to assess their health and abundance helps inform conservation strategies and prevent overexploitation.

b. **Data Collection:** Gathering data on plant distribution, population size, and reproductive success provides valuable information for conservation planning.

3. Processing

Sustainable Processing Practices:

a. **Eco-friendly Techniques:** Using environmentally friendly processing methods (e.g., solvent-free extraction, energy-efficient technologies) reduces the environmental impact of medicinal plant processing.

b. **Waste Management:** Implementing waste management practices to recycle or dispose of processing by-products minimizes environmental pollution and supports sustainability.

Quality Control:

a. **Maintaining Genetic Integrity:** Ensuring that processing methods do not alter the genetic or chemical composition of medicinal plants helps maintain the quality and efficacy of medicinal products.

Conservation in Processing:

a. **Utilizing By-products:** Finding uses for by-products and waste materials from processing can contribute to the conservation of resources and reduce waste.

4. Storage

Preservation Techniques:

   a. **Proper Storage Conditions:** Maintaining appropriate storage conditions (e.g., temperature, humidity, light) helps preserve the quality and efficacy of medicinal plant materials.

   b. **Container Selection:** Using suitable containers (e.g., airtight, light-proof) prevents contamination and degradation of stored plant materials.

Long-term Storage:

   a. **Seed Storage:** Storing seeds in seed banks under controlled conditions ensures the long-term preservation of genetic material for future cultivation.

   b. **Herbarium Specimens:** Preserving plant specimens in herbaria provides valuable records of plant species and helps in research and conservation efforts.

Multiple Choice Questions (MCQs) - Objective

1. What is the first step in the production of drugs from natural sources?

   A) Processing

   B) Collection

   C) Storage

   D) Cultivation

2. Which factor is **not** a key consideration in the selection of species for cultivation?

   A) Therapeutic potential

   B) Soil type adaptability

   C) Harvesting method

   D) Climate suitability

3. What is the primary purpose of soil testing in the cultivation of medicinal plants?

A) To determine the plant's flowering time

B) To assess the soil's fertility and nutrient content

C) To increase moisture content

D) To optimize harvesting methods

4. What is the role of irrigation in the cultivation of medicinal plants?

A) To increase soil acidity

B) To ensure adequate water supply for plant growth

C) To enhance photosynthesis

D) To prevent soil erosion

5. Why is timing critical during the collection of medicinal plants?

A) To avoid pest infestation

B) To ensure the plant parts contain the highest concentration of active compounds

C) To increase the plant's growth rate

D) To decrease the plant's water content

6. Which method is commonly used for the extraction of active compounds from raw medicinal materials?

A) Titration

B) Percolation

C) Grinding

D) Air drying

7. What is the primary goal of proper storage conditions for medicinal drugs?

A) To improve the color of the drug

B) To prevent degradation and maintain quality

C) To reduce the drug's potency

D) To increase the drug's moisture content

8. What role do plant hormones like auxins play in medicinal plant cultivation?

A) They inhibit plant growth

B) They promote cell elongation and root development

C) They decrease the plant's size

D) They increase the plant's moisture content

9. What is the significance of polyploidy in medicinal plants?

    A) It reduces plant growth

    B) It can increase the size and yield of the plant

    C) It decreases the production of secondary metabolites

    D) It has no effect on the plant's medicinal properties

10. Why is mutation breeding used in medicinal plant cultivation?

    A) To increase soil acidity

    B) To develop new plant varieties with improved traits

    C) To decrease plant height

    D) To prevent seed germination

11. What is the purpose of hybridization in medicinal plants?

    A) To create uniform plant varieties with enhanced traits

    B) To reduce the plant's growth rate

    C) To increase soil pH

    D) To decrease the plant's secondary metabolites

12. What is the primary concern when collecting wild medicinal plants?

    A) Reducing the plant's water content

    B) Preventing overharvesting and ensuring sustainability

    C) Increasing the plant's flowering time

    D) Reducing the plant's size

13. What is the role of berberine in Goldenseal (Hydrastis canadensis)?

    A) It enhances photosynthesis

    B) It provides antimicrobial and anti-inflammatory properties

    C) It increases the plant's growth rate

    D) It decreases the plant's water content

14. Which plant hormone is commonly used to regulate fruit ripening in medicinal plants?

A) Auxins

B) Cytokinins

C) Ethylene

D) Gibberellins

15. What is the primary benefit of organic farming in medicinal plant cultivation?

A) It increases the plant's moisture content

B) It reduces the use of synthetic chemicals and supports environmental health

C) It enhances the plant's flowering time

D) It increases soil acidity

16. What is a significant advantage of using tissue culture in medicinal plant propagation?

A) It reduces the plant's size

B) It allows for the rapid multiplication of plants with desired traits

C) It decreases the plant's secondary metabolite production

D) It increases soil erosion

17. How does proper packaging help in the storage of medicinal drugs?

A) It increases the drug's water content

B) It protects the drugs from environmental factors and contamination

C) It decreases the drug's potency

D) It enhances the drug's color

18. What is the primary reason for using steam distillation in the extraction of essential oils from plants like Lavender?

A) To increase the plant's size

B) To preserve the volatile compounds in the essential oils

C) To reduce the plant's moisture content

D) To enhance the plant's flowering time

19. What is a key factor in determining the optimal harvest time for medicinal plants?

    A) The plant's color

    B) The highest concentration of active compounds

    C) The plant's height

    D) The plant's water content

20. What is the role of seed banks in the conservation of medicinal plants?

    A) To reduce soil pH

    B) To preserve genetic diversity for future cultivation

    C) To decrease the plant's growth rate

    D) To increase the plant's size

Short Answer Type Questions (Subjective)

1. Explain the importance of soil preparation in the cultivation of medicinal plants.

2. Describe the role of genetic improvement in the cultivation of medicinal plants.

3. What are the key factors to consider when selecting the optimal harvest time for medicinal plants?

4. How do plant hormones like gibberellins and cytokinins influence the growth of medicinal plants?

5. Discuss the significance of sustainable cultivation practices in the production of medicinal plants.

6. What are the main steps involved in the processing of medicinal plant materials?

7. Explain the impact of polyploidy on the yield and quality of medicinal plants.

8. How does hybridization contribute to the development of new medicinal plant varieties?

9. Describe the role of ethical collection practices in the conservation of wild medicinal plants.

10. What are the challenges associated with the storage of medicinal drugs, and how can they be addressed?

11. How does the use of tissue culture enhance the propagation of medicinal plants?

12. Discuss the importance of proper packaging in maintaining the quality of stored medicinal drugs.

13. What are the advantages and limitations of using organic farming methods in medicinal plant cultivation?

14. How does mutation breeding help in improving the traits of medicinal plants?

15. Describe the process of steam distillation and its application in the extraction of essential oils from medicinal plants.

16. What are the benefits of establishing seed banks for the conservation of medicinal plants?

17. How does the timing of collection affect the medicinal value of plant materials?

18. Explain the role of berberine in the pharmacology of Goldenseal (Hydrastis canadensis).

19. How do environmental factors like climate and soil conditions influence the cultivation of medicinal plants?

20. Discuss the importance of conservation storage in maintaining the genetic diversity of medicinal plants.

Long Answer Type Questions (Subjective)

1. Discuss the various factors influencing the cultivation of medicinal plants and their impact on the yield and quality of the final product.

2. Explain the process of collecting medicinal plant materials and the ethical considerations that must be taken into account to ensure sustainability.

3. Describe the different methods used in the processing of medicinal plant materials and the importance of standardization in ensuring the quality of the final product.

4. Analyze the role of plant hormones in the cultivation of medicinal plants, providing examples of how they can be used to enhance growth and yield.

5. Discuss the significance of polyploidy and hybridization in the development of new medicinal plant varieties, including their advantages and challenges.

6. Explain the various storage methods used for medicinal drugs and the factors that influence the stability and shelf life of these products.

7. Discuss the importance of conservation in the cultivation, collection, processing, and storage of medicinal plants, providing examples of conservation practices.

8. Analyze the impact of environmental factors such as climate, soil conditions, and water management on the successful cultivation of medicinal plants.

9. Explain the pharmacological properties of Ginseng (Panax ginseng) and Cannabis (Cannabis sativa), including their active compounds, mechanisms of action, and therapeutic uses.

10. Discuss the role of mutation breeding in the cultivation of medicinal plants and how it can be used to develop plants with improved traits.

Answer Key for MCQs

1. (D) Cultivation

2. (C) Harvesting method

3. (B) To assess the soil's fertility and nutrient content

4. (B) To ensure adequate water supply for plant growth

5. (B) To ensure the plant parts contain the highest concentration of active compounds:

6. (B) Percolation

7. (B) To prevent degradation and maintain quality

8. (B) They promote cell elongation and root development

9. (B) It can increase the size and yield of the plant

10. (B) To develop new plant varieties with improved traits

11. (A) To create uniform plant varieties with enhanced traits

12. (B) Preventing overharvesting and ensuring sustainability

13. (B) It provides antimicrobial and anti-inflammatory properties

14. (C) Ethylene

15. (B) It reduces the use of synthetic chemicals and supports environmental health:

16. (B) It allows for the rapid multiplication of plants with desired traits

17. (B) It protects the drugs from environmental factors and contamination

18. (B) To preserve the volatile compounds in the essential oils

19. (B) The highest concentration of active compounds

20. (B) To preserve genetic diversity for future cultivation

CHAPTER – 6

PLANT TISSUE CULTURE IN DETAIL

INTRODUCTION:

Plant tissue culture is a method of growing plant cells, tissues, or organs under sterile conditions on a nutrient culture medium. It plays a crucial role in plant research and agriculture, offering techniques for plant propagation, genetic modification, and conservation.

Key Concepts in Plant Tissue Culture

1. **Sterile Environment**:
   a. A sterile environment is essential to prevent contamination by microorganisms. This is usually achieved through autoclaving, use of laminar flow hoods, and sterilization of tools and surfaces with alcohol or other disinfectants.

2. **Culture Media**:
   a. The culture medium provides the necessary nutrients for the plant tissues to grow. It typically contains a carbon source (like sucrose), inorganic salts, vitamins, amino acids, and plant hormones such as auxins, cytokinins, and gibberellins. The choice of medium depends on the type of tissue being cultured and the desired outcome (e.g., root induction, shoot proliferation).

3. **Explants**:
   a. An explant is the piece of plant tissue used to initiate the culture. It can be taken from various parts of the plant, such as leaves, stems, roots, or even flowers. The choice of explant affects the success of the culture and the type of plant development.

4. **Totipotency**:

a. Plant cells exhibit totipotency, the ability of a single cell to regenerate into a whole plant. This property is fundamental to tissue culture techniques, as it allows for the regeneration of plants from a small number of cells.

5. **Stages of Plant Tissue Culture**:
   a. **Initiation**: Selection and sterilization of explants, followed by their placement on the culture medium.
   b. **Multiplication**: Induction of shoot or root proliferation using specific hormones in the medium.
   c. **Rooting**: Transfer of shoots to a medium that promotes root formation.
   d. **Acclimatization**: Gradual adaptation of the cultured plantlets to external conditions, usually by transferring them to soil or a suitable substrate.

6. **Applications**:
   a. **Micropropagation**: Rapid multiplication of plants through tissue culture, producing large numbers of identical plants (clones).
   b. **Genetic Engineering**: Introduction of new traits by inserting genes into plant tissues in vitro, followed by regeneration of the genetically modified plants.
   c. **Conservation**: Preservation of endangered plant species through tissue culture and cryopreservation techniques.
   d. **Secondary Metabolite Production**: Culturing plant tissues to produce valuable compounds like alkaloids, flavonoids, and terpenoids.

7. **Advantages**:
   a. **Disease-Free Plants**: Tissue culture can produce plants free from pathogens.

b. **Year-Round Production**: Unlike traditional methods, tissue culture allows for continuous plant production regardless of the season.

c. **Genetic Uniformity**: The plants produced are genetically identical to the parent plant, ensuring uniformity in crop quality.

8. **Challenges**:

   a. **Contamination**: Maintaining sterility is challenging and essential to avoid culture loss.

   b. **Cost**: Tissue culture requires specialized equipment and skilled personnel, making it more expensive than conventional propagation methods.

   c. **Somaclonal Variation**: Sometimes, genetic variations may occur in the cultured plants, leading to unintended changes in the plant characteristics.

HISTORICAL DEVELOPMENT OF PLANT TISSUE CULTURE

The historical development of plant tissue culture is marked by significant milestones that have shaped the field into a vital component of modern plant biology and agriculture. Here's a detailed overview of its evolution:

1. Early Theoretical Foundations (19th Century)

a. **1838-1839**: The concept of cell theory was proposed by botanists Matthias Schleiden and Theodor Schwann. They stated that all living organisms are composed of cells, and the cell is the fundamental unit of life. This theory laid the groundwork for the idea that individual plant cells could potentially grow and regenerate into whole plants.

b. **1902**: German botanist Gottlieb Haberlandt, often referred to as the "Father of Plant Tissue Culture," proposed the idea of totipotency in plant cells. He attempted to culture isolated plant cells in vitro, but his experiments were unsuccessful due to the lack of a suitable culture medium and knowledge of plant hormones.

2. Development of Techniques and Media (1920s-1930s)

a. **1922**: The first successful plant tissue culture was achieved by American botanist Ross Granville Harrison, who cultured frog nerve fibers in vitro, which indirectly influenced plant tissue culture research.

b. **1920s**: F. C. Steward and his colleagues successfully cultured carrot root tissues and obtained a mass of undifferentiated cells known as callus. This success highlighted the importance of nutrients and hormones in culture media.

c. **1934**: Philip White developed a simple nutrient medium that allowed the continuous culture of tomato roots. His work demonstrated that plant tissues could be maintained in vitro for extended periods.

3. Discovery of Plant Hormones and Their Role (1930s-1950s)

a. **1939**: The discovery of the first plant hormone, auxin (indole-3-acetic acid, IAA), by Kenneth Thimann and Fritz Went, provided a breakthrough in plant tissue culture. Auxins were found to be essential for root formation and callus induction.

b. **1950s**: The discovery of cytokinins, another class of plant hormones, by Folke Skoog and Carlos O. Miller, further advanced tissue culture techniques. Cytokinins promote cell division and shoot formation, complementing the role of auxins.

4. Advancements in Culture Techniques and Applications (1950s-1970s)

a. **1950s**: F. C. Steward and colleagues developed methods for somatic embryogenesis, where embryos are formed from somatic cells in culture. This demonstrated that plant cells could undergo complete differentiation in vitro.

b. **1962**: Toshio Murashige and Folke Skoog developed the Murashige and Skoog (MS) medium, which became the most widely used culture medium in plant tissue culture. The MS medium, rich in nutrients and hormones, is suitable for a wide range of plant species.

c. **1960s**: The development of micropropagation techniques, especially by Georges Morel, allowed for the mass production of disease-free plants, particularly orchids.

5. Modern Developments and Biotechnology (1980s-Present)

a. **1980s**: The advent of genetic engineering and recombinant DNA technology enabled the introduction of foreign genes into plant cells in vitro, followed by the regeneration of genetically modified plants. Plant tissue culture became a key tool in the production of genetically modified crops (GMOs).

b. **1980s-1990s**: Cryopreservation techniques were developed for the long-term storage of plant tissues at ultra-low temperatures, facilitating the conservation of endangered plant species and valuable genetic resources.

c. **1990s-Present**: Tissue culture has expanded into various applications, including the production of secondary metabolites, development of transgenic plants, and use in functional genomics. Tissue culture techniques have also been integrated into commercial agriculture for large-scale production of crops, ornamental plants, and trees.

TYPES OF CULTURES

Plant tissue culture encompasses various types of cultures, each tailored to specific research objectives, plant species, and desired outcomes. Here's a detailed overview of the different types of cultures used in plant tissue culture:

1. Callus Culture

a. **Description**: Callus culture involves the growth of unorganized, undifferentiated plant cells or tissues on a nutrient medium. Callus is typically induced from an explant (e.g., leaf, stem, or root tissue) by placing it on a medium containing high concentrations of auxins and cytokinins.

b. **Applications**:

   i.   **Genetic Manipulation**: Used as a starting point for genetic transformation and somatic embryogenesis.

   ii. **Secondary Metabolite Production**: Callus cultures are used to produce valuable secondary metabolites, such as alkaloids, flavonoids, and terpenoids.

c. **Example**: Callus cultures of Catharanthus roseus are used to produce vincristine and vinblastine, which are important anticancer compounds.

2. Suspension Culture

a. **Description**: Suspension culture involves the cultivation of single cells or small clusters of cells in a liquid medium. The callus is first dispersed into individual cells, which are then suspended in a liquid culture medium that is continuously agitated to maintain cell separation and aeration.

b. **Applications**:

   i.   **Mass Production of Cells**: Ideal for large-scale production of plant cells for secondary metabolite extraction.

   ii. **Protoplast Culture**: Used to generate and culture protoplasts (plant cells without cell walls) for fusion experiments and genetic engineering.

c. **Example**: Suspension cultures of Taxus species are used to produce paclitaxel, an important anticancer drug.

3. Organ Culture

a. **Description**: Organ culture involves the culture of isolated plant organs, such as roots, shoots, leaves, or flower buds, on a nutrient medium. The goal is to study the development and differentiation of specific plant organs in vitro.

b. **Types of Organ Cultures**:

   i.   **Root Culture**: Culturing isolated roots to study root growth, development, and nutrient uptake.

ii. **Shoot Tip Culture**: Culturing shoot apices or meristems to propagate plants vegetatively, often used for micropropagation and virus elimination.

iii. **Leaf Culture**: Culturing leaves to study leaf development or induce callus formation.

c. **Applications**:

i. **Micropropagation**: Shoot tip culture is commonly used to propagate large numbers of disease-free plants.

ii. **Research**: Organ cultures are used to study specific physiological and developmental processes.

d. **Example**: Shoot tip culture is extensively used for the micropropagation of orchids and bananas.

4. Protoplast Culture

a. **Description**: Protoplast culture involves the culture of plant cells that have had their cell walls enzymatically removed, leaving behind the plasma membrane-bound protoplast. Protoplasts can be cultured to regenerate into whole plants or be used in somatic hybridization.

b. **Applications**:

i. **Somatic Hybridization**: Fusion of protoplasts from different species to create somatic hybrids with desirable traits.

ii. **Genetic Engineering**: Direct uptake of DNA, RNA, or other macromolecules into protoplasts for genetic modification.

c. **Example**: Protoplast fusion has been used to create somatic hybrids between different species of Brassica (e.g., cabbage and radish).

5. Embryo Culture

a. **Description**: Embryo culture involves the isolation and in vitro culture of plant embryos, either zygotic (from fertilization) or somatic (from somatic cells). The goal is often to rescue embryos that might not develop in vivo due to incompatibility or environmental stress.

b. **Applications**:

    i. **Embryo Rescue**: Used to overcome barriers in interspecific and intergeneric hybridization, allowing the development of hybrid plants.

    ii. **Somatic Embryogenesis**: Inducing somatic cells to form embryos that can develop into complete plants, used in clonal propagation and genetic engineering.

c. **Example**: Embryo rescue techniques are used to produce hybrids in crops like wheat and barley, where normal embryo development is hindered by cross-species incompatibility.

6. Anther and Pollen Culture

a. **Description**: Anther or pollen culture involves culturing anthers or isolated pollen grains to produce haploid plants through androgenesis. These haploid plants can then be treated to double their chromosome number, resulting in homozygous diploid plants.

b. **Applications**:

    i. **Breeding**: Production of homozygous lines in a single generation, which is valuable in plant breeding programs.

    ii. **Genetic Studies**: Haploid plants are used in genetic studies to investigate gene expression and inheritance.

c. **Example**: Anther culture is widely used in crops like rice, wheat, and tobacco to produce homozygous lines for breeding.

7. Somatic Embryogenesis

a. **Description**: Somatic embryogenesis is the process by which somatic cells (non-reproductive cells) develop into embryos that can grow into complete plants. This process can occur directly from the explant or indirectly through callus formation.

b. **Applications**:

i. **Clonal Propagation**: Rapid multiplication of plants with desirable traits.

ii. **Synthetic Seed Production**: Somatic embryos can be encapsulated to create synthetic seeds for storage and planting.

c. **Example**: Somatic embryogenesis is used in the clonal propagation of high-value crops like coffee, oil palm, and conifers.

8. Meristem Culture

a. **Description**: Meristem culture involves the culture of the shoot apical meristem or axillary buds to produce virus-free plants. The meristem is the growing tip of a plant, and because viruses often do not invade this region, plants regenerated from meristem cultures are typically free of pathogens.

b. **Applications**:

i. **Virus Elimination**: Producing virus-free planting material for vegetatively propagated crops like potatoes, bananas, and strawberries.

ii. **Micropropagation**: Mass propagation of elite varieties.

c. **Example**: Meristem culture is commonly used to produce virus-free potato plants.

9. Hairy Root Culture

a. **Description**: Hairy root culture is induced by infecting plant tissues with Agrobacterium rhizogenes, which causes the formation of rapidly growing roots that can be cultured in vitro. These roots have a high capacity for secondary metabolite production.

b. **Applications**:

i. **Secondary Metabolite Production**: Used to produce valuable compounds like alkaloids and terpenoids.

ii. **Genetic Studies**: Studying root development and gene expression.

c. **Example**: Hairy root cultures of *Solanum lycopersicum* (tomato) are used to produce valuable compounds like solasodine.

NUTRITIONAL REQUIREMENTS OF PLANT TISSUE CULTURE

The nutritional requirements of plant tissue culture are critical for the successful growth and development of plant tissues, organs, or cells in vitro. The culture medium must provide all the essential nutrients, vitamins, growth regulators, and other compounds necessary to support various physiological processes. Below is a detailed overview of the nutritional requirements in plant tissue culture:

1. Macronutrients

Macronutrients are required in large quantities for plant growth and development. They provide the essential elements that are involved in the formation of cellular structures and metabolic functions.

a. **Nitrogen (N)**:
   i. **Forms**: Provided as nitrate (NO_3^-) or ammonium (NH_4^+) salts, often as potassium nitrate (KNO_3) and ammonium nitrate (NH_4NO_3).
   ii. **Function**: Essential for the synthesis of amino acids, proteins, nucleic acids, and chlorophyll.

b. **Phosphorus (P)**:
   i. **Forms**: Supplied as phosphate ions ($H_2PO_4^-$), commonly as potassium dihydrogen phosphate (KH_2PO_4).
   ii. **Function**: Vital for energy transfer (ATP), nucleic acids, and phospholipids.

c. **Potassium (K)**:
   i. **Forms**: Supplied as potassium nitrate (KNO_3) or potassium chloride (KCl).
   ii. **Function**: Regulates osmotic balance, enzyme activation, and photosynthesis.

d. **Calcium (Ca):**
   i.   **Forms**: Supplied as calcium chloride ($CaCl_2$) or calcium nitrate $[Ca(NO_3)_2]$.
   ii. **Function**: Important for cell wall stability, membrane integrity, and signaling.

e. **Magnesium (Mg):**
   i.   **Forms**: Provided as magnesium sulfate ($MgSO_4$).
   ii. **Function**: Central component of chlorophyll and a cofactor for many enzymes.

f. **Sulfur (S):**
   i.   **Forms**: Supplied as sulfate ions (SO_4^{2-}), commonly as magnesium sulfate ($MgSO_4$).
   ii. **Function**: Integral to the synthesis of sulfur-containing amino acids (cysteine and methionine) and vitamins.

2. Micronutrients

Micronutrients are required in smaller quantities but are equally essential for plant growth and development, often acting as cofactors in enzymatic reactions.

a. **Iron (Fe):**
   i.   **Forms**: Usually provided as ferrous sulfate ($FeSO_4$) or chelated forms like ferric ethylenediaminetetraacetic acid (Fe-EDTA).
   ii. **Function**: Crucial for chlorophyll synthesis, respiration, and electron transport.

b. **Manganese (Mn):**
   i.   **Forms**: Supplied as manganese sulfate ($MnSO_4$).
   ii. **Function**: Activates enzymes involved in photosynthesis and nitrogen metabolism.

c. **Zinc (Zn):**
   i.   **Forms**: Provided as zinc sulfate ($ZnSO_4$).

ii. **Function**: Required for protein synthesis, hormone regulation, and enzyme activation.

d. **Copper (Cu)**:

i. **Forms**: Supplied as copper sulfate ($CuSO_4$).

ii. **Function**: Involved in lignin synthesis and acts as a cofactor for oxidative enzymes.

e. **Molybdenum (Mo)**:

i. **Forms**: Supplied as ammonium molybdate $[(NH_4)_6Mo_7O_{24}]$.

ii. **Function**: Essential for nitrogen fixation and nitrate reduction.

f. **Boron (B)**:

i. **Forms**: Provided as boric acid (H_3BO_3).

ii. **Function**: Important for cell wall synthesis, membrane function, and reproductive development.

3. Vitamins

Vitamins are organic compounds that are required in small amounts and serve as coenzymes or precursors for enzyme systems.

a. **Thiamine (Vitamin B1)**:

i. **Function**: Acts as a coenzyme in carbohydrate metabolism and is essential for energy production.

b. **Nicotinic Acid (Niacin)**:

i. **Function**: Precursor for NAD+ and NADP+, which are involved in redox reactions and energy metabolism.

c. **Pyridoxine (Vitamin B6)**:

i. **Function**: Involved in amino acid metabolism and the synthesis of neurotransmitters.

d. **Inositol**:

i. **Function**: Important for cell membrane integrity and cell signaling.

e. **Biotin (Vitamin H)**:

i.   **Function**: Essential for fatty acid synthesis and amino acid metabolism.

4. Carbohydrates

Carbohydrates are provided as an energy source, as plant tissues in vitro typically cannot photosynthesize efficiently due to the controlled environment.

a. **Sucrose**:

   i.   **Common Concentration**: Typically used at 2-3% (w/v).

   ii. **Function**: Serves as the primary energy source and osmotic regulator in the culture medium.

b. **Other Sugars**: Glucose, fructose, and maltose can also be used, but sucrose is the most common due to its efficiency.

5. Growth Regulators

Growth regulators, or plant hormones, are critical for controlling cell division, elongation, differentiation, and organogenesis in plant tissue culture.

a. **Auxins**:

   i.   **Examples**: Indole-3-acetic acid (IAA), 2,4-dichlorophenoxyacetic acid (2,4-D), and naphthalene acetic acid (NAA).

   ii. **Function**: Promote cell division, root initiation, and callus formation.

b. **Cytokinins**:

   i.   **Examples**: Kinetin, benzylaminopurine (BAP), and zeatin.

   ii. **Function**: Stimulate cell division, shoot initiation, and delay senescence.

c. **Gibberellins**:

   i.   **Examples**: Gibberellic acid (GA_3).

   ii. **Function**: Promote stem elongation, seed germination, and breaking dormancy.

d. **Abscisic Acid (ABA)**:

i. **Function**: Involved in stress responses, seed dormancy, and regulation of stomatal closure.

e. **Ethylene**:

i. **Function**: Regulates fruit ripening, leaf abscission, and response to stress, although often it is undesirable in culture as it can inhibit growth.

6. Gelling Agents

Gelling agents solidify the culture medium, providing support for the plant tissues.

a. **Agar**:

i. **Source**: Extracted from red algae.

ii. **Function**: The most common gelling agent, used to create a semi-solid medium for plant tissue culture.

b. **Alternative Gelling Agents**:

i. **Examples**: Gelrite, Phytagel.

ii. **Function**: Used when a clear medium or different gelling properties are desired.

7. pH Adjusters

The pH of the culture medium is adjusted to an optimal level, typically between 5.6 and 5.8, to ensure nutrient availability and proper physiological functioning.

a. **Common Agents**:

i. **Examples**: Hydrochloric acid (HCl) or sodium hydroxide (NaOH).

ii. **Function**: Adjust the pH of the medium to the desired level before sterilization.

GROWTH AND THEIR MAINTENANCE

Growth and maintenance are critical aspects of plant tissue culture, as they ensure the successful development, multiplication, and sustainability of cultured plant tissues, organs, or cells. Proper management of the culture environment and regular maintenance practices are essential for achieving desired outcomes, whether it be callus formation, organogenesis, or somatic embryogenesis. Below is a detailed explanation of growth and maintenance in plant tissue culture:

1. Factors Influencing Growth in Plant Tissue Culture

1.1. Culture Medium

The culture medium is the foundation for plant tissue growth in vitro. It must provide all essential nutrients, vitamins, and growth regulators to support cellular functions.

a. **Balanced Nutrient Supply**: The composition of the medium must be tailored to the specific needs of the plant species and the type of tissue being cultured.

b. **Growth Regulators**: The correct balance of auxins, cytokinins, gibberellins, and other growth regulators is crucial for determining the growth pattern (e.g., shoot vs. root formation).

c. **Carbohydrate Source**: Sucrose is commonly used as an energy source, and its concentration can influence growth rates and morphogenesis.

1.2. Physical Environment

The physical environment in which cultures are maintained plays a significant role in growth.

a. **Temperature**: Most plant tissues grow optimally at temperatures between 25°C and 28°C. Deviations can lead to stress or suboptimal growth.

b. **Light**: Light quality, intensity, and photoperiod influence photosynthesis and photomorphogenesis. Some cultures require light for shoot induction, while others may require darkness for callus formation.

c. **Humidity**: High relative humidity (around 70-80%) is maintained to prevent desiccation of cultures, especially when cultured in a semi-solid medium.

d. **Aeration**: Gas exchange is necessary to provide oxygen and remove ethylene and other gaseous byproducts. Proper sealing of culture vessels is crucial to maintain an optimal gas environment.

1.3. pH

The pH of the culture medium is adjusted to between 5.6 and 5.8 before sterilization. This pH range is optimal for nutrient availability and enzyme activity, promoting healthy growth.

2. Maintenance of Cultures

Regular maintenance is essential to sustain healthy growth and prevent contamination or degeneration of the cultures.

2.1. Subculturing

Subculturing involves transferring growing tissues, cells, or organs to fresh medium at regular intervals. This prevents nutrient depletion, waste accumulation, and maintains the growth potential of the culture.

a. **Frequency**: Subculturing frequency depends on the growth rate of the culture. Fast-growing cultures may need to be subcultured every 4-6 weeks.

b. **Techniques**: Sterile techniques must be strictly followed to avoid contamination. The explants or tissues are carefully excised and transferred to fresh medium under aseptic conditions.

2.2. Monitoring and Contamination Control

Continuous monitoring of cultures is necessary to detect any signs of contamination or abnormal growth early.

a. **Visual Inspection**: Regular checks for microbial contamination (bacterial, fungal) and physiological disorders are essential. Contaminated cultures must be discarded immediately to prevent the spread to other cultures.

b. **Sterility Maintenance**: All tools, culture media, and workspaces must be sterilized before use. Regular cleaning and sterilization protocols help minimize contamination risks.

2.3. Environmental Control

Maintaining the physical environment within optimal parameters is crucial for sustained growth.

a. **Temperature Control**: Growth chambers or culture rooms should have precise temperature control to avoid fluctuations that could stress the cultures.

b. **Light Regulation**: Light intensity and photoperiod must be controlled using programmable timers and light sources suitable for the plant species.

c. **Humidity and Ventilation**: Proper ventilation and humidity control are essential to prevent fungal growth and desiccation.

2.4. Record Keeping

3. Long-term Maintenance and Storage

For long-term maintenance, cultures may need to be stored or preserved.

3.1. Slow Growth Storage

Reducing the growth rate by lowering the temperature (e.g., 4-10°C) or reducing light intensity can extend the interval between subculturing, making maintenance easier.

a. **Objective**: Slow down metabolism to minimize the need for frequent subculturing, commonly used for germplasm storage or conserving valuable genotypes.

3.2. Cryopreservation

Cryopreservation involves storing plant tissues or cells at ultra-low temperatures (typically in liquid nitrogen at -196°C) for long-term preservation.

a. **Process**: Tissues are treated with cryoprotectants before being frozen rapidly. Upon thawing, the tissues can be cultured again, resuming normal growth.

b. **Application**: Used for conserving genetic material, rare species, or valuable germplasm over long periods without regular maintenance.

APPLICATIONS OF PLANT TISSUE CULTURE IN PHARMACOGNOSY

Plant tissue culture has numerous applications in pharmacognosy, which is the study of medicinal drugs derived from plants and other natural sources. These applications are essential for the production of medicinal compounds, the conservation of endangered species, and the development of novel pharmaceuticals. Below is a detailed overview of the applications of plant tissue culture in pharmacognosy:

1. Production of Secondary Metabolites

One of the primary applications of plant tissue culture in pharmacognosy is the production of secondary metabolites, which are bioactive compounds responsible for the therapeutic properties of medicinal plants.

1.1. In Vitro Production

Plant tissue culture techniques such as cell suspension cultures, callus cultures, and organ cultures (like root or shoot cultures) are employed to produce secondary metabolites in vitro.

a. **Example**: Production of alkaloids, flavonoids, terpenoids, and phenolic compounds, which are used in various pharmaceutical applications.

b. **Advantages**: This approach allows for the production of bioactive compounds in a controlled environment, independent of seasonal variations, and without the need for extensive cultivation of the whole plant.

1.2. Elicitation

Elicitation is a technique used to enhance the production of secondary metabolites in cultured plant cells by introducing biotic or abiotic elicitors.

a. **Example**: Jasmonic acid, salicylic acid, or yeast extract can be used as elicitors to increase the yield of specific compounds like taxol from Taxus spp. cultures.

b. **Benefits**: This method increases the concentration of desired metabolites, making the process more efficient and economically viable.

2. Conservation of Medicinal Plants

Plant tissue culture plays a critical role in the conservation of endangered and medicinally important plant species.

2.1. Micropropagation

Micropropagation is the process of rapidly multiplying plant material to produce a large number of offspring in a relatively short period.

a. **Application**: Used for the conservation and mass propagation of rare or endangered medicinal plants like Rauwolfia serpentina and Digitalis spp.

b. **Benefits**: Ensures the availability of medicinal plants for future generations and reduces the pressure on wild populations.

2.2. Germplasm Conservation

Plant tissue culture techniques are employed to conserve germplasm of medicinal plants, ensuring their genetic diversity is preserved.

a. **Cryopreservation**: Storage of plant tissues at ultra-low temperatures (e.g., liquid nitrogen) for long-term conservation.

b. **Benefits**: Provides a long-term solution for preserving the genetic material of important medicinal plants, especially those at risk of extinction.

3. Genetic Improvement of Medicinal Plants

Tissue culture techniques facilitate the genetic improvement of medicinal plants to enhance the yield of bioactive compounds or improve resistance to diseases and environmental stress.

3.1. Somaclonal Variation

Somaclonal variation refers to the genetic variation observed in plants regenerated from tissue cultures, which can be exploited for plant improvement.

a. **Application**: Used to develop plant varieties with enhanced secondary metabolite production, improved growth rates, or increased resistance to pests and diseases.

b. **Example**: Development of high-yielding Catharanthus roseus varieties that produce increased levels of vincristine and vinblastine, important anti-cancer alkaloids.

3.2. Genetic Engineering

Genetic transformation techniques, such as Agrobacterium-mediated transformation or biolistic methods, are used to introduce new traits into medicinal plants.

a. **Application**: Engineering plants to produce higher levels of therapeutic compounds or to introduce new biosynthetic pathways for novel drug production.

b. **Example**: Transgenic Artemisia annua plants engineered to produce higher levels of artemisinin, an important anti-malarial compound.

4. Disease-Free Plant Production

Plant tissue culture techniques are used to produce disease-free and genetically uniform plant material, which is crucial for the consistent production of medicinal compounds.

4.1. Meristem Culture

Meristem culture is a technique used to produce virus-free plants by culturing the meristematic tissue, which is usually free from viruses and other pathogens.

a. **Application**: Producing disease-free planting material for medicinal plants like ginger (Zingiber officinale) and potato (Solanum tuberosum), which are prone to viral infections.

b. **Benefits**: Ensures the availability of healthy plant material, leading to higher yields of medicinal compounds and reducing the risk of disease transmission.

5. Biosynthesis and Pathway Studies

Plant tissue culture allows researchers to study the biosynthesis of secondary metabolites and the pathways involved in their production.

5.1. Studying Metabolic Pathways

Cultured cells, tissues, or organs can be used to investigate the biosynthetic pathways of various secondary metabolites.

a. **Application**: Understanding the biosynthesis of important drugs like morphine from Papaver somniferum or quinine from Cinchona spp.

b. **Benefits**: Provides insights into the regulation of metabolic pathways, enabling the manipulation of cultures to enhance the production of specific compounds.

5.2. Mutagenesis and Selection

Plant tissue culture is used in combination with mutagenesis (induced by chemicals or radiation) to create mutants with altered metabolic pathways.

a. **Application**: Selecting mutants that produce higher levels of desired secondary metabolites or novel compounds with potential therapeutic applications.

b. **Example**: Developing mutants of Mentha species that produce higher levels of essential oils with improved therapeutic properties.

6. Large-Scale Cultivation of Medicinal Plants

Plant tissue culture techniques are increasingly being used for the large-scale cultivation of medicinal plants, especially those that are difficult to grow under conventional agricultural practices.

6.1. Bioreactor Systems

Large-scale bioreactor systems are used to cultivate plant cells or tissues in a controlled environment, facilitating the production of medicinal compounds.

a. **Application**: Commercial production of plant-derived pharmaceuticals, such as paclitaxel (Taxol) from Taxus spp. using cell suspension cultures in bioreactors.

b. **Advantages**: Offers a scalable and sustainable approach to producing high-value medicinal compounds without the need for extensive land use or natural resources.

EDIBLE VACCINES

Edible vaccines represent a novel approach in plant tissue culture, where plants are genetically engineered to produce specific antigens, which can stimulate an immune response when consumed. This concept leverages plant tissue culture techniques to develop vaccines that are cost-effective, easy to administer, and can be distributed without the need for cold chain logistics. Here's a detailed explanation of edible vaccines in the context of plant tissue culture:

1. Introduction to Edible Vaccines

Edible vaccines are vaccines produced in genetically modified plants, which, when ingested, trigger an immune response in the human body. These vaccines are designed to combat various infectious diseases by delivering the necessary antigens directly through the consumption of the plant or its products, such as fruits, leaves, or seeds.

2. Development of Edible Vaccines Using Plant Tissue Culture

2.1. Genetic Engineering of Plants

The development of edible vaccines begins with the genetic modification of plants to express specific antigens.

a. **Gene Selection**: The gene encoding the antigen of interest (e.g., viral, bacterial, or parasitic antigens) is identified and isolated.

b. **Transformation Techniques**: The selected gene is inserted into the plant genome using transformation techniques such as Agrobacterium-mediated transformation or biolistics (gene gun).

    i. **Agrobacterium-mediated Transformation**: This is a common method where the gene of interest is inserted into the T-DNA region of the Ti plasmid, which is then introduced into plant cells by the bacterium Agrobacterium tumefaciens.

    ii. **Biolistics**: Also known as particle bombardment, this method involves coating tiny metal particles with DNA and shooting them into plant tissues, where the DNA integrates into the plant genome.

2.2. Plant Tissue Culture Techniques

Once the plant cells are transformed, plant tissue culture techniques are used to regenerate whole plants from the modified cells.

a. **Callus Formation**: Transformed cells are cultured on a medium containing growth regulators to induce callus formation, a mass of undifferentiated cells.

b. **Regeneration**: The callus is then transferred to a medium with a specific balance of auxins and cytokinins to promote shoot and root formation, regenerating the plant.

c. **Selection**: Transgenic plants are selected based on their ability to express the introduced gene, usually confirmed by molecular techniques like PCR, Southern blotting, or ELISA.

3. Types of Edible Vaccines

Different types of plants have been used to produce edible vaccines, depending on the target antigen and the desired mode of delivery.

3.1. Transgenic Fruits and Vegetables

Common food crops like bananas, potatoes, tomatoes, and lettuce have been used to produce edible vaccines.

a. **Bananas**: Used for vaccines against diseases like Hepatitis B and Rotavirus, as they are easily consumed and accepted, especially by children.

b. **Potatoes**: Modified to express antigens against diseases such as cholera, making them an effective vehicle for oral immunization.

c. **Tomatoes and Lettuce**: Also used for expressing antigens, particularly for mucosal immunization, where the vaccine is delivered directly to the mucosal tissues (e.g., in the gastrointestinal tract).

3.2. Transgenic Seeds and Grains

Seeds and grains like rice and maize are also used for edible vaccines.

a. **Rice**: Engineered to produce antigens for diseases like cholera and Hepatitis B, rice is stable and can be stored for long periods, making it suitable for vaccine distribution.

b. **Maize**: Used to produce vaccines against diseases like enterotoxigenic Escherichia coli (ETEC) infections.

4. Mechanism of Action of Edible Vaccines

When the transgenic plant or plant product containing the vaccine antigen is consumed, the antigen is delivered to the immune system via the mucosal surfaces of the digestive tract.

a. **Immune Response**: The antigen is taken up by M cells in the gut-associated lymphoid tissue (GALT), where it is processed and presented to immune cells, leading to the activation of both humoral (antibody-mediated) and cellular immune responses.

b. **Mucosal Immunity**: Edible vaccines are particularly effective in stimulating mucosal immunity, which is the first line of defense against many pathogens that enter the body through mucosal surfaces.

5. Advantages of Edible Vaccines

5.1. Cost-Effectiveness

Edible vaccines are cheaper to produce than traditional vaccines because they do not require expensive purification processes, sterile injections, or cold chain logistics.

5.2. Ease of Administration

These vaccines are administered orally, eliminating the need for needles, which reduces the risk of needle-associated infections and increases compliance, especially in children.

5.3. Stability and Storage

Edible vaccines can be stored and transported without the need for refrigeration, making them ideal for use in developing countries where cold chain infrastructure may be lacking.

5.4. Mass Immunization

The ease of administration and production scalability make edible vaccines suitable for large-scale immunization programs, especially in resource-limited settings.

6. Challenges and Considerations

Despite the potential benefits, there are several challenges and considerations in the development and use of edible vaccines.

6.1. Dosage Control

Ensuring a consistent dosage of the antigen in each plant product is challenging, as natural variations in plant growth can affect antigen expression levels.

6.2. Regulatory Approval

Edible vaccines must undergo rigorous testing and regulatory approval to ensure their safety, efficacy, and stability, similar to traditional vaccines.

6.3. Public Acceptance

Public acceptance of genetically modified organisms (GMOs) remains a significant hurdle, as concerns about the safety and ethics of consuming transgenic plants persist.

CLASSIFICATION:

Plant tissue culture can be classified based on the type of explant used, the culture technique, and the purpose of the culture. Here is a detailed classification with examples:

1. Based on the Type of Explant Used

1.1. Meristem Culture

a. **Definition**: This involves culturing the meristematic tissue (the actively dividing cells at the tips of roots and shoots).

b. **Purpose**: Primarily used for producing virus-free plants.

c. **Example: Banana (Musa spp.)** - Meristem culture is used to eliminate viral infections and produce disease-free planting material.

1.2. Callus Culture

a. **Definition**: Involves the growth of unorganized, undifferentiated mass of cells (callus) derived from plant explants.

b. **Purpose**: Used for genetic transformation, somaclonal variation, and production of secondary metabolites.

c. **Example: Tobacco (Nicotiana tabacum)** - Used in callus culture for studying plant genetics and for transformation experiments.

1.3. Suspension Culture

a. **Definition**: Involves the culture of single cells or small cell aggregates suspended in a liquid medium.

b. **Purpose**: Used for large-scale production of secondary metabolites and for studying cell behavior in liquid environments.

c. **Example: Catharanthus roseus (Periwinkle)** - Used to produce alkaloids like vincristine and vinblastine.

1.4. Protoplast Culture

a. **Definition**: Involves the culture of plant cells without cell walls, known as protoplasts.

b. **Purpose**: Used for somatic hybridization and genetic engineering.

c. **Example: Brassica spp. (Cabbage family)** - Protoplast fusion used to create hybrid plants with desirable traits.

1.5. Organ Culture

a. **Definition**: Involves the culture of isolated organs such as roots, shoots, or embryos.

b. **Purpose**: Used for studying the development of specific organs or for the production of secondary metabolites.

c. **Example: Datura spp. (Jimsonweed)** - Root cultures are used for the production of tropane alkaloids.

1.6. Embryo Culture

a. **Definition**: Involves the culture of isolated embryos, either zygotic or somatic.

b. **Purpose**: Used for overcoming seed dormancy, embryo rescue, and for hybridization between distant species.

c. **Example: Orchid species** - Embryo culture is used to rescue hybrid embryos that fail to develop in natural conditions.

2. Based on the Culture Technique

2.1. Static Culture

a. **Definition**: The explant is placed on a solid medium, and the culture remains stationary.

b. **Purpose**: Used for shoot and root formation, callus induction, and organ culture.

c. **Example: Rose (Rosa spp.)** - Used for the propagation of shoots and roots in horticulture.

2.2. Liquid Culture

a. **Definition**: The explant is placed in a liquid medium, often agitated to keep cells in suspension.

b. **Purpose**: Used for cell suspension cultures, protoplast cultures, and mass propagation.

c. **Example: Ginseng (Panax ginseng)** - Liquid culture is used for the large-scale production of ginsenosides, bioactive compounds.

3. Based on the Purpose of the Culture

3.1. Micropropagation

a. **Definition**: The process of rapidly multiplying plant material under sterile conditions to produce a large number of progeny.

b. **Purpose**: Used for clonal propagation of plants, especially in commercial horticulture and agriculture.

c. **Example: Orchid (Orchidaceae family)** - Micropropagation is widely used for mass production of orchids.

3.2. Anther and Pollen Culture

a. **Definition**: Involves the culture of anthers or isolated pollen grains to produce haploid plants.

b. **Purpose**: Used for plant breeding, developing homozygous lines, and genetic studies.

c. **Example: Wheat (Triticum aestivum)** - Anther culture is used to develop haploid plants, which are then doubled to produce homozygous lines.

3.3. Somatic Embryogenesis

a. **Definition**: The process of developing embryos from somatic or non-reproductive cells.

b. **Purpose**: Used for clonal propagation, synthetic seed production, and genetic transformation.

c. **Example: Carrot (Daucus carota)** - Somatic embryogenesis is used to produce synthetic seeds and for plant regeneration.

3.4. Somaclonal Variation

a. **Definition**: Refers to the genetic variation observed among plants regenerated from tissue culture.

b. **Purpose**: Exploited for developing new plant varieties with desirable traits.

c. **Example: Sugarcane (Saccharum spp.)** - Somaclonal variation is used to develop new varieties with improved yield and disease resistance.

3.5. Synthetic Seed Production

a. **Definition**: Involves encapsulating somatic embryos or other tissues in a gel-like substance to produce "seeds" that can be stored and planted.

b. **Purpose**: Used for the storage, handling, and propagation of elite genotypes.

c. **Example: Alfalfa (Medicago sativa)** - Synthetic seeds are produced for easier distribution and storage of high-value cultivars.

4. Based on the Plant Part Used

4.1. Leaf Culture

a. **Definition**: The culture of leaf explants to regenerate plants.

b. **Purpose**: Used for clonal propagation, secondary metabolite production, and genetic studies.

c. **Example: Begonia spp.** - Leaf culture is commonly used for the propagation of ornamental plants.

4.2. Root Culture

a. **Definition**: Involves the culture of roots, either for regeneration or secondary metabolite production.

b. **Purpose**: Used for the production of bioactive compounds and studying root development.

c. **Example: Licorice (Glycyrrhiza glabra)** - Root culture is used to produce glycyrrhizin, a medicinal compound.

5. Based on the Regeneration Method

5.1. Direct Organogenesis

a. **Definition**: Direct regeneration of organs like shoots or roots from explants without an intermediate callus stage.

b. **Purpose**: Used for rapid plant regeneration and avoiding somaclonal variation.

c. **Example: Basil (Ocimum basilicum)** - Direct shoot regeneration from leaf explants for micropropagation.

5.2. Indirect Organogenesis

a. **Definition**: Regeneration of organs via an intermediate callus phase.

b. **Purpose**: Used for genetic transformation and plant breeding.

c. **Example: Tobacco (Nicotiana tabacum)** - Indirect organogenesis through callus culture for genetic studies.

Multiple Choice Questions (MCQs) - Objective

1. What is a sterile environment in plant tissue culture primarily used for?

   A) Promoting plant growth

   B) Preventing contamination by microorganisms

   C) Enhancing photosynthesis

   D) Increasing plant yield

2. Which of the following is the most commonly used sugar in plant tissue culture media?

   A) Glucose

   B) Fructose

   C) Sucrose

   D) Maltose

3. What does the term "totipotency" refer to in plant tissue culture?

   A) The ability of a cell to differentiate into multiple types

   B) The ability of a single cell to regenerate into a whole plant

   C) The ability of a plant to produce secondary metabolites

   D) The ability of a plant to grow in any soil type

4. Which plant tissue culture technique involves the use of liquid medium with continuous agitation?

A) Callus culture

B) Suspension culture

C) Organ culture

D) Embryo culture

5. What is the primary purpose of using auxins in plant tissue culture?

A) Promoting shoot formation

B) Inducing root formation and callus induction

C) Enhancing fruit ripening

D) Delaying senescence

6. Which plant hormone is commonly used to stimulate shoot proliferation in tissue culture?

A) Gibberellins

B) Ethylene

C) Cytokinins

D) Auxins

7. What is the main advantage of using micropropagation in plant tissue culture?

A) Increasing the size of the plants

B) Producing large numbers of genetically identical plants

C) Enhancing the color of flowers

D) Improving seed germination

8. Which of the following culture types is used to study root growth and development in vitro?

A) Leaf culture

B) Callus culture

C) Root culture

D) Suspension culture

9. What is the significance of the Murashige and Skoog (MS) medium in plant tissue culture?

A) It is used for genetic transformation

B) It is the most widely used culture medium for a wide range of plants

C) It is used for cryopreservation

D) It is specifically for protoplast culture

10. Which plant tissue culture technique is used to produce haploid plants through androgenesis?

A) Meristem culture

B) Anther and pollen culture

C) Protoplast culture

D) Embryo culture

11. What is the main purpose of cryopreservation in plant tissue culture?

A) Enhancing plant growth

B) Long-term preservation of plant tissues at ultra-low temperatures

C) Inducing flowering

D) Improving soil fertility

12. In the context of plant tissue culture, what is an explant?

A) A nutrient medium

B) A piece of plant tissue used to initiate a culture

C) A type of gelling agent

D) A growth regulator

13. Which of the following is a common application of somatic embryogenesis in plant tissue culture?

A) Production of haploid plants

B) Clonal propagation and synthetic seed production

C) Genetic modification

D) Virus elimination

14. What is the role of gelling agents like agar in plant tissue culture?

A) To provide nutrients to the plant

B) To solidify the culture medium and provide support

C) To increase the pH of the medium

D) To enhance photosynthesis

15. What is the primary goal of using genetic engineering in plant tissue culture?

A) Increasing the size of the plant

B) Introducing new traits or improving existing ones

C) Enhancing root growth

D) Reducing the growth rate

16. Which plant is widely used in genetic transformation studies due to its model organism status in plant tissue culture?

A) Catharanthus roseus

B) Begonia spp.

C) Nicotiana tabacum (Tobacco)

D) Musa spp. (Banana)

17. What is the primary benefit of using tissue culture for the production of secondary metabolites?

A) Enhancing flower color

B) Producing bioactive compounds in a controlled environment

C) Increasing plant size

D) Improving seed germination

18. Which plant is known for its production of the anti-cancer alkaloids vincristine and vinblastine?

A) Basil (Ocimum basilicum)

B) Licorice (Glycyrrhiza glabra)

C) Catharanthus roseus (Periwinkle)

D) Banana (Musa spp.)

19. What is the role of anther culture in plant breeding?

A) To produce virus-free plants

B) To produce homozygous lines in a single generation

C) To enhance root formation

D) To increase flower production

20. What is a significant challenge associated with the development of edible vaccines?

    A) High production costs

    B) Dosage control and public acceptance

    C) Limited plant species

    D) Difficulty in genetic modification

Short Answer Type Questions (Subjective)

1. Explain the concept of totipotency and its importance in plant tissue culture.
2. Describe the role of culture media in plant tissue culture and list its main components.
3. What are the applications of micropropagation in agriculture and horticulture?
4. How does the use of plant hormones like auxins and cytokinins influence tissue culture outcomes?
5. Discuss the importance of cryopreservation in the conservation of plant germplasm.
6. Explain the process of somatic embryogenesis and its applications in plant tissue culture.
7. What are the advantages of using suspension culture for the production of secondary metabolites?
8. How does genetic engineering complement plant tissue culture in developing transgenic plants?
9. Describe the process of anther culture and its significance in plant breeding.
10. What are the key factors that influence the growth and maintenance of plant tissues in vitro?
11. Explain the use of Meristem culture in producing virus-free plants.

12. Discuss the role of gelling agents in plant tissue culture and how they contribute to culture stability.

13. How is the Murashige and Skoog (MS) medium significant in plant tissue culture?

14. What are the challenges faced in maintaining sterility during plant tissue culture?

15. How do elicitors enhance the production of secondary metabolites in plant tissue culture?

16. Describe the pharmacological importance of Catharanthus roseus in cancer treatment.

17. Explain the concept of somaclonal variation and its applications in plant breeding.

18. What are the potential advantages and limitations of using edible vaccines?

19. Discuss the role of plant tissue culture in the production of disease-free planting material.

20. How do protoplast cultures contribute to somatic hybridization and genetic engineering?

Long Answer Type Questions (Subjective)

1. Discuss the historical development of plant tissue culture and how key milestones have shaped the field.

2. Explain the various types of cultures in plant tissue culture, providing examples of their applications and benefits.

3. Analyze the nutritional requirements of plant tissue culture and how they contribute to successful in vitro plant growth.

4. How do plant tissue culture techniques contribute to the conservation of endangered plant species and the production of secondary metabolites?

5. Discuss the applications of plant tissue culture in pharmacognosy, focusing on the production of secondary metabolites and the conservation of medicinal plants.

6. Explain the process of developing edible vaccines using plant tissue culture and the challenges associated with their production and implementation.

7. How does genetic engineering in conjunction with plant tissue culture lead to the development of transgenic plants with desirable traits?

8. Describe the process of micropropagation and its significance in commercial horticulture and agriculture.

9. Analyze the role of somatic embryogenesis in plant tissue culture, including its applications in clonal propagation and synthetic seed production.

Answer Key for MCQs

1. (B) Preventing contamination by microorganisms

2. (C) Sucrose

3. (B) The ability of a single cell to regenerate into a whole plant

4. (B) Suspension culture

5. (B) Inducing root formation and callus induction

6. (C) Cytokinins

7. (B) Producing large numbers of genetically identical plants

8. (C) Root culture

9. (B) It is the most widely used culture medium for a wide range of plants

10.(B) Anther and pollen culture

11.(B) Long-term preservation of plant tissues at ultra-low temperatures

12.(B) A piece of plant tissue used to initiate a culture

13.(B) Clonal propagation and synthetic seed production

14.(B) To solidify the culture medium and provide support

15.(B) Introducing new traits or improving existing ones

16.(C) Nicotiana tabacum (Tobacco)

17.(B) Producing bioactive compounds in a controlled environment

18.(C) Catharanthus roseus (Periwinkle)

19.(B) To produce homozygous lines in a single generation

20.(B) Dosage control and public acceptance

CHAPTER – 7

PHARMACOGNOSY IN VARIOUS SYSTEMS OF MEDICINE

INTRODUCTION:

Pharmacognosy is the study of medicinal drugs derived from plants or other natural sources. It involves understanding the origin, chemical properties, and therapeutic potential of natural substances. In various systems of medicine, pharmacognosy plays a crucial role in identifying and utilizing natural remedies. Here's an introduction to how pharmacognosy is integrated into different systems of medicine:

1. Traditional Chinese Medicine (TCM)

a. **Principles**: TCM emphasizes the balance of Qi (energy), Yin, and Yang. It uses herbal medicine, acupuncture, and dietary therapy.

b. **Pharmacognosy Role**: In TCM, pharmacognosy involves identifying and categorizing herbs used in formulas, understanding their effects on the body's energy balance, and their roles in treating various ailments.

2. Ayurveda

a. **Principles**: Ayurveda is based on the balance of the three doshas (Vata, Pitta, Kapha). It uses herbal remedies, dietary recommendations, and lifestyle adjustments.

b. **Pharmacognosy Role**: Ayurvedic pharmacognosy focuses on the medicinal plants used to balance the doshas and their specific therapeutic properties, ensuring that the herbs used are authentic and effective.

3. Homeopathy

a. **Principles**: Homeopathy is based on the principle of "like cures like," using highly diluted substances to stimulate the body's healing response.

b. **Pharmacognosy Role**: Pharmacognosy in homeopathy involves sourcing and preparing the natural substances used in remedies, ensuring their purity and potency.

4. Unani Medicine

a. **Principles**: Unani medicine is based on the balance of four humors (blood, phlegm, yellow bile, and black bile) and uses herbal medicines, dietary practices, and therapeutic techniques.

b. **Pharmacognosy Role**: Unani pharmacognosy focuses on identifying and standardizing herbs and natural substances used to maintain or restore humoral balance.

5. Naturopathy

a. **Principles**: Naturopathy promotes self-healing through natural methods, including herbal medicine, nutrition, and lifestyle changes.

b. **Pharmacognosy Role**: In naturopathy, pharmacognosy involves the study and application of natural substances to support the body's healing processes, ensuring their efficacy and safety.

6. Western Herbal Medicine

a. **Principles**: Western herbal medicine uses a scientific approach to the study of medicinal plants, focusing on their pharmacological effects and clinical applications.

b. **Pharmacognosy Role**: Pharmacognosy here involves the detailed analysis of plant constituents, extraction methods, and their therapeutic actions based on clinical research.

7. Integrative Medicine

a. **Principles**: Integrative medicine combines conventional Western medicine with complementary therapies, including herbal medicine, to provide holistic care.

b. **Pharmacognosy Role**: In integrative medicine, pharmacognosy supports the integration of herbal remedies with conventional treatments, ensuring that herbal treatments are evidence-based and safe.

Key Concepts in Pharmacognosy

a. **Botanical Identification**: Correctly identifying and classifying medicinal plants.

b. **Phytochemistry**: Studying the chemical compounds in plants and their effects on health.

c. **Pharmacology**: Understanding how plant compounds interact with the body.

d. **Ethnobotany**: Exploring traditional uses of plants and their cultural significance.

e. **Quality Control**: Ensuring the purity, potency, and safety of herbal products.

AYURVEDA SYSTEMS

1. Role in Allopathy

Pharmacognosy in allopathy (conventional Western medicine) plays a crucial role in integrating natural substances into modern therapeutic practices. Here's how pharmacognosy contributes:

a. **Drug Discovery**: Many modern pharmaceuticals have origins in traditional herbal medicine. Pharmacognosy helps in identifying, isolating, and characterizing bioactive compounds from natural sources, which can lead to the development of new drugs.

b. **Standardization**: Pharmacognosy ensures that natural products used in medicine meet specific quality and safety standards. This involves detailed analysis of plant constituents and their consistency across different batches.

c. **Pharmacokinetics and Pharmacodynamics**: Understanding how natural compounds are absorbed, distributed, metabolized, and excreted in the body (pharmacokinetics) and their effects on the body (pharmacodynamics) is crucial for integrating herbal medicines into conventional treatments.

d. **Toxicology**: Pharmacognosy assesses the safety of natural substances, identifying potential toxic effects and interactions with other drugs.

e. **Clinical Research**: Pharmacognosy supports clinical trials to evaluate the efficacy and safety of herbal medicines, contributing to evidence-based medicine.

2. Role in Ayurveda

Pharmacognosy in Ayurveda (an ancient system of medicine originating from India) plays a vital role in maintaining and enhancing the efficacy of Ayurvedic treatments. Here's how pharmacognosy contributes to Ayurveda:

a. **Identification and Classification**: Ayurvedic pharmacognosy involves the detailed identification and classification of medicinal plants used in Ayurvedic formulations. This ensures the correct plant species are used and maintains the integrity of traditional remedies.

b. **Quality Control**: Ensuring the quality, purity, and potency of Ayurvedic herbs is essential. Pharmacognosy provides methods for standardizing herbal products to ensure they are free from contaminants and consistent in their therapeutic effects.

c. **Formulation Development**: Ayurveda often uses complex formulations containing multiple herbs. Pharmacognosy aids in understanding the interactions between these herbs, optimizing their efficacy, and ensuring that formulations are safe and effective.

d. **Phytochemical Analysis**: Pharmacognosy involves studying the chemical compounds in Ayurvedic herbs, such as alkaloids, flavonoids, saponins, and essential oils. This analysis helps in understanding the therapeutic actions of herbs and supporting traditional knowledge with scientific evidence.

e. **Ethnobotany**: Ayurvedic pharmacognosy often involves studying traditional uses of plants within local cultures. This knowledge is used to guide the selection and use of herbs in Ayurvedic practice.

f. **Clinical Efficacy**: Research supported by pharmacognosy helps validate traditional Ayurvedic practices by assessing the clinical efficacy of herbal medicines, contributing to evidence-based Ayurvedic medicine.

g. **Safety Assessment**: Pharmacognosy plays a role in evaluating the safety of Ayurvedic remedies, including assessing potential side effects, interactions with other drugs, and long-term safety.

Comparative Insights

a. **Integration with Modern Science**: In allopathy, pharmacognosy is primarily used to integrate natural substances into modern drug development and therapy. In Ayurveda, pharmacognosy supports traditional practices by providing scientific validation and ensuring the quality and safety of herbal medicines.

b. **Focus Areas**: While allopathy focuses on isolating and studying individual compounds for drug development, Ayurveda often uses complex mixtures of herbs and focuses on holistic healing.

c. **Research Approaches**: Allopathic pharmacognosy emphasizes clinical trials and standardized testing, while Ayurvedic pharmacognosy often combines traditional knowledge with modern scientific techniques to validate and enhance traditional remedies.

UNANI SYSTEMS

1. Role of Pharmacognosy in Allopathy

In allopathy (conventional Western medicine), pharmacognosy is essential in the integration of natural substances into modern pharmaceutical practices. Key roles include:

    a. **Drug Discovery and Development**: Many pharmaceutical drugs are derived from natural sources. Pharmacognosy involves the discovery of new bioactive compounds from plants and other natural sources, which can be developed into new medications.

    b. **Standardization and Quality Control**: Pharmacognosy ensures that herbal and natural products meet specific quality standards. This includes verifying the identity, purity, potency, and consistency of natural substances used in medicine.

    c. **Pharmacokinetics and Pharmacodynamics**: Studying how natural compounds are absorbed, metabolized, and excreted (pharmacokinetics) and their effects on the body (pharmacodynamics) helps integrate these compounds into therapeutic practices.

    d. **Safety and Toxicology**: Pharmacognosy evaluates the safety of natural products, identifying potential toxic effects, interactions with other medications, and ensuring overall safety for patients.

    e. **Clinical Research and Evidence-Based Medicine**: Pharmacognosy supports the development of clinical trials to assess the efficacy and safety of herbal and natural medicines, contributing to evidence-based practices.

2. Role of Pharmacognosy in Unani Medicine

Unani medicine, a traditional system of medicine with origins in Greece and developed further in the Islamic world, relies heavily on pharmacognosy. Here's how pharmacognosy contributes:

    a. **Identification and Classification**: Unani pharmacognosy involves identifying and classifying medicinal plants and substances used in Unani formulations. This ensures that the correct plant species are used and maintains the integrity of Unani remedies.

b. **Standardization and Quality Control**: Pharmacognosy provides methods for standardizing and controlling the quality of herbal products used in Unani medicine. This includes ensuring the purity, potency, and consistency of the herbal ingredients.

c. **Phytochemical Analysis**: The study of chemical compounds in Unani herbs, such as alkaloids, glycosides, and essential oils, helps understand their therapeutic effects. Pharmacognosy supports this analysis to validate the traditional uses of these herbs.

d. **Formulation Development**: Unani medicine often uses complex herbal formulations. Pharmacognosy helps in understanding the interactions between different herbs in these formulations, optimizing their efficacy and safety.

e. **Ethnobotany and Traditional Knowledge**: Pharmacognosy involves studying the traditional uses of plants in Unani medicine and validating these practices with modern scientific methods. This helps bridge traditional knowledge with contemporary research.

f. **Safety and Toxicology**: Pharmacognosy assesses the safety of Unani herbal remedies, including evaluating potential side effects, interactions with other drugs, and long-term safety.

g. **Clinical Efficacy**: Research supported by pharmacognosy helps in evaluating the clinical efficacy of Unani herbal medicines, contributing to evidence-based Unani practice.

Comparative Insights

a. **Integration with Modern Science**: In allopathy, pharmacognosy is focused on integrating natural substances into modern drug development and therapeutic practices. In Unani medicine, pharmacognosy supports the traditional system by validating and ensuring the quality of herbal remedies.

b. **Research Focus**: Allopathic pharmacognosy emphasizes drug development and standardization, whereas Unani pharmacognosy focuses on validating traditional uses and ensuring the efficacy and safety of complex herbal formulations.

c. **Approach to Herbal Medicine**: Allopathic pharmacognosy often involves isolating and studying individual compounds, while Unani pharmacognosy may focus more on the holistic use of complex mixtures of herbs.

SIDDHA SYSTEMS

1. **Role of Pharmacognosy in Allopathy**

In allopathy (conventional Western medicine), pharmacognosy plays a crucial role in the integration of natural substances into modern therapeutic practices. Key contributions include:

a. **Drug Discovery and Development**: Many pharmaceutical drugs have been derived from natural sources. Pharmacognosy helps in identifying, isolating, and characterizing bioactive compounds from plants and other natural sources, leading to the development of new medications.

b. **Standardization and Quality Control**: Pharmacognosy ensures that natural products used in medicine meet specific quality standards. This involves analyzing plant constituents and ensuring consistency in their therapeutic effects.

c. **Pharmacokinetics and Pharmacodynamics**: Understanding how natural compounds are absorbed, distributed, metabolized, and excreted in the body (pharmacokinetics) and their effects on the body (pharmacodynamics) is essential for integrating herbal medicines into conventional treatments.

d. **Safety and Toxicology**: Pharmacognosy assesses the safety of natural substances, including identifying potential toxic effects and interactions with other medications, ensuring that herbal medicines are safe for patient use.

e. **Clinical Research**: Pharmacognosy supports clinical trials to evaluate the efficacy and safety of herbal medicines, contributing to evidence-based practices and helping integrate these treatments into conventional medical systems.

2. Role of Pharmacognosy in Siddha Medicine

Siddha medicine is an ancient system of traditional medicine that originated in South India and is based on the principles of balancing the body's three humors (Vata, Pitta, and Kapha). Pharmacognosy plays a significant role in Siddha medicine in the following ways:

a. **Identification and Classification**: Siddha pharmacognosy involves the identification and classification of medicinal plants and minerals used in Siddha formulations. Accurate identification ensures the use of the correct plant species and maintains the authenticity of traditional remedies.

b. **Standardization and Quality Control**: Ensuring the quality and purity of herbal and mineral ingredients is crucial in Siddha medicine. Pharmacognosy provides methods for standardizing these ingredients, ensuring they meet specific quality standards and are free from contaminants.

c. **Phytochemical Analysis**: The study of chemical compounds in Siddha herbs, including alkaloids, flavonoids, and essential oils, helps understand their therapeutic properties. Pharmacognosy supports this analysis to validate traditional uses with scientific evidence.

d. **Formulation Development**: Siddha medicine often uses complex formulations containing multiple herbs and minerals. Pharmacognosy helps in understanding the interactions between these components, optimizing their efficacy, and ensuring safety.

e. **Ethnobotany and Traditional Knowledge**: Pharmacognosy involves studying traditional uses of plants and minerals within Siddha medicine. This knowledge is used to guide the selection and use of ingredients in Siddha formulations, combining traditional wisdom with modern scientific methods.

f. **Safety and Toxicology**: Pharmacognosy assesses the safety of Siddha remedies, including evaluating potential side effects, interactions with other drugs, and ensuring the long-term safety of herbal and mineral ingredients.

g. **Clinical Efficacy**: Research supported by pharmacognosy helps evaluate the clinical efficacy of Siddha medicines, contributing to evidence-based practice and supporting the integration of Siddha treatments into modern healthcare.

Comparative Insights

a. **Integration with Modern Science**: In allopathy, pharmacognosy focuses on integrating natural substances into modern drug development and therapy. In Siddha medicine, pharmacognosy supports traditional practices by ensuring the quality, efficacy, and safety of herbal and mineral remedies.

b. **Research Focus**: Allopathic pharmacognosy emphasizes drug development, standardization, and clinical research, while Siddha pharmacognosy focuses on validating traditional uses, optimizing formulations, and ensuring the safety and efficacy of complex remedies.

c. **Approach to Herbal Medicine**: Allopathic pharmacognosy often involves isolating and studying individual compounds, whereas Siddha pharmacognosy may focus on the holistic use of complex mixtures of herbs and minerals.

HOMEOPATHY SYSTEMS

1. **Role of Pharmacognosy in Allopathy**

In allopathy (conventional Western medicine), pharmacognosy contributes significantly to the integration of natural substances into modern therapeutic practices. Key roles include:

a. **Drug Discovery and Development**: Pharmacognosy plays a critical role in discovering new drugs from natural sources. Many pharmaceuticals are derived from plants, and pharmacognosy helps in identifying, isolating, and characterizing bioactive compounds that can lead to new drug development.

b. **Standardization and Quality Control**: Ensuring the quality, purity, and consistency of natural products is essential. Pharmacognosy involves developing and applying methods for standardizing herbal medicines to meet specific quality standards, ensuring that they are effective and safe for use.

c. **Pharmacokinetics and Pharmacodynamics**: Understanding how natural compounds are absorbed, distributed, metabolized, and excreted (pharmacokinetics) and their effects on the body (pharmacodynamics) is crucial for integrating herbal remedies into conventional treatments and ensuring their therapeutic efficacy.

d. **Safety and Toxicology**: Pharmacognosy evaluates the safety of natural substances, including potential toxic effects and interactions with other medications. This helps in ensuring that herbal medicines are safe for patients and do not cause adverse effects.

e. **Clinical Research**: Pharmacognosy supports clinical trials and research to evaluate the efficacy and safety of herbal medicines. This contributes to evidence-based medicine by providing scientific validation for traditional remedies and facilitating their integration into modern healthcare practices.

2. Role of Pharmacognosy in Homeopathy

Homeopathy is a system of medicine based on the principle of "like cures like," where highly diluted substances are used to stimulate the body's healing response. In homeopathy, pharmacognosy plays the following roles:

a. **Source Identification**: Pharmacognosy helps in identifying the natural sources of homeopathic remedies. This includes plants, minerals, and animal substances used to prepare homeopathic medicines.

b. **Preparation and Potentization**: In homeopathy, natural substances are subjected to a process called potentization, which involves serial dilution and succussion (vigorous shaking). Pharmacognosy ensures that the original substance is correctly identified and prepared according to homeopathic principles, maintaining the integrity of the remedy.

c. **Standardization**: Although homeopathic remedies are highly diluted, pharmacognosy helps in standardizing the source material to ensure consistency in the preparation process. This includes verifying the authenticity of the source material and ensuring it meets specific quality criteria.

d. **Phytochemical Analysis**: Pharmacognosy involves studying the chemical composition of plants and other substances used in homeopathic remedies. This analysis helps in understanding the potential therapeutic effects of the original substances, even though they are used in highly diluted forms.

e. **Safety and Toxicology**: Pharmacognosy assesses the safety of homeopathic remedies by ensuring that the source materials are free from contaminants and harmful substances. It also involves studying potential interactions with other medications, even though homeopathic remedies are used in highly diluted forms.

f. **Clinical Efficacy**: Pharmacognosy supports research to evaluate the efficacy of homeopathic remedies, although this is often more challenging due to the highly diluted nature of the remedies. Research helps in validating the therapeutic potential of homeopathic treatments and contributes to evidence-based homeopathy.

Comparative Insights

a. **Integration with Modern Science**: In allopathy, pharmacognosy focuses on integrating natural substances into modern drug development and therapeutic practices. In homeopathy, pharmacognosy supports the identification, preparation, and standardization of natural substances used in remedies, ensuring they meet quality standards.

b. **Research Focus**: Allopathic pharmacognosy emphasizes drug development, standardization, and clinical research. Homeopathic pharmacognosy focuses on the preparation and standardization of remedies, safety, and understanding the potential therapeutic effects of highly diluted substances.

c. **Approach to Natural Substances**: Allopathic pharmacognosy often involves studying and utilizing individual compounds from natural sources. In contrast, homeopathic pharmacognosy deals with the preparation of highly diluted substances, ensuring that the source materials are authentic and free from contaminants.

CHINESE SYSTEMS

1. **Role of Pharmacognosy in Allopathy**

In allopathy (conventional Western medicine), pharmacognosy plays a key role in integrating natural substances into modern therapeutic practices. Key roles include:

a. **Drug Discovery and Development**: Pharmacognosy is critical for discovering new drugs from natural sources. Many modern pharmaceuticals have origins in traditional herbal remedies, and pharmacognosy helps in identifying, isolating, and characterizing bioactive compounds from plants and other natural sources.

b. **Standardization and Quality Control**: Ensuring the quality, purity, and consistency of natural products is crucial. Pharmacognosy provides methods for standardizing herbal medicines, ensuring they meet specific quality standards and are effective and safe for patient use.

c. **Pharmacokinetics and Pharmacodynamics**: Understanding how natural compounds are absorbed, distributed, metabolized, and excreted (pharmacokinetics) and their effects on the body (pharmacodynamics) is essential for integrating herbal medicines into conventional treatments.

d. **Safety and Toxicology**: Pharmacognosy evaluates the safety of natural substances, identifying potential toxic effects and interactions with other medications, thus ensuring the safety of herbal medicines.

e. **Clinical Research**: Pharmacognosy supports clinical trials and research to evaluate the efficacy and safety of herbal medicines, contributing to evidence-based medicine and facilitating the integration of these treatments into modern healthcare practices.

2. Role of Pharmacognosy in Traditional Chinese Medicine (TCM)

Traditional Chinese Medicine (TCM) is an ancient system of medicine that uses herbal remedies, acupuncture, and other modalities to restore balance and health. Pharmacognosy plays a significant role in TCM through the following aspects:

a. **Identification and Classification**: Pharmacognosy helps in the accurate identification and classification of medicinal herbs used in TCM. This involves verifying the correct plant species and ensuring that traditional remedies are authentic.

b. **Quality Control and Standardization**: Ensuring the quality and purity of herbal ingredients is vital in TCM. Pharmacognosy provides methods for standardizing these ingredients to maintain their efficacy and safety. This includes checking for contaminants and ensuring that herbs meet specific quality criteria.

c. **Phytochemical Analysis**: Pharmacognosy involves studying the chemical constituents of TCM herbs, such as alkaloids, flavonoids, saponins, and essential oils. This analysis helps to understand the therapeutic properties of the herbs and validate traditional uses with scientific evidence.

d. **Formulation and Synergy**: TCM often uses complex formulations containing multiple herbs. Pharmacognosy helps in understanding the interactions between these herbs and optimizing their combinations to enhance therapeutic efficacy and safety.

e. **Ethnobotany and Traditional Knowledge**: Pharmacognosy supports the study of traditional uses of plants in TCM, integrating traditional knowledge with modern scientific methods. This helps to guide the selection and use of herbs in TCM formulations.

f. **Safety and Toxicology**: Pharmacognosy assesses the safety of TCM herbs, including identifying potential side effects and interactions with other drugs. This ensures that TCM remedies are safe for use and do not cause adverse effects.

g. **Clinical Efficacy**: Research supported by pharmacognosy helps evaluate the clinical efficacy of TCM herbs and formulations. This research contributes to evidence-based TCM practices and supports the integration of TCM treatments into modern healthcare.

Comparative Insights

a. **Integration with Modern Science**: In allopathy, pharmacognosy focuses on integrating natural substances into modern drug development and therapeutic practices. In TCM, pharmacognosy supports the traditional use of herbs by ensuring the quality, efficacy, and safety of these natural remedies.

b. **Research Focus**: Allopathic pharmacognosy emphasizes drug discovery, standardization, and clinical research. TCM pharmacognosy focuses on the identification, standardization, and formulation of herbal remedies, as well as understanding the synergy between multiple herbs.

c. **Approach to Herbal Medicine**: Allopathic pharmacognosy often involves isolating and studying individual compounds from natural sources. In TCM, pharmacognosy deals with complex herbal formulations and the holistic use of multiple herbs in combination.

CLASSIFICATION:

Pharmacognosy, the study of natural products used in medicine, is classified differently depending on the system of medicine. Here's an overview of how pharmacognosy is classified in various systems of medicine, along with examples:

1. Allopathy (Conventional Western Medicine)

Classification in Allopathy:

a. **Botanical Pharmacognosy**: Focuses on plant-derived substances used in medicine.

   i. **Example**: **Quinine** from *Cinchona* bark, used to treat malaria.

b. **Phytochemistry**: Study of the chemical compounds in plants.

   i. **Example**: **Taxol** from *Taxus brevifolia* (Pacific yew), used in cancer treatment.

c. **Pharmacognostic Techniques**: Methods used to identify and standardize natural substances.

   i. **Example**: High-performance liquid chromatography (HPLC) for identifying active components in herbal extracts.

d. **Pharmacokinetics and Pharmacodynamics**: Understanding how natural compounds affect the body and are processed by it.

i. **Example**: **Digitalis** from *Digitalis purpurea* (foxglove), used in heart conditions.

2. Ayurveda

Classification in Ayurveda:

a. **Dravya (Substances)**: Classification based on the source and nature of substances.

   i. **Example**: **Ashwagandha** (*Withania somnifera*), classified as a "Rasayana" (rejuvenative) herb.

b. **Guna (Qualities)**: Classification based on physical and chemical properties.

   i. **Example**: **Turmeric** (*Curcuma longa*), known for its anti-inflammatory properties.

c. **Virya (Potency)**: Classification based on the action of the substance (e.g., heating or cooling effects).

   i. **Example**: **Ginger** (*Zingiber officinale*), which has a warming effect.

d. **Vipaka (Metabolic Effect)**: Classification based on the metabolic effect after digestion.

   i. **Example**: **Neem** (*Azadirachta indica*), known for its bitter taste and detoxifying effect.

3. Siddha Medicine

Classification in Siddha Medicine:

a. **Viridh (Category of Drugs)**: Classification based on the type of substance.

   i. **Example**: **Andrographis paniculata** (Kalmegh), used for liver disorders.

b. **Uzhir (Body Parts)**: Classification based on the part of the plant used.

   i. **Example**: **Pippali** (*Piper longum*), used primarily for its fruit.

c. **Mura (Dosage Forms)**: Classification based on how the substance is prepared and administered.

   i. **Example: Chooranam** (powdered form of medicinal herbs) used for various conditions.

4. Traditional Chinese Medicine (TCM)

Classification in TCM:

a. **Herb Classification**: Based on the herb's nature, flavor, and its effects on the body.

   i. **Example: Ginseng** (*Panax ginseng*), classified as a "Yang tonic" and used for energy and vitality.

b. **Five Flavors**: Classification based on the taste and its therapeutic effects.

   i. **Example: Licorice root** (*Glycyrrhiza uralensis*), sweet in flavor and used to harmonize other herbs.

c. **Meridian (Channel) Theory**: Classification based on the specific meridian or organ system the herb affects.

   i. **Example: Gingko biloba** affects the lung and heart meridians.

d. **Nature and Temperature**: Classification based on the herb's thermal nature (cold, hot, neutral).

   i. **Example: Peppermint** (*Mentha piperita*), which is cooling.

5. Homeopathy

Classification in Homeopathy:

a. **Materia Medica**: Classification based on the source material of homeopathic remedies.

   i. **Example: Arnica montana**, derived from the Arnica plant, used for trauma and bruising.

b. **Potentization**: Classification based on the degree of dilution and succussion (shaking).

   i. **Example: Belladonna** in various potencies (e.g., 30C, 200C).

c. **Remedy Types**: Classification based on the type of substance used (plant, mineral, animal).

   i.   **Example: Sulphur**, a mineral remedy used for skin conditions.

Multiple Choice Questions (MCQs) - Objective

1. What is the primary focus of pharmacognosy in Traditional Chinese Medicine (TCM)?

   A) Balance of Qi and blood

   B) Identifying and categorizing herbs used in formulas

   C) Diagnosing diseases

   D) Balancing the doshas

2. In Ayurveda, what is the role of pharmacognosy in relation to the three doshas?

   A) Balancing Yin and Yang

   B) Balancing the three doshas (Vata, Pitta, Kapha)

   C) Strengthening the immune system

   D) Enhancing mental clarity

3. Which system of medicine uses the principle "like cures like"?

   A) Ayurveda

   B) Homeopathy

   C) Unani

   D) Siddha

4. In Unani medicine, what does pharmacognosy primarily focus on?

   A) Balancing Qi

   B) Standardizing herbs and natural substances

   C) Enhancing spiritual well-being

   D) Creating new synthetic drugs

5. What is a key role of pharmacognosy in allopathic medicine?

   A) Integrating natural substances into modern drug development

B) Balancing Yin and Yang

C) Identifying toxic plants

D) Enhancing energy levels

6. Which herbal component in Ayurveda is classified as a "Rasayana" (rejuvenative) herb?

   A) Neem

   B) Ashwagandha

   C) Ginkgo biloba

   D) Belladonna

7. What is the primary use of Arnica montana in allopathic medicine?

   A) Treating digestive issues

   B) Reducing bruising and muscle soreness

   C) Enhancing memory

   D) Treating skin infections

8. Which active constituent of Taxus baccata is used in cancer treatment?

   A) Atropine

   B) Quinine

   C) Paclitaxel

   D) Sulphur

9. What is the main pharmacological action of Quinine derived from Cinchona bark?

   A) Antimalarial

   B) Anti-inflammatory

   C) Antioxidant

   D) Sedative

10. In Siddha medicine, what is the role of pharmacognosy in the preparation of remedies?

   A) Creating synthetic drugs

   B) Ensuring the safety and efficacy of herbal and mineral ingredients

C) Enhancing mental clarity

D) Promoting physical strength

11. Which system of medicine uses the concept of "Virya" (potency) in classifying medicinal plants?

A) Ayurveda

B) Allopathy

C) Homeopathy

D) TCM

12. What is the primary therapeutic use of Ginkgo biloba in allopathic medicine?

A) Enhancing physical strength

B) Treating fever

C) Improving cognitive function and memory

D) Reducing anxiety

13. Which natural substance is used in Homeopathy for treating trauma and bruising?

A) Ginkgo biloba

B) Sulphur

C) Arnica montana

D) Neem

14. In Unani medicine, what is the significance of phytochemical analysis in pharmacognosy?

A) Developing synthetic drugs

B) Understanding therapeutic effects of herbs

C) Promoting mental clarity

D) Enhancing spiritual well-being

15. What is the role of pharmacognosy in integrative medicine?

A) Balancing the doshas

B) Supporting the integration of herbal remedies with conventional treatments

C) Enhancing energy levels

D) Diagnosing diseases

16. In which system of medicine is Ashwagandha primarily used as an adaptogen?

A) Ayurveda

B) TCM

C) Homeopathy

D) Unani

17. What is the primary pharmacological action of Sulphur in allopathic medicine?

A) Treating fever

B) Antimicrobial and keratinolytic

C) Enhancing cognitive function

D) Sedative

18. Which system of medicine emphasizes the balance of Qi (energy), Yin, and Yang?

A) Ayurveda

B) TCM

C) Siddha

D) Homeopathy

19. What is the main role of potentization in homeopathic pharmacognosy?

A) Enhancing drug absorption

B) Preparing and diluting natural substances to stimulate healing

C) Identifying toxic plants

D) Standardizing herbal remedies

20. Which active constituent is responsible for the neuroprotective effects of Ashwagandha?

A) Quinine

B) Paclitaxel

C) Withanolides

D) Sulphur

Short Answer Type Questions (Subjective)

1. Explain the role of pharmacognosy in Traditional Chinese Medicine (TCM).

2. How does pharmacognosy support drug discovery in allopathic medicine?

3. What is the significance of pharmacognosy in Ayurveda?

4. Describe the therapeutic uses of Ashwagandha in Ayurveda.

5. How is pharmacognosy applied in the preparation of homeopathic remedies?

6. Discuss the role of phytochemical analysis in Unani medicine.

7. What are the key pharmacological actions of Quinine derived from Cinchona bark?

8. How does pharmacognosy contribute to the development of new drugs in allopathy?

9. Explain the role of Arnica montana in homeopathic and allopathic medicine.

10. How does pharmacognosy support the standardization of herbal medicines?

11. What is the importance of potentization in homeopathy?

12. Discuss the role of pharmacognosy in the identification and classification of medicinal plants in Ayurveda.

13. What are the therapeutic benefits of Ginkgo biloba in allopathic medicine?

14. How is Sulphur used in allopathic and Siddha medicine?

15. What is the role of pharmacognosy in ensuring the safety of herbal remedies?

16. Explain the concept of "Virya" (potency) in Ayurvedic pharmacognosy.

17. Describe the pharmacological properties of paclitaxel derived from Taxus baccata.

18. How does pharmacognosy contribute to the safety and efficacy of Siddha medicine?

19. What is the significance of pharmacognosy in integrative medicine?

20. Discuss the use of Neem in Ayurveda and its pharmacological actions.

Long Answer Type Questions (Subjective)

1. Discuss the role of pharmacognosy in various systems of medicine, focusing on its application in Ayurveda, TCM, and allopathy.

2. Explain the importance of pharmacognosy in drug discovery and development in allopathic medicine, providing examples of key drugs derived from natural sources.

3. Analyze the role of pharmacognosy in homeopathy, including the process of potentization and its impact on remedy preparation.

4. How does pharmacognosy support the safety, efficacy, and standardization of herbal medicines in Unani medicine?

5. Discuss the therapeutic uses of Ashwagandha and Ginkgo biloba in different systems of medicine, highlighting their pharmacological actions.

6. Explain the significance of pharmacognosy in Siddha medicine, including its role in the preparation and standardization of herbal and mineral remedies.

7. How does pharmacognosy contribute to the integration of herbal remedies in modern healthcare practices, particularly in integrative medicine?

8. Describe the pharmacological properties and therapeutic uses of Quinine and Paclitaxel, and their significance in allopathic medicine.

9. Discuss the role of pharmacognosy in ensuring the quality, purity, and safety of herbal products across different systems of medicine.

Answer Key for MCQs

1. (B) Identifying and categorizing herbs used in formulas
2. (B) Balancing the three doshas (Vata, Pitta, Kapha)
3. (B) Homeopathy
4. (B) Standardizing herbs and natural substances
5. (A) Integrating natural substances into modern drug development
6. (B) Ashwagandha

7. (B) Reducing bruising and muscle soreness

8. (C) Paclitaxel

9. (A) Antimalarial

10.(B) Ensuring the safety and efficacy of herbal and mineral ingredients

11.(A) Ayurveda

12.(C) Improving cognitive function and memory

13.(C) Arnica montana

14.(B) Understanding therapeutic effects of herbs

15.(B) Supporting the integration of herbal remedies with conventional treatments

16.(A) Ayurveda

17.(B) Antimicrobial and keratinolytic

18.(B) TCM

19.(B) Preparing and diluting natural substances to stimulate healing

20. (C) Withanolides

CHAPTER – 8

INTRODUCTION TO SECONDARY METABOLITES

INTRODUCTION:

Secondary metabolites are organic compounds produced by plants, fungi, bacteria, and marine organisms that are not directly involved in the normal growth, development, or reproduction of an organism. Unlike primary metabolites, which are essential for basic life processes, secondary metabolites have diverse roles, often related to defense, competition, and interaction with the environment.

Key Features of Secondary Metabolites:

1. **Diversity and Complexity**:
    a. Secondary metabolites are structurally diverse, including alkaloids, terpenoids, phenolics, glycosides, and polyketides.
    b. They are often complex molecules with specific functional groups that contribute to their biological activity.

2. **Ecological Functions**:
    a. **Defense**: Many secondary metabolites serve as defense mechanisms against herbivores, pathogens, and competitors. For example, alkaloids in plants deter herbivores, and antibiotics produced by fungi and bacteria inhibit the growth of competing microorganisms.
    b. **Attraction**: Some secondary metabolites attract pollinators or seed dispersers, aiding in plant reproduction.
    c. **Communication**: Certain metabolites are involved in signaling between organisms, such as in symbiotic relationships.

3. **Economic and Pharmaceutical Importance**:

a. Many secondary metabolites have medicinal properties and are used in pharmaceuticals. For example, the alkaloid morphine is a potent analgesic, and the terpenoid artemisinin is used to treat malaria.

b. They are also important in agriculture, food, and cosmetic industries as pesticides, flavoring agents, and fragrances.

4. **Biosynthesis**:

   a. The biosynthesis of secondary metabolites involves complex enzymatic pathways often derived from primary metabolic routes like glycolysis, the citric acid cycle, or the shikimate pathway.

   b. These pathways are tightly regulated and can be influenced by environmental factors, developmental stages, and stress conditions.

5. **Classification**:

   a. **Alkaloids**: Nitrogen-containing compounds often with pharmacological effects (e.g., morphine, quinine).

   b. **Terpenoids**: Derived from isoprene units, they include essential oils, resins, and steroids (e.g., menthol, taxol).

   c. **Phenolics**: Compounds with one or more hydroxyl groups attached to an aromatic ring (e.g., flavonoids, tannins).

   d. **Glycosides**: Compounds where a sugar is bound to a non-carbohydrate moiety, often with medicinal properties (e.g., digitalis).

   e. **Polyketides**: Produced by the polymerization of acetyl and propionyl subunits, including antibiotics like erythromycin.

6. **Role in Evolution**:

   a. Secondary metabolites have played a significant role in the evolution of plants and microorganisms, contributing to the survival and adaptation of species in various ecological niches.

b. They have co-evolved with other organisms, influencing plant-insect interactions, microbial competition, and symbiotic relationships.

ALKALOIDS

1. Definition of Alkaloids: Alkaloids are a large and diverse group of naturally occurring organic compounds that mostly contain basic nitrogen atoms. These compounds are primarily found in plants, although they can also be present in fungi, bacteria, and animals. Alkaloids often have significant pharmacological effects on humans and animals, which has led to their extensive use in medicine.

2. Classification of Alkaloids: Alkaloids can be classified based on their chemical structure, origin, and biosynthetic pathways:

a. **Based on Structure**:
   i. **Heterocyclic Alkaloids**: These contain a nitrogen atom within a ring structure (e.g., pyridine, quinoline).
   ii. **Non-Heterocyclic Alkaloids** (Protoalkaloids): These have a nitrogen atom outside the ring structure (e.g., ephedrine, colchicine).

b. **Based on Origin**:
   i. **True Alkaloids**: Derived from amino acids and contain a nitrogen atom in a heterocyclic ring (e.g., morphine, quinine).
   ii. **Protoalkaloids**: Derived from amino acids but do not have the nitrogen atom in a heterocyclic ring (e.g., mescaline).
   iii. **Pseudoalkaloids**: Not derived from amino acids but resemble alkaloids in structure and function (e.g., caffeine, theobromine).

c. **Based on Biosynthesis**:
   i. **Pyrrolidine Alkaloids**: Derived from ornithine (e.g., hygrine).
   ii. **Pyridine and Piperidine Alkaloids**: Derived from lysine (e.g., nicotine).

iii. **Indole Alkaloids**: Derived from tryptophan (e.g., strychnine, vinblastine).

iv. **Isoquinoline Alkaloids**: Derived from tyrosine (e.g., morphine, papaverine).

v. **Terpenoid Alkaloids**: Derived from terpenoid pathways (e.g., aconitine).

vi. **Steroidal Alkaloids**: Derived from steroidal pathways (e.g., solanine).

3. Properties of Alkaloids:

a. **Physical Properties**:

   i. **Solubility**: Alkaloids are generally soluble in organic solvents such as alcohol, ether, and chloroform. They are usually sparingly soluble in water, but their salts (e.g., hydrochlorides, sulfates) are often more water-soluble.

   ii. **State**: Most alkaloids are solid at room temperature, except for a few like coniine and nicotine, which are liquids.

   iii. **Color**: Alkaloids are typically colorless, although some (e.g., berberine) are brightly colored.

   iv. **Taste**: Alkaloids generally have a bitter taste.

b. **Chemical Properties**:

   i. **Basicity**: Alkaloids are basic due to the presence of a nitrogen atom. The degree of basicity varies depending on the structure of the alkaloid.

   ii. **Formation of Salts**: Alkaloids can form salts with acids, which are typically more soluble in water and are used for medicinal purposes.

   iii. **Reactivity**: Alkaloids react with acids, alcohols, and oxidizing agents, which can be utilized in their extraction and identification.

4. Tests for Identification of Alkaloids: Several qualitative tests can be used to identify the presence of alkaloids in a sample:

a. **Dragendorff's Test:**

   i.   **Reagent**: A solution of potassium bismuth iodide (Dragendorff's reagent).

   ii. **Procedure**: A few drops of Dragendorff's reagent are added to the extract of the sample.

   iii. **Result**: The formation of an orange-red precipitate indicates the presence of alkaloids.

b. **Mayer's Test:**

   i.   **Reagent**: A solution of potassium mercuric iodide (Mayer's reagent).

   ii. **Procedure**: A few drops of Mayer's reagent are added to the extract.

   iii. **Result**: The formation of a creamy white precipitate indicates the presence of alkaloids.

c. **Wagner's Test:**

   i.   **Reagent**: A solution of iodine in potassium iodide (Wagner's reagent).

   ii. **Procedure**: A few drops of Wagner's reagent are added to the extract.

   iii. **Result**: The formation of a reddish-brown precipitate indicates the presence of alkaloids.

d. **Hager's Test:**

   i.   **Reagent**: A solution of picric acid.

   ii. **Procedure**: A few drops of picric acid solution are added to the extract.

   iii. **Result**: The formation of a yellow precipitate indicates the presence of alkaloids.

e. **Tannic Acid Test**:

   i. **Reagent**: A solution of tannic acid.

   ii. **Procedure**: A few drops of tannic acid solution are added to the extract.

   iii. **Result**: The formation of a buff-colored precipitate indicates the presence of alkaloids.

GLYCOSIDES

1. Definition of Glycosides: Glycosides are organic compounds formed by the combination of a sugar (glycone) with a non-sugar moiety (aglycone or genin) through a glycosidic bond. The glycone part is typically glucose, but it can be other sugars as well. The aglycone part, which determines the pharmacological activity, can be a variety of chemical groups like alcohols, phenols, or steroids.

2. Classification of Glycosides: Glycosides are classified based on the chemical nature of the aglycone, the type of glycosidic bond, and the biological activity:

a. **Based on the Aglycone**:

   i. **Phenolic Glycosides**: The aglycone is a phenolic compound (e.g., arbutin).

   ii. **Alcoholic Glycosides**: The aglycone is an alcohol (e.g., salicin).

   iii. **Anthraquinone Glycosides**: The aglycone is an anthraquinone (e.g., senna glycosides).

   iv. **Cardiac Glycosides**: The aglycone is a steroidal compound with potent cardiac activity (e.g., digoxin).

   v. **Cyanogenic Glycosides**: The aglycone contains a cyanide group, which can release cyanide upon hydrolysis (e.g., amygdalin).

   vi. **Saponin Glycosides**: The aglycone is a triterpenoid or steroidal compound that forms soapy froths in water (e.g., glycyrrhizin).

   vii. **Coumarin Glycosides**: The aglycone is a coumarin derivative (e.g., scopoletin).

viii. **Flavonoid Glycosides**: The aglycone is a flavonoid (e.g., quercetin glycosides).

b. **Based on the Glycosidic Bond**:

i. **O-Glycosides**: The glycosidic bond is formed with an oxygen atom (e.g., salicin).

ii. **C-Glycosides**: The glycosidic bond is formed with a carbon atom (e.g., aloin).

iii. **N-Glycosides**: The glycosidic bond is formed with a nitrogen atom (e.g., adenosine).

iv. **S-Glycosides**: The glycosidic bond is formed with a sulfur atom (e.g., sinigrin).

c. **Based on Biological Activity**:

i. **Cardioactive Glycosides**: Affect heart function (e.g., digoxin, digitoxin).

ii. **Laxative Glycosides**: Induce bowel movements (e.g., senna glycosides).

iii. **Anti-inflammatory Glycosides**: Reduce inflammation (e.g., salicin).

iv. **Antioxidant Glycosides**: Prevent oxidative damage (e.g., quercetin glycosides).

3. **Properties of Glycosides:**

a. **Physical Properties**:

i. **Solubility**: Glycosides are generally soluble in water and alcohol, making them extractable by these solvents. Their solubility is influenced by the sugar component, which is hydrophilic.

ii. **Taste**: Most glycosides are bitter, although some, like saponins, can be sweet.

iii. **Crystalline Nature**: Many glycosides are crystalline solids, although they can also be amorphous.

iv. **Stability**: Glycosides are usually stable in dry conditions but can be hydrolyzed in the presence of acids, bases, or enzymes.

b. **Chemical Properties**:

i. **Hydrolysis**: Glycosides can be hydrolyzed by acids, bases, or specific enzymes (glycosidases) to yield the sugar and aglycone components.

ii. **Reaction with Fehling's Solution**: The glycone part of glycosides, upon hydrolysis, can reduce Fehling's solution if it contains a free aldehyde or ketone group.

4. Tests for Identification of Glycosides: Various qualitative tests are used to detect the presence of glycosides in plant extracts:

a. **General Test for Glycosides (Baljet Test):**

i. **Reagent**: Picric acid in an alkaline medium.

ii. **Procedure**: The extract is treated with Baljet's reagent.

iii. **Result**: The appearance of a yellow to orange color indicates the presence of glycosides.

b. **Borntrager's Test** (For Anthraquinone Glycosides):

i. **Reagent**: Dilute sulfuric acid and benzene or chloroform, followed by ammonia.

ii. **Procedure**: The extract is boiled with dilute sulfuric acid, cooled, and shaken with an organic solvent. The organic layer is separated and treated with ammonia.

iii. **Result**: A pink, red, or violet color in the ammoniacal layer indicates the presence of anthraquinone glycosides.

c. **Keller-Killiani Test** (For Cardiac Glycosides):

i. **Reagent**: Ferric chloride and concentrated sulfuric acid.

ii. **Procedure**: The extract is treated with a mixture of ferric chloride and sulfuric acid.

iii. **Result**: A blue or green color at the interface indicates the presence of deoxy sugars in cardiac glycosides.

d. **Legal's Test** (For Cardiac Glycosides):

i. **Reagent**: Pyridine, sodium nitroprusside, and sodium hydroxide.

ii. **Procedure**: The extract is treated with pyridine and sodium nitroprusside, followed by sodium hydroxide.

iii. **Result**: The formation of a pink to red color indicates the presence of cardiac glycosides.

e. **Foam Test** (For Saponin Glycosides):

i. **Reagent**: Water.

ii. **Procedure**: The extract is shaken with water in a test tube.

iii. **Result**: The formation of persistent froth indicates the presence of saponins.

FLAVONOIDS

1. Definition of Flavonoids: Flavonoids are a large group of polyphenolic compounds found in plants, characterized by their basic structure of a 15-carbon skeleton consisting of two benzene rings (A and B) connected by a three-carbon bridge that forms an oxygenated heterocyclic ring (C). They play various roles in plants, such as pigmentation, UV filtration, symbiotic nitrogen fixation, and defense against pathogens.

2. Classification of Flavonoids: Flavonoids are classified based on their chemical structure, particularly the degree of oxidation and the pattern of substitution in the heterocyclic ring:

a. **Flavones:** Characterized by a double bond between C2 and C3 and a keto group at C4 (e.g., apigenin, luteolin).

b. **Flavonols:** Similar to flavones but with a hydroxyl group at C3 (e.g., quercetin, kaempferol).

c. **Flavanones:** Lack the double bond between C2 and C3, leading to a saturated ring (e.g., naringenin, hesperidin).

d. **Flavanonols**: Like flavanones but with a hydroxyl group at C3 (e.g., taxifolin).

e. **Flavanols (Catechins)**: Have a hydroxyl group at C3 but lack the double bond between C2 and C3, and the C4 carbon is bonded to a hydroxyl group (e.g., catechin, epicatechin).

f. **Isoflavonoids**: Have the B ring attached at C3 instead of C2, typical in legumes (e.g., genistein, daidzein).

g. **Anthocyanins**: Pigmented flavonoids responsible for red, purple, and blue colors in plants (e.g., cyanidin, delphinidin).

h. **Chalcones**: Precursors to flavonoids with an open-chain structure between the two benzene rings (e.g., phloretin).

3. **Properties of Flavonoids:**

a. **Physical Properties**:

   i. **Solubility**: Flavonoids are generally soluble in organic solvents like ethanol and methanol. Some flavonoid glycosides are water-soluble.

   ii. **Color**: Flavonoids can be colorless, pale yellow, or deeply colored, depending on their specific structure.

   iii. **State**: Flavonoids are typically crystalline solids.

   iv. **Stability**: Flavonoids are sensitive to light, heat, and pH, which can lead to degradation or color changes.

b. **Chemical Properties**:

   i. **Acid-Base Reactions**: Flavonoids can act as weak acids and may react with bases to form salts.

   ii. **Chelation**: Flavonoids can chelate metal ions due to their polyphenolic structure.

   iii. **Antioxidant Activity**: Flavonoids are potent antioxidants, capable of scavenging free radicals due to their phenolic hydroxyl groups.

4. Tests for Identification of Flavonoids: Several qualitative tests are used to detect the presence of flavonoids in plant extracts:

a. **Shinoda Test:**
   i. **Reagent**: Magnesium turnings and concentrated hydrochloric acid.
   ii. **Procedure**: The extract is mixed with magnesium turnings, and a few drops of concentrated hydrochloric acid are added.
   iii. **Result**: The appearance of a red, pink, or orange color indicates the presence of flavonoids.

b. **Ferric Chloride Test:**
   i. **Reagent**: 1% ferric chloride solution.
   ii. **Procedure**: A few drops of ferric chloride solution are added to the extract.
   iii. **Result**: The formation of a greenish, bluish, or black color indicates the presence of flavonoids, particularly flavonols.

c. **Lead Acetate Test:**
   i. **Reagent**: 10% lead acetate solution.
   ii. **Procedure**: The extract is treated with lead acetate solution.
   iii. **Result**: The formation of a yellow precipitate indicates the presence of flavonoids.

d. **Sodium Hydroxide Test:**
   i. **Reagent**: Dilute sodium hydroxide solution.
   ii. **Procedure**: The extract is treated with dilute sodium hydroxide solution.
   iii. **Result**: The solution turns yellow, which disappears upon the addition of an acid, indicating the presence of flavonoids.

e. **Alkaline Reagent Test:**
   i. **Reagent**: 10% sodium hydroxide solution.
   ii. **Procedure**: The extract is treated with sodium hydroxide solution.

iii.   **Result**: The appearance of an intense yellow color that becomes colorless on adding dilute acid indicates the presence of flavonoids.

TANNINS

1. Definition of Tannins

Tannins are a diverse group of high molecular weight polyphenolic compounds widely distributed in the plant kingdom. They are characterized by their ability to bind and precipitate proteins and other macromolecules. Tannins play crucial roles in plant physiology, including defense against herbivores and pathogens, regulation of growth, and protection against UV radiation. Due to their astringent properties, tannins are extensively used in the leather industry for tanning hides, as well as in traditional medicine and the production of certain beverages like tea and wine.

2. Classification of Tannins

Tannins can be broadly classified into two main categories based on their chemical structure and reactivity:

A. Hydrolyzable Tannins

Hydrolyzable tannins are esters of gallic acid or ellagic acid with a sugar moiety, typically glucose. They can be hydrolyzed into their constituent phenolic acids and sugars under acidic or enzymatic conditions.

  a. **Gallotannins**

      i.   **Structure**: Composed of gallic acid units esterified to a sugar core, usually β-D-glucose.

     ii.   **Examples**: Pentagalloyl glucose, tannic acid.

   iii.   **Properties**: Exhibit strong protein-binding capacity and antioxidant activity.

  b. **Ellagitannins**

i. **Structure**: Formed by the oxidative coupling of gallic acid units, leading to the formation of hexahydroxydiphenoyl (HHDP) groups attached to the sugar core.

ii. **Examples**: Castalagin, vescalagin.

iii. **Properties**: More complex structures compared to gallotannins, with enhanced antioxidant and antimicrobial properties.

B. Condensed Tannins (Proanthocyanidins)

Condensed tannins, also known as proanthocyanidins, are polymers of flavan-3-ol units such as catechin and epicatechin. Unlike hydrolyzable tannins, condensed tannins are not readily hydrolyzed by acids or enzymes.

a. **Structure**: Composed of flavan-3-ol monomers linked primarily through C4→C8 or C4→C6 bonds, forming linear or branched polymers.

b. **Examples**: Catechin, epicatechin, procyanidins.

c. **Properties**: Known for their strong antioxidant activity, ability to bind proteins, and contribution to the astringency of foods and beverages.

C. Other Classifications

While the above two categories cover the primary types of tannins, some classifications also consider:

a. **Phlorotannins**: Found in brown algae, composed of phloroglucinol units.

b. **Complex Tannins**: Mixtures of hydrolyzable and condensed tannins or tannins bound with other plant constituents.

3. Properties of Tannins

A. Physical Properties

a. **Solubility**:

i. **Hydrolyzable Tannins**: Soluble in water and ethanol, especially under acidic conditions.

ii. **Condensed Tannins**: Soluble in aqueous and alcoholic solutions but less so in alkaline conditions.

b. **Color**:

    i.   Typically colorless to pale yellow in solution. Upon oxidation, especially in the presence of metals, they can develop deeper colors.

c. **Taste**:

    i.   Possess a characteristic astringent taste, which is due to their ability to precipitate salivary proteins.

d. **State**:

    i.   Usually found as amorphous solids or crystalline powders depending on the specific tannin.

B. Chemical Properties

a. **Protein Precipitation**:

    i.   Tannins can bind to proteins and precipitate them, a property exploited in leather tanning and in certain biological assays.

b. **Antioxidant Activity**:

    i.   The polyphenolic structure allows tannins to scavenge free radicals, thereby acting as antioxidants.

c. **Metal Chelation**:

    i.   Tannins can chelate metal ions such as Fe^{2+} and Al^{3+}, forming stable complexes that can influence plant physiology and soil chemistry.

d. **Hydrolyzability**:

    i.   Hydrolyzable tannins can be broken down into smaller molecules like gallic acid and ellagic acid upon hydrolysis.

    ii.   Condensed tannins resist hydrolysis and are more stable under various conditions.

e. **Reactivity with Bases and Acids**:

    i.   Tannins can react with bases to form salts and with acids to remain in their esterified forms or undergo hydrolysis.

4. Tests for Identification of Tannins

Several qualitative and quantitative tests are employed to detect and characterize tannins in plant extracts:

A. Ferric Chloride Test

    a. **Reagent**: 1% Ferric chloride (FeCl₃) solution.

    b. **Procedure**: Add a few drops of ferric chloride solution to the plant extract.

    c. **Result**:

        i. **Hydrolyzable Tannins**: May produce a greenish or blue-black color.

        ii. **Condensed Tannins**: Typically yield a blue or greenish-black coloration.

    d. **Principle**: Tannins form colored complexes with iron ions due to the formation of ferric tannate complexes.

B. Gelatin Test

    a. **Reagent**: Gelatin solution.

    b. **Procedure**: Add gelatin solution to the plant extract and gently heat.

    c. **Result**:

        i. **Positive for Tannins**: The mixture becomes turbid or precipitates upon cooling due to tannin-protein (gelatin) binding.

    d. **Principle**: Tannins precipitate proteins like gelatin, indicating their presence.

C. Hide Powder Test

    a. **Reagent**: Hide powder (animal skin powder).

    b. **Procedure**: Mix hide powder with the plant extract and shake.

    c. **Result**:

        i. **Positive for Tannins**: A precipitate forms as tannins bind to the hide powder proteins.

    d. **Principle**: Tannins interact with the proteins in hide powder, causing precipitation.

D. Lead Acetate Test

a. **Reagent**: 5% Lead acetate solution.

b. **Procedure**: Add lead acetate solution to the plant extract.

c. **Result**:

   i. **Positive for Tannins**: A black or blue-black precipitate forms.

d. **Principle**: Tannins form insoluble complexes with lead ions.

E. Reaction with Sodium Nitroprusside

a. **Reagent**: Sodium nitroprusside solution.

b. **Procedure**: Add sodium nitroprusside to the extract.

c. **Result**:

   i. **Positive for Tannins**: A violet or purple color develops.

d. **Principle**: Tannins react with sodium nitroprusside to form colored complexes.

F. UV-Visible Spectroscopy

a. **Procedure**: Measure the absorbance of the extract in the UV-visible range.

b. **Result**:

   i. **Characteristic Peaks**: Tannins exhibit specific absorbance peaks, typically around 280 nm due to their polyphenolic structure.

c. **Principle**: The conjugated double bonds in tannins absorb UV light, providing a spectral signature for identification.

G. Quantitative Methods

a. **Folin-Ciocalteu Method**: Measures the total phenolic content, which correlates with tannin concentration.

b. **Butanol-HCl Method**: Specifically used for quantifying proanthocyanidins (condensed tannins).

VOLATILE OIL

Volatile oils, also known as essential oils, are complex mixtures of volatile, aromatic compounds derived from plants. These oils are called "volatile" because they evaporate readily at room temperature, releasing their distinctive fragrances. They are primarily responsible for the characteristic aroma of many plants and have been used for centuries in perfumery, medicine, and food flavoring.

Volatile oils are typically obtained from plant materials through processes like distillation, expression, or solvent extraction. They contain a wide range of chemical constituents, including terpenes, phenolic compounds, esters, aldehydes, and ketones, which contribute to their diverse therapeutic and aromatic properties.

Classification of Volatile Oils

Volatile oils can be classified based on different criteria such as their chemical composition, plant source, or method of extraction. The most common classification is based on their chemical composition:

A. Terpene-Based Volatile Oils

a. **Monoterpenes (C10H16)**

    i.   **Structure**: Composed of two isoprene units (C5H8).

    ii.   **Examples**: Limonene (citrus oils), Pinene (pine oil), Menthol (peppermint oil).

    iii.   **Properties**: Often responsible for the characteristic scents of fruits and flowers; have antimicrobial, anti-inflammatory, and bronchodilatory effects.

b. **Sesquiterpenes (C15H24)**

    i.   **Structure**: Composed of three isoprene units.

    ii.   **Examples**: Bisabolol (chamomile oil), Farnesene (ginger oil).

    iii.   **Properties**: Known for anti-inflammatory, antibacterial, and sedative properties.

c. **Diterpenes (C20H32)**

    i.   **Structure**: Composed of four isoprene units.

ii. **Examples**: Phytol (found in chlorophyll), Retinol (vitamin A precursor).

iii. **Properties**: Less volatile compared to mono- and sesquiterpenes, often have antioxidant and anticancer properties.

B. Phenylpropanoids

a. **Structure**: Derived from the phenylpropane skeleton (C6-C3).

b. **Examples**: Eugenol (clove oil), Anethole (anise oil), Cinnamaldehyde (cinnamon oil).

c. **Properties**: Exhibit strong antimicrobial, analgesic, and antioxidant activities.

C. Alcohols, Aldehydes, and Ketones

a. **Alcohols**

i. **Examples**: Linalool (lavender oil), Geraniol (rose oil), Citronellol (lemongrass oil).

ii. **Properties**: Typically have antiseptic, antifungal, and calming effects.

b. **Aldehydes**

i. **Examples**: Citral (lemon oil), Cinnamaldehyde (cinnamon oil).

ii. **Properties**: Known for their potent antimicrobial and anti-inflammatory properties.

c. **Ketones**

i. **Examples**: Menthone (peppermint oil), Camphor (camphor oil).

ii. **Properties**: Often have mucolytic, sedative, and healing properties.

D. Esters

a. **Structure**: Formed by the reaction between an acid and an alcohol.

b. **Examples**: Linalyl acetate (lavender oil), Methyl salicylate (wintergreen oil).

c. **Properties**: Typically responsible for the pleasant, fruity aromas and are known for their anti-inflammatory, antispasmodic, and calming effects.

E. Oxides and Ethers

   a. **Examples**: 1,8-Cineole (eucalyptus oil), Safrole (sassafras oil).

   b. **Properties**: Often have expectorant, decongestant, and antimicrobial effects.

3. Properties of Volatile Oils

A. Physical Properties

   a. **Volatility**: Volatile oils evaporate easily at room temperature, making them suitable for aromatherapy and perfumery.

   b. **Solubility**:

      i. **Insoluble in Water**: Volatile oils are hydrophobic and do not mix well with water.

      ii. **Soluble in Organic Solvents**: They are soluble in alcohol, ether, chloroform, and other organic solvents.

   c. **Odor**: Characteristic and often strong, determined by the specific mix of constituents in the oil.

   d. **Refractive Index**: Volatile oils typically have a high refractive index, which can be used as a quality control parameter.

   e. **Optical Rotation**: Many volatile oils are optically active, exhibiting either levorotatory or dextrorotatory properties.

   f. **Density**: Generally lighter than water, though some oils (e.g., clove oil) may be denser.

B. Chemical Properties

   a. **Prone to Oxidation**: Exposure to air, light, and heat can lead to oxidation, altering the oil's scent and therapeutic properties.

   b. **Reactivity**:

      i. **Terpenes**: Can undergo rearrangements and oxidations.

      ii. **Phenylpropanoids**: Can form phenols, ethers, and esters.

   c. **Therapeutic Activities**: Many volatile oils have antimicrobial, anti-inflammatory, analgesic, and antioxidant properties.

4. Tests for Identification of Volatile Oils

Several tests are used to identify and analyze volatile oils, each targeting specific physical or chemical properties of the oil:

A. Solubility Test

    a. **Reagents**: Organic solvents like alcohol, ether, and chloroform.

    b. **Procedure**: Mix the volatile oil with the solvent.

    c. **Result**:

        i. **Positive**: The oil dissolves completely in the organic solvent, indicating its lipophilic nature.

    d. **Principle**: Volatile oils are soluble in organic solvents but insoluble in water.

B. Thin Layer Chromatography (TLC)

    a. **Reagents**: Silica gel plates, suitable solvent system, and visualizing agents (e.g., iodine vapors).

    b. **Procedure**: Apply a small amount of oil on the TLC plate, develop it in a solvent system, and visualize the spots.

    c. **Result**:

        i. **Positive**: The presence of specific spots with distinct Rf values corresponding to the components of the volatile oil.

    d. **Principle**: Different components of the volatile oil migrate at different rates on the TLC plate, allowing separation and identification.

C. Optical Rotation Test

    a. **Instrument**: Polarimeter.

    b. **Procedure**: Measure the optical rotation of the oil sample.

    c. **Result**:

        i. **Positive**: Specific optical rotation value indicating the presence of chiral molecules in the oil.

    d. **Principle**: Volatile oils with chiral components rotate plane-polarized light, and this rotation can be quantified.

D. Refractive Index Measurement

a. **Instrument**: Refractometer.

b. **Procedure**: Measure the refractive index of the oil at a specific temperature (usually 20°C).

c. **Result**:

   i. **Positive**: A specific refractive index value characteristic of the volatile oil.

d. **Principle**: The refractive index provides information about the purity and composition of the oil.

E. Specific Gravity Test

a. **Instrument**: Pycnometer or hydrometer.

b. **Procedure**: Measure the specific gravity of the oil relative to water.

c. **Result**:

   i. **Positive**: A specific gravity value within the expected range for the oil.

d. **Principle**: The specific gravity is a measure of the oil's density compared to water.

F. Chemical Tests for Specific Constituents

a. **Terpenes (e.g., Liebermann-Burchard Test)**

   i. **Reagents**: Acetic anhydride and concentrated sulfuric acid.

   ii. **Procedure**: Add reagents to the oil sample.

   iii. **Result**:

   1. **Positive**: A color change (e.g., green, blue) indicating the presence of terpenes.

   iv. **Principle**: Terpenes react with the reagents to produce characteristic colors.

b. **Phenols (e.g., Ferric Chloride Test)**

   i. **Reagents**: 1% Ferric chloride solution.

   ii. **Procedure**: Add ferric chloride to the oil sample.

iii. **Result**:

> 1. **Positive**: A color change (e.g., violet, blue) indicating the presence of phenolic compounds like eugenol.

iv. **Principle**: Phenols form colored complexes with ferric ions.

c. **Esters (e.g., Hydroxamic Acid Test)**

  i. **Reagents**: Hydroxylamine solution, ethanol, and sodium hydroxide.

  ii. **Procedure**: Heat the oil with the reagents and add ferric chloride.

  iii. **Result**:

> 1. **Positive**: A deep red or burgundy color indicates the presence of esters.

  iv. **Principle**: Esters react with hydroxylamine to form hydroxamic acids, which then react with ferric chloride to form colored complexes.

G. Gas Chromatography-Mass Spectrometry (GC-MS)

a. **Instrument**: GC-MS system.

b. **Procedure**: Inject the volatile oil into the GC-MS system, which separates and identifies the individual components.

c. **Result**:

  i. **Positive**: A detailed profile of the oil's components, including their retention times and mass spectra.

d. **Principle**: GC separates the volatile components based on their boiling points, and MS identifies them based on their mass-to-charge ratios.

RESINS

1. Definition of Resins

Resins are complex mixtures of hydrocarbons secreted by certain plants, particularly conifers. They are amorphous, solid or semi-solid substances that are typically insoluble in water but soluble in organic solvents like alcohol, ether, and chloroform. Resins are produced by plants as a response to injury or as a protective mechanism against herbivores and pathogens. They often harden upon exposure to air, forming a protective barrier over wounds in plants.

Resins have a wide range of applications, including in varnishes, adhesives, incense, and traditional medicine, where they are used for their antimicrobial, anti-inflammatory, and analgesic properties.

2. Classification of Resins

Resins can be classified based on their chemical composition, physical properties, or origin. The most common classifications are based on their chemical composition and the presence of other associated compounds.

A. Based on Chemical Composition

a. **Pure Resins**

   i. **Definition**: Resins composed primarily of resin acids and resin alcohols.

   ii. **Examples**: Colophony (rosin), Amber.

   iii. **Properties**: Hard and brittle, insoluble in water, soluble in organic solvents.

b. **Gum Resins**

   i. **Definition**: Mixtures of resins and gum (a water-soluble polysaccharide).

   ii. **Examples**: Myrrh, Asafoetida.

   iii. **Properties**: Partially soluble in water (due to the gum content) and fully soluble in organic solvents.

c. **Oleoresins**

   i. **Definition**: Mixtures of resins and volatile oils.

   ii. **Examples**: Turpentine, Ginger oleoresin.

   iii. **Properties**: Sticky and viscous; aromatic due to the volatile oil content.

d. **Oleo-gum Resins**

   i. **Definition**: Mixtures of resins, volatile oils, and gums.

ii. **Examples**: Frankincense, Myrrh.

iii. **Properties**: Have a combination of properties from both gum resins and oleoresins.

e. **Balsams**

i. **Definition**: Resins that contain a high percentage of benzoic acid or cinnamic acid esters.

ii. **Examples**: Balsam of Peru, Balsam of Tolu.

iii. **Properties**: Aromatic and viscous; often used in perfumery and medicine.

B. Based on Physical Properties

a. **Hard Resins**

i. **Examples**: Amber, Copal.

ii. **Properties**: Hard, brittle, and non-tacky.

b. **Soft Resins**

i. **Examples**: Pine resin, Mastic.

ii. **Properties**: Soft, sticky, and tacky.

C. Based on Plant Source

a. **Coniferous Resins**

i. **Examples**: Pine resin, Spruce resin.

ii. **Properties**: Typically derived from coniferous trees; often contain a high proportion of diterpenoid acids.

b. **Angiosperm Resins**

i. **Examples**: Myrrh, Frankincense.

ii. **Properties**: Derived from flowering plants; often used in incense and traditional medicine.

3. Properties of Resins

A. Physical Properties

a. **Appearance**: Resins can be clear, opaque, or translucent. Their color ranges from pale yellow to dark brown.

b. **Solubility**:

  i. **Insoluble in Water**: Resins are generally hydrophobic and do not dissolve in water.

  ii. **Soluble in Organic Solvents**: They are soluble in alcohol, ether, and chloroform.

c. **Texture**: Resins can be brittle or soft and sticky, depending on their composition.

d. **Odor**: Many resins have a characteristic aromatic odor due to the presence of volatile oils or aromatic acids.

e. **Melting Point**: Resins typically soften upon heating and do not have a sharp melting point.

B. Chemical Properties

a. **Complex Mixtures**: Resins are composed of various chemical constituents, including resin acids, resin alcohols, esters, and terpenoids.

b. **Reactivity**:

  i. **Oxidation**: Resins can oxidize upon exposure to air, leading to hardening.

  ii. **Polymerization**: Some resins can undergo polymerization, which increases their hardness and durability.

c. **Therapeutic Properties**: Resins often exhibit antimicrobial, anti-inflammatory, and analgesic properties, making them valuable in traditional medicine.

4. Tests for Identification of Resins

Several tests are used to identify and analyze resins, focusing on their solubility, chemical reactions, and physical properties:

A. Solubility Test

a. **Reagents**: Organic solvents like alcohol, ether, and chloroform.

b. **Procedure**: Mix the resin with the solvent.

c. **Result**:

i. **Positive**: The resin dissolves in the organic solvent, indicating its resinous nature.

d. **Principle**: Resins are soluble in organic solvents but insoluble in water.

B. Acetone Solubility Test

a. **Reagents**: Acetone.

b. **Procedure**: Dissolve the resin in acetone and allow it to evaporate.

c. **Result**:

  i. **Positive**: A residue is left behind after evaporation, indicating the presence of resin acids.

d. **Principle**: Resin acids are soluble in acetone, and their presence can be confirmed by the residue left after evaporation.

C. Ferric Chloride Test

a. **Reagents**: Ferric chloride solution.

b. **Procedure**: Add ferric chloride to an alcoholic solution of the resin.

c. **Result**:

  i. **Positive**: A green or bluish color indicates the presence of phenolic compounds within the resin.

d. **Principle**: Phenolic compounds in resins form colored complexes with ferric chloride.

D. Saponification Test

a. **Reagents**: Sodium hydroxide (NaOH) or potassium hydroxide (KOH).

b. **Procedure**: Heat the resin with a solution of NaOH or KOH.

c. **Result**:

  i. **Positive**: The formation of a soap-like substance indicates the presence of resin acids.

d. **Principle**: Resin acids react with alkali to form soap-like compounds through saponification.

E. Libermann-Burchard Test

a. **Reagents**: Acetic anhydride and concentrated sulfuric acid.

b. **Procedure**: Add reagents to the resin.

c. **Result**:

    i. **Positive**: A green or bluish-green color indicates the presence of terpenoids in the resin.

d. **Principle**: Terpenoids react with acetic anhydride and sulfuric acid to form colored complexes.

F. Melting Point Test

a. **Procedure**: Heat a small amount of resin and observe the temperature at which it softens or melts.

b. **Result**:

    i. **Observation**: The resin softens and eventually melts at a characteristic temperature range.

c. **Principle**: The melting point or softening range can provide information about the purity and type of resin.

G. Gas Chromatography-Mass Spectrometry (GC-MS)

a. **Instrument**: GC-MS system.

b. **Procedure**: Inject the resin into the GC-MS system, which separates and identifies the individual components.

c. **Result**:

    i. **Positive**: A detailed profile of the resin's components, including their retention times and mass spectra.

d. **Principle**: GC separates the volatile components of the resin, while MS identifies them based on their mass-to-charge ratios.

CLASSIFICATION:

Secondary metabolites are organic compounds produced by plants, fungi, bacteria, and other organisms that are not directly involved in the normal growth, development, or reproduction of the organism. Unlike primary metabolites, which are essential for basic cellular functions, secondary metabolites often play roles in defense, competition, and interactions with the environment.

Secondary metabolites can be classified into several major groups based on their chemical structure and biosynthetic origins:

1. Alkaloids

a. **Definition**: Nitrogen-containing compounds, typically derived from amino acids.

b. **Functions**: Often act as defense compounds, toxins, or have pharmacological effects on animals and humans.

c. **Examples**:

    i. **Morphine** from *Papaver somniferum* (Opium poppy)

    ii. **Quinine** from *Cinchona* species (used for treating malaria)

    iii. **Caffeine** from *Coffea arabica* (Coffee)

2. Terpenoids (Isoprenoids)

a. **Definition**: Largest group of secondary metabolites, composed of isoprene units (C5H8).

b. **Functions**: Play roles in plant growth regulation, defense, and attraction of pollinators.

c. **Examples**:

    i. **Menthol** from *Mentha* species (Peppermint)

    ii. **Taxol** from *Taxus brevifolia* (used in cancer treatment)

    iii. **Carotenoids** like **β-Carotene** in carrots (precursor of Vitamin A)

3. Phenolic Compounds

a. **Definition**: Compounds that have at least one aromatic ring with one or more hydroxyl groups.

b. **Functions**: Provide UV protection, defense against pathogens, and contribute to the color and flavor of plants.

c. **Examples**:

    i. **Flavonoids** like **Quercetin** in onions and apples

ii.   **Tannins** in tea and wine, which have astringent properties

iii.   **Lignin** in the cell walls of woody plants, providing structural support

4. Glycosides

a. **Definition**: Compounds in which a sugar is bound to a non-sugar moiety (aglycone) through a glycosidic bond.

b. **Functions**: Often involved in plant defense, pigmentation, and signaling.

c. **Examples**:

i.   **Saponins** like **Diosgenin** from *Dioscorea* species (used in the synthesis of steroids)

ii.   **Cardiac glycosides** like **Digoxin** from *Digitalis purpurea* (used to treat heart conditions)

iii.   **Anthraquinone glycosides** like **Aloin** in Aloe vera (used as a laxative)

5. Tannins

a. **Definition**: Polyphenolic compounds capable of binding and precipitating proteins.

b. **Functions**: Defense against herbivores and pathogens, antioxidant properties.

c. **Examples**:

i.   **Ellagitannins** in pomegranates

ii.   **Condensed tannins** in grapes, which contribute to the astringency of red wine

iii.   **Gallotannins** in oak trees, used in leather tanning

6. Volatile Oils (Essential Oils)

a. **Definition**: Mixtures of volatile, aromatic compounds, often terpenoids or phenylpropanoids.

b. **Functions**: Serve as attractants for pollinators, defense mechanisms, or allelopathic agents.

c. **Examples**:

    i.   **Eugenol** from cloves (*Syzygium aromaticum*)

    ii.   **Limonene** from citrus fruits (*Citrus* species)

    iii. **Thymol** from thyme (*Thymus vulgaris*)

7. Resins

a. **Definition**: Complex mixtures of terpenoids and other secondary metabolites that are secreted by plants, especially trees.

b. **Functions**: Protect plants from herbivores and pathogens, used in traditional medicine and industry.

c. **Examples**:

    i.   **Rosin** from pine trees (*Pinus* species)

    ii.   **Myrrh** from *Commiphora* species

    iii. **Frankincense** from *Boswellia* species

8. Coumarins

a. **Definition**: Benzopyrone compounds derived from the phenylpropanoid pathway.

b. **Functions**: Antimicrobial, anti-inflammatory, and anticoagulant properties.

c. **Examples**:

    i.   **Coumarin** from sweet clover (*Melilotus officinalis*)

    ii.   **Aesculetin** from *Aesculus hippocastanum* (Horse chestnut)

    iii. **Umbelliferone** from *Umbelliferae* family plants

9. Lignans

a. **Definition**: Phenolic compounds derived from phenylpropanoid precursors that are linked by a β,β'-linkage.

b. **Functions**: Antioxidant, anticancer, and antiviral properties.

c. **Examples**:

    i.   **Podophyllotoxin** from *Podophyllum* species (used in cancer therapy)

ii. **Sesamin** from sesame seeds (*Sesamum indicum*)

iii. **Matairesinol** from flax seeds (*Linum usitatissimum*)

Multiple Choice Questions (MCQs)

1. What are secondary metabolites?

    a. Compounds essential for growth and development

    b. Compounds involved in normal cellular functions

    c. Organic compounds not directly involved in growth, development, or reproduction

    d. Inorganic compounds with no biological role

2. Which of the following is a major group of secondary metabolites?

    a. Proteins

    b. Lipids

    c. Alkaloids

    d. Carbohydrates

3. Alkaloids are primarily classified based on which characteristic?

    a. Color

    b. Solubility

    c. Nitrogen content and biosynthesis

    d. Presence of oxygen

4. Which of the following is a true alkaloid?

    a. Caffeine

    b. Quinine

    c. Ephedrine

    d. Colchicine

5. Which pathway is primarily involved in the biosynthesis of terpenoids?

    a. Shikimate pathway

    b. Glycolysis

c. Citric acid cycle

d. Mevalonate pathway

6. Which test is used to identify the presence of anthraquinone glycosides?

a. Dragendorff's Test

b. Mayer's Test

c. Borntrager's Test

d. Hager's Test

7. What is the primary function of tannins in plants?

a. Photosynthesis

b. Respiration

c. Defense against herbivores and pathogens

d. Energy storage

8. Which class of secondary metabolites is responsible for the characteristic aroma of many plants?

a. Alkaloids

b. Glycosides

c. Volatile oils

d. Tannins

9. Which secondary metabolite is known for its anticancer properties and is derived from the Pacific yew tree?

a. Quinine

b. Taxol

c. Morphine

d. Caffeine

10. Which of the following is a phenolic compound that contributes to the color and flavor of plants?

a. Glycosides

b. Tannins

c. Flavonoids

d. Alkaloids

11. Which test is used to detect the presence of flavonoids?

    a. Ferric Chloride Test

    b. Shinoda Test

    c. Wagner's Test

    d. Legal's Test

12. What is the chemical nature of eugenol?

    a. Alkaloid

    b. Terpene

    c. Phenolic compound

    d. Glycoside

13. Which of the following secondary metabolites is used in the treatment of malaria?

    a. Morphine

    b. Quinine

    c. Caffeine

    d. Menthol

14. Which secondary metabolite is commonly found in tea and wine and has astringent properties?

    a. Flavonoids

    b. Alkaloids

    c. Tannins

    d. Glycosides

15. Which test is used to detect the presence of saponin glycosides?

    a. Foam Test

    b. Keller-Killiani Test

    c. Shinoda Test

    d. Dragendorff's Test

16. Which secondary metabolite is known for its hepatoprotective properties?

    a. Sesamin

    b. Caffeine

    c. Podophyllotoxin

    d. Quercetin

17. Limonene, a compound with a characteristic citrus aroma, belongs to which class of secondary metabolites?

    a. Alkaloids

    b. Terpenoids

    c. Phenolic compounds

    d. Glycosides

18. Which compound is a potent central nervous system stimulant found in coffee beans?

    a. Limonene

    b. Caffeine

    c. Quinine

    d. Eugenol

19. Which secondary metabolite is a precursor to Vitamin A?

    a. Limonene

    b. Quercetin

    c. β-Carotene

    d. Flavonoids

20. Which test involves the use of magnesium turnings and concentrated hydrochloric acid to detect flavonoids?

    a. Shinoda Test

    b. Mayer's Test

    c. Borntrager's Test

    d. Hager's Test

Short Answer Type Questions (Subjective)

1. What are secondary metabolites, and how do they differ from primary metabolites?
2. Discuss the role of alkaloids in plant defense mechanisms.
3. Describe the classification of glycosides based on the nature of the aglycone.
4. Explain the significance of terpenoids in medicine.
5. What are phenolic compounds, and what role do they play in plants?
6. How are tannins classified, and what are their main properties?
7. Describe the process of biosynthesis of secondary metabolites.
8. Explain the importance of flavonoids in human health.
9. Discuss the pharmacological properties of eugenol.
10. What are volatile oils, and how are they extracted from plants?
11. Explain the role of secondary metabolites in the evolution of plants.
12. How are resins classified, and what are their common applications?
13. Describe the chemical properties of alkaloids.
14. What tests are used to identify the presence of tannins in plant extracts?
15. Discuss the role of secondary metabolites in pharmaceutical industries.
16. Explain the pharmacological effects of caffeine on the human body.
17. How do secondary metabolites contribute to the ecological functions of plants?
18. What is the role of coumarins in medicine?
19. Describe the significance of sesamin in modern pharmacology.
20. What are the potential therapeutic uses of podophyllotoxin?

Long Answer Type Questions (Subjective)

1. Discuss the classification, properties, and significance of alkaloids in various fields such as medicine and agriculture.
2. Explain the role of secondary metabolites in plant defense and adaptation, providing examples of different classes of secondary metabolites.

3. Describe the process of biosynthesis of terpenoids and their applications in the pharmaceutical and cosmetic industries.

4. Discuss the pharmacological properties, traditional uses, and modern applications of tannins.

5. Explain the significance of volatile oils in traditional and modern medicine, including their extraction methods and applications.

6. Analyze the role of glycosides in plant metabolism and human medicine, including their classification and identification tests.

7. Discuss the role of flavonoids in plants and their importance in human health, providing examples of common flavonoids and their sources.

8. Describe the pharmacological properties, traditional uses, and modern applications of resins in various industries.

9. Explain the role of secondary metabolites in drug discovery and development, with examples of important drugs derived from natural sources.

10. Discuss the significance of secondary metabolites in the cosmetic industry, focusing on the applications of terpenoids, phenolics, and volatile oils.

Answer Key for MCQs

1. (c) Organic compounds not directly involved in growth, development, or reproduction

2. (c) Alkaloids

3. (c) Nitrogen content and biosynthesis

4. (b) Quinine

5. (d) Mevalonate pathway

6. (c) Borntrager's Test

7. (c) Defense against herbivores and pathogens

8. (c) Volatile oils

9. (b) Taxol

10.(c) Flavonoids

11.(b) Shinoda Test

12.(c) Phenolic compound

13.(b) Quinine

14.(c) Tannins

15.(a) Foam Test

16.(a) Sesamin

17.(b) Terpenoids

18.(b) Caffeine

19.(c) β-Carotene

20.(a) Shinoda Test

CHAPTER – 9

FIBERS

INTRODUCTION:

Fibers are elongated, thread-like structures that play a crucial role in both plant and animal kingdoms. They are primarily composed of long-chain molecules and are classified based on their origin, composition, and function. Fibers are integral to various industries, including textiles, paper, and biomedical applications.

Classification of Fibers

Fibers can be broadly classified into two categories:

1. **Natural Fibers:**
   a. **Plant-based Fibers:** Derived from plants, these fibers are primarily composed of cellulose. Examples include cotton, jute, hemp, flax, and sisal.
   b. **Animal-based Fibers:** These fibers are obtained from animals and are primarily composed of proteins such as keratin or fibroin. Examples include wool (from sheep), silk (from silkworms), and mohair (from angora goats).
   c. **Mineral-based Fibers:** Derived from minerals, these fibers include asbestos, which was historically used for its fire-resistant properties.

2. **Synthetic Fibers:**
   a. **Cellulosic Fibers:** These are semi-synthetic fibers derived from natural cellulose, such as rayon and acetate.
   b. **Non-cellulosic Fibers:** These fully synthetic fibers are made from petrochemicals and include nylon, polyester, acrylic, and spandex.

Structure and Properties

1. **Physical Structure:** Fibers generally have a high length-to-diameter ratio. Their structure can be smooth or crimped, influencing the texture and strength of the fiber. The alignment of polymer chains within the fiber contributes to its tensile strength and elasticity.

2. **Chemical Composition:** The chemical composition varies depending on the type of fiber. For instance, plant fibers are rich in cellulose, animal fibers in proteins, and synthetic fibers in various polymers like polyamide (nylon) or polyethylene terephthalate (polyester).

3. **Mechanical Properties:** Fibers exhibit different mechanical properties, including tensile strength, elasticity, and flexibility. Natural fibers like cotton have high moisture absorbency, while synthetic fibers like polyester are known for their durability and resistance to environmental conditions.

Functions and Uses

1. **Textiles:** Fibers are the building blocks of the textile industry. They are spun into yarns and woven or knitted into fabrics used for clothing, upholstery, and various industrial applications.

2. **Paper Manufacturing:** Plant fibers, particularly those from trees (wood pulp), are essential in paper production.

3. **Biomedical Applications:** Certain fibers, like those used in sutures or tissue engineering, are designed for biocompatibility and bioresorbability.

4. **Composite Materials:** Fibers like glass and carbon are used to reinforce composite materials, providing strength and rigidity to products like aircraft, automobiles, and sporting goods.

Processing of Fibers

The processing of fibers involves several steps:

1. **Harvesting:** For natural fibers, this includes the collection of raw materials (e.g., cotton bolls, sheep wool).

2. **Ginning or Scouring:** Removing impurities from plant or animal fibers.

3. **Spinning:** Transforming fibers into yarn or thread.

4. **Weaving or Knitting:** Creating fabrics from yarns.

5. **Finishing:** Treating fabrics to enhance properties such as water resistance, colorfastness, or softness.

COTTON

Cotton (Gossypium herbaceum)

- **Biological**   **Source:**
  Cotton is derived from the hairs surrounding the seeds of the plant *Gossypium herbaceum* and other species of the genus *Gossypium*, belonging to the family Malvaceae. It is primarily cultivated in tropical and subtropical regions.

- **Chemical Nature:**
  Cotton fibers are almost pure cellulose, which is a polysaccharide composed of glucose units. The cellulose content in cotton is around 90-95%. It also contains small amounts of waxes, proteins, and pectins.

- **Uses:**
    1. **Medical Uses:**
       Cotton is widely used in the pharmaceutical industry, mainly in the form of absorbent cotton wool, which is sterilized and used for wound dressings, swabs, and surgical procedures. It is highly absorbent and is used for cleaning wounds, applying antiseptics, and as a padding material in medical treatments.

    2. **Industrial Uses:**
       Cotton fibers are extensively used in the textile industry to produce fabrics, threads, and garments. It is known for its durability, comfort, and breathability.

    3. **Other Uses:**

Cottonseed oil, extracted from cotton seeds, is used in cooking and food products. Cottonseed meal, a byproduct of oil extraction, is used as animal feed. Cotton linters (short fibers) are used in making paper, plastics, and other industrial products.

Jute (Corchorus capsularis and Corchorus olitorius)

- **Biological Source**:

  Jute is obtained from the bark of the plants *Corchorus capsularis* and *Corchorus olitorius*, which belong to the family Malvaceae (or Tiliaceae in some classifications). These plants are primarily cultivated in tropical regions, especially in India, Bangladesh, and China.

- **Chemical Nature**:

  Jute is composed mainly of cellulose and lignin. The fibers contain around 60-65% cellulose, 20-22% hemicellulose, and 10-12% lignin. Jute is known for its strength, durability, and biodegradable nature, making it an eco-friendly fiber.

- **Uses**:

  1. **Medical Uses**:

     Although jute itself is not directly used in mainstream pharmaceuticals, it has some applications in traditional medicine. The leaves of *Corchorus olitorius* are used in some traditional medicines for their anti-inflammatory, antioxidant, and antimicrobial properties. In folk medicine, it is also used as a remedy for fever, dysentery, and constipation.

  2. **Industrial Uses**:

     Jute is widely used in the production of sacking, hessian cloth, ropes, and other types of packaging materials. It is commonly used for making eco-friendly bags, mats, and other products due to its biodegradable nature.

3. **Other Uses**:

    The leaves and shoots of *Corchorus olitorius* are consumed as a vegetable in some countries, particularly in Africa and Asia. They are rich in vitamins, minerals, and fiber. The mucilage from the leaves is sometimes used to treat skin irritations.

Hemp (Cannabis sativa)

- **Biological Source**:

Hemp is obtained from the plant *Cannabis sativa*, which belongs to the family Cannabaceae. It is primarily cultivated for its fibers, seeds, and medicinal compounds. Hemp is a variety of *Cannabis* that contains low levels of the psychoactive compound tetrahydrocannabinol (THC), generally less than 0.3%.

- **Chemical Nature**:

Hemp contains a variety of chemical compounds, including cannabinoids, terpenes, flavonoids, and other secondary metabolites. Key constituents include:

1. **Cannabinoids**: The most notable are cannabidiol (CBD) and tetrahydrocannabinol (THC). CBD is non-psychoactive and has various medicinal properties, while THC has psychoactive effects but is present in low amounts in industrial hemp.

2. **Hemp Fibers**: The fibers are primarily composed of cellulose, hemicellulose, and lignin, which give them strength and durability.

3. **Hemp Seed Oil**: Hemp seeds are rich in essential fatty acids, such as omega-3 and omega-6, and contain proteins, vitamins, and minerals.

- **Uses**:
    1. **Medical Uses**:

- **CBD**: Hemp is widely used for its cannabidiol (CBD) content, which has numerous therapeutic benefits, including anti-inflammatory, analgesic, anti-anxiety, and neuroprotective effects. CBD is used in the treatment of conditions like epilepsy, anxiety, chronic pain, and certain neurological disorders.
- **Hemp Seed Oil**: Rich in essential fatty acids, hemp seed oil is used as a dietary supplement and in skincare products for its moisturizing and anti-inflammatory properties.

2. **Industrial Uses**:
   - **Hemp Fiber**: Hemp fibers are strong and durable, making them ideal for producing textiles, ropes, paper, bioplastics, and construction materials like hempcrete. It is also used in the automotive industry for manufacturing composites.
   - **Biofuel**: Hemp can be used to produce biodiesel and ethanol, providing a renewable energy source.

3. **Nutritional Uses**:

   Hemp seeds are considered a superfood due to their high content of essential fatty acids, protein, and fiber. They are used in a variety of food products such as hemp seed oil, protein powder, and nutritional supplements.

4. **Cosmetic Uses**:

   Hemp seed oil is commonly used in skincare and hair care products due to its moisturizing properties and ability to improve skin elasticity and reduce inflammation.

Multiple Choice Questions (Objective)

1. Which of the following is a natural fiber derived from plants?

   A) Nylon

B) Polyester

C) Cotton

D) Spandex

2. What is the primary chemical component of cotton fibers?

A) Keratin

B) Cellulose

C) Polyamide

D) Fibroin

3. Which fiber is derived from the bast of the hemp plant?

A) Silk

B) Jute

C) Hemp

D) Sisal

4. Which synthetic fiber is made from polyamide?

A) Acrylic

B) Nylon

C) Polyester

D) Rayon

5. What natural fiber is primarily composed of keratin?

A) Wool

B) Cotton

C) Nylon

D) Sisal

6. Which fiber is known for its strength and durability, and is commonly used in ropes and canvas?

A) Cotton

B) Wool

C) Hemp

D) Polyester

7. Which of the following fibers is classified as a semi-synthetic fiber?

A) Nylon

B) Polyester

C) Acetate

D) Glass Fiber

8. What is the main application of surgical cotton?

A) Wound dressings

B) Sutures

C) Prosthetics

D) Compression garments

9. Which fiber is primarily used in the production of biodegradable geotextiles?

A) Jute

B) Silk

C) Nylon

D) Spandex

10. Which fiber is derived from the leaves of the Agave sisalana plant?

A) Cotton

B) Hemp

C) Sisal

D) Wool

11. Which fiber is known for its use in bulletproof vests due to its high tensile strength?

A) Silk

B) Kevlar (Aramid)

C) Wool

D) Polyester

12. What is the primary use of rayon in the medical field?

A) Sutures

B) Surgical dressings

C) Dental floss

D) Bandages

13. Which synthetic fiber is known for its exceptional elasticity and is widely used in compression garments?

A) Nylon

B) Polyester

C) Spandex (Lycra)

D) Acrylic

14. Which fiber is primarily used in the production of surgical sutures and is derived from the silkworm?

A) Wool

B) Silk

C) Hemp

D) Cotton

15. What is the main component of acrylic fibers?

A) Polyacrylonitrile

B) Cellulose

C) Polyethylene

D) Polyamide

16. Which natural fiber is obtained from the fleece of sheep?

A) Silk

B) Wool

C) Cotton

D) Cashmere

17. Which fiber is commonly used in the production of vascular grafts?

A) Nylon

B) Silk

C) Polyester

D) Cotton

18. Which fiber is known for its use in thermal insulating garments and is derived from the undercoat of goats?

    A) Silk

    B) Mohair

    C) Cashmere

    D) Wool

19. Which fiber is considered a natural mineral fiber?

    A) Wool

    B) Asbestos

    C) Cotton

    D) Kevlar

20. Which synthetic fiber is used in the production of stretchable electronics due to its elasticity?

    A) Spandex (Lycra)

    B) Nylon

    C) Rayon

    D) Polyester

Short Answer Type Questions (Subjective)

1. What are the primary differences between natural and synthetic fibers?
2. Explain the chemical composition and structure of cotton fibers.
3. What are the main uses of jute in the textile industry?
4. Describe the process of producing nylon and its applications in the medical field.
5. How is silk produced, and what are its primary medical applications?
6. Discuss the environmental impact of synthetic fibers like polyester.
7. Explain the significance of cellulose in plant-based fibers like cotton and hemp.

8. What are the unique properties of spandex that make it suitable for medical applications?

9. Describe the role of rayon in medical textiles.

10. What are the main characteristics of wool that make it suitable for orthopedic supports?

11. How is sisal harvested, and what are its primary industrial uses?

12. What are the benefits of using biodegradable fibers like jute in environmental applications?

13. Explain the chemical nature of polyester and its uses in biomedical applications.

14. What makes carbon fibers suitable for use in orthopedic implants?

15. How is asbestos different from other natural fibers in terms of health risks?

16. Describe the applications of glass fibers in medical devices.

17. What is the significance of using biodegradable sutures in surgery?

18. How does cashmere compare to wool in terms of softness and warmth?

19. Explain the process of converting cellulose into acetate fibers.

20. What are the potential medical applications of triacetate fibers?

Long Answer Type Questions (Subjective)

1. Discuss the classification of fibers based on their origin and chemical composition, providing examples for each category.

2. Explain the process of harvesting and processing cotton, and discuss its various applications in the medical and textile industries.

3. Describe the chemical composition, properties, and applications of hemp fibers in both industrial and medical fields.

4. Discuss the role of synthetic fibers like nylon, polyester, and spandex in medical applications, focusing on their chemical structure and biocompatibility.

5. Explain the environmental impact of synthetic fibers and discuss the efforts being made to develop sustainable alternatives.

6. Analyze the advantages and disadvantages of using natural fibers like wool and silk in medical applications, including their biocompatibility and biodegradability.

7. Describe the production process of rayon and its role in medical textiles and drug delivery systems.

8. Discuss the significance of using biodegradable fibers like jute and sisal in environmental conservation and medical applications.

9. Explain the chemical and structural differences between acetate and triacetate fibers and their respective uses in medical textiles.

10. Discuss the health risks associated with asbestos fibers and the measures taken to mitigate these risks in industrial and medical settings.

Answer Key for MCQs

1. C) Cotton
2. B) Cellulose
3. C) Hemp
4. B) Nylon
5. A) Wool
6. C) Hemp
7. C) Acetate
8. A) Wound dressings
9. A) Jute
10. C) Sisal
11. B) Kevlar (Aramid)
12. B) Surgical dressings
13. C) Spandex (Lycra)
14. B) Silk

15.A) Polyacrylonitrile

16.B) Wool

17.C) Polyester

18.C) Cashmere

19.B) Asbestos

20.A) Spandex (Lycra)

CHAPTER – 10

HALLUCINOGENS, TERATOGENS, NATURAL ALLERGENS

INTRODUCTION:

1. Hallucinogens:

Definition: Hallucinogens are a class of drugs that alter perception, mood, and various cognitive processes, leading to changes in sensory experiences and thought patterns. They can cause hallucinations, which are false perceptions of reality.

Types of Hallucinogens:

    a. **Classic Hallucinogens:** These include substances like LSD (lysergic acid diethylamide), psilocybin (magic mushrooms), and mescaline (from peyote cactus). They primarily affect serotonin receptors in the brain.

    b. **Dissociative Hallucinogens:** Such as PCP (phencyclidine) and ketamine, which can cause a sense of detachment from the environment and oneself.

    c. **Deliriants:** These include drugs like diphenhydramine and atropine, which can cause delirium and confusion.

Mechanism of Action: Hallucinogens often work by affecting neurotransmitter systems in the brain. For example, classic hallucinogens primarily interact with serotonin receptors (5-HT2A receptors), while dissociatives affect NMDA (N-methyl-D-aspartate) receptors.

Uses and Effects:

    a. **Therapeutic Uses:** Some hallucinogens have been studied for their potential therapeutic benefits in treating mental health conditions like depression and PTSD.

    b. **Recreational Use:** Many are used recreationally for their ability to produce altered states of consciousness.

c. **Adverse Effects:** Can include anxiety, paranoia, and impaired judgment. In severe cases, hallucinogens can lead to lasting psychological issues.

2. Teratogens:

Definition: Teratogens are substances that cause developmental abnormalities in a fetus or embryo when a pregnant woman is exposed to them. They can lead to birth defects or developmental disorders.

Types of Teratogens:

a. **Pharmaceutical Drugs:** Certain medications, such as thalidomide (which caused limb abnormalities) and some anti-seizure drugs, are known teratogens.

b. **Environmental Factors:** Exposure to radiation, certain chemicals (like mercury), and infectious agents (like rubella) can be teratogenic.

c. **Substances of Abuse:** Alcohol (leading to fetal alcohol syndrome) and tobacco can also act as teratogens.

Mechanism of Action: Teratogens can disrupt normal fetal development by causing genetic mutations, interfering with cell division, or affecting the normal growth of tissues and organs.

Effects and Prevention:

a. **Effects:** Birth defects can range from minor to severe and include physical abnormalities, developmental delays, and cognitive impairments.

b. **Prevention:** Avoiding known teratogens during pregnancy, regular prenatal care, and proper management of health conditions can help minimize risk.

3. Natural Allergens:

Definition: Natural allergens are substances originating from natural sources that can trigger allergic reactions in susceptible individuals. These reactions occur when the immune system overreacts to these harmless substances.

Types of Natural Allergens:

a. **Pollen:** Pollen from trees, grasses, and weeds is a common allergen that can cause seasonal allergic rhinitis (hay fever).

b. **Mold:** Mold spores found in damp environments can trigger allergic reactions and asthma.

c. **Animal Dander:** Proteins found in the skin, saliva, and urine of animals like cats and dogs can cause allergic reactions.

d. **Foods:** Certain foods such as peanuts, shellfish, and eggs can be allergens, causing food allergies.

Mechanism of Action: Allergens typically provoke an immune response involving IgE antibodies. This response leads to the release of histamines and other chemicals that cause symptoms of an allergic reaction.

Effects and Management:

a. **Effects:** Allergic reactions can range from mild (sneezing, itching) to severe (anaphylaxis, a life-threatening reaction).

b. **Management:** Avoidance of known allergens, use of antihistamines, and allergen immunotherapy (allergy shots) can help manage and reduce allergic symptoms.

CLASSIFICATION:

1. Hallucinogens

A. Classic Hallucinogens

a. **LSD (Lysergic Acid Diethylamide):** A potent hallucinogen that alters perception and mood, often leading to visual and auditory hallucinations.

b. **Psilocybin:** Found in certain species of mushrooms, it produces effects similar to LSD, including altered perceptions and mood changes.

c. **Mescaline:** Derived from the peyote cactus, it induces visual and auditory hallucinations.

B. Dissociative Hallucinogens

a. **PCP (Phencyclidine):** Originally developed as an anesthetic, it can cause detachment from reality, hallucinations, and a sense of floating.

b. **Ketamine:** Used medically as an anesthetic, it can produce dissociative effects and hallucinations, sometimes used in the treatment of depression.

C. Deliriants

a. **Diphenhydramine:** An antihistamine that, at high doses, can cause delirium and hallucinations.

b. **Atropine:** Found in plants like belladonna, it can cause delirium, hallucinations, and confusion at high doses.

2. Teratogens

A. Pharmaceutical Teratogens

a. **Thalidomide:** Caused severe limb defects in children born to mothers who took it during pregnancy.

b. **Valproic Acid:** An anticonvulsant that can cause neural tube defects and other developmental issues.

B. Environmental Teratogens

a. **Radiation:** Exposure to high levels of radiation can cause developmental abnormalities and increase the risk of cancer in the offspring.

b. **Mercury:** Exposure to mercury, especially in high levels, can cause neurological and developmental problems in the fetus.

C. Substances of Abuse

a. **Alcohol:** Can cause fetal alcohol syndrome, leading to physical and cognitive abnormalities.

b. **Tobacco:** Can lead to low birth weight, premature birth, and developmental problems.

3. Natural Allergens

A. Pollen Allergens

a. **Tree Pollen:** Common in spring; examples include oak, birch, and cedar pollen.

b. **Grass Pollen:** Common in summer; examples include Bermuda grass and Timothy grass.

c. **Weed Pollen:** Common in late summer and fall; examples include ragweed and sagebrush.

B. Mold Allergens

a. **Aspergillus:** A common mold found in soil and decaying vegetation.

b. **Penicillium:** Often found in damp buildings and on food, it can trigger allergic reactions.

C. Animal Dander Allergens

a. **Cat Dander:** Proteins found in cat saliva, skin, and urine.

b. **Dog Dander:** Proteins found in dog saliva, skin, and urine.

D. Food Allergens

a. **Peanuts:** A common allergen that can cause severe allergic reactions, including anaphylaxis.

b. **Shellfish:** Includes allergens from crustaceans (e.g., shrimp) and mollusks (e.g., clams).

Multiple Choice Questions (MCQs)

1. What is the primary action of classic hallucinogens like LSD?

    a) Inhibiting NMDA receptors

    b) Agonizing serotonin receptors

    c) Blocking dopamine receptors

    d) Inhibiting GABA receptors

2. Which of the following is a dissociative hallucinogen?

    a) LSD

    b) Psilocybin

    c) PCP

    d) Mescaline

3. Which substance is known to cause fetal alcohol syndrome when consumed during pregnancy?

a) Tobacco

b) Alcohol

c) Mercury

d) Thalidomide

4. Which of the following is NOT a known teratogen?

a) Valproic Acid

b) LSD

c) Psilocybin

d) Atropine

5. Which allergen is commonly found in cat dander?

a) Can f 1

b) Fel d 1

c) Ara h 1

d) Tropomyosin

6. What is the primary mechanism by which hallucinogens like LSD produce their effects?

a) Inhibition of dopamine receptors

b) Stimulation of NMDA receptors

c) Agonism of 5-HT2A receptors

d) Blocking of acetylcholine receptors

7. Which of the following is a natural allergen found in peanuts?

a) Ara h 1

b) Fel d 1

c) Can f 1

d) Penicillium

8. Which drug was withdrawn from the market due to its teratogenic effects causing severe limb defects?

a) Valproic Acid

b) Thalidomide

c) Alcohol

d) Atropine

9. Which of the following is a common mold allergen?

a) Limonene

b) Tropomyosin

c) Aspergillus fumigatus

d) Fel d 1

10. What is the primary health risk associated with mercury exposure during pregnancy?

a) Hallucinations

b) Allergic reactions

c) Developmental and neurological issues

d) Respiratory infections

11. Which hallucinogen is derived from magic mushrooms?

a) LSD

b) Mescaline

c) Psilocybin

d) PCP

12. What is a major allergen found in dog dander?

a) Ara h 1

b) Fel d 1

c) Tropomyosin

d) Can f 1

13. Which drug is used to treat multiple myeloma but is also a known teratogen?

a) Valproic Acid

b) Thalidomide

c) Ketamine

d) Psilocybin

14. What is the major allergen found in shellfish?

   a) Fel d 1

   b) Tropomyosin

   c) Ara h 1

   d) Can f 1

15. Which of the following hallucinogens is known to cause dissociative effects?

   a) Psilocybin

   b) Ketamine

   c) LSD

   d) Thalidomide

16. What is the primary pharmacological action of diphenhydramine?

   a) Serotonin receptor agonism

   b) Antihistamine

   c) NMDA receptor antagonism

   d) Dopamine receptor antagonism

17. Which compound in tobacco smoke is primarily responsible for its stimulant effects?

   a) Atropine

   b) Nicotine

   c) Caffeine

   d) LSD

18. Which of the following teratogens is associated with neural tube defects?

   a) Thalidomide

   b) Alcohol

   c) Valproic Acid

   d) Mercury

19. Which of the following molds is often associated with allergic bronchopulmonary aspergillosis (ABPA)?

   a) Penicillium chrysogenum

b) Aspergillus fumigatus

c) Aspergillus niger

d) Aspergillus flavus

20. Which hallucinogen was historically used as an anesthetic and is known for causing dissociative effects?

a) LSD

b) PCP

c) Psilocybin

d) Mescaline

Short Answer Type Questions (Subjective)

1. Define hallucinogens and explain the different types of hallucinogens.

2. Discuss the mechanism of action of LSD and its effects on the brain.

3. What are teratogens? Provide examples of pharmaceutical and environmental teratogens.

4. Explain how mercury acts as a teratogen and its effects on fetal development.

5. Describe the health risks associated with fetal alcohol syndrome.

6. What are natural allergens? List and describe the types of allergens that can cause respiratory issues.

7. Discuss the role of Fel d 1 in cat allergies and the common symptoms associated with it.

8. Explain the use of thalidomide in modern medicine and its teratogenic risks.

9. Describe the pharmacological effects of ketamine as a dissociative hallucinogen.

10. What is the primary mechanism by which penicillin can cause allergic reactions in some individuals?

11. How does valproic acid affect fetal development, and what are the associated risks?

12. Discuss the role of nicotine in tobacco and its effects on the central nervous system.

13. What are the therapeutic uses of psilocybin, and what are its potential risks?

14. Explain the allergic reactions caused by peanut allergens and the management of such allergies.

15. Describe the effects of Atropine and its use in medicine.

16. How does exposure to Aspergillus fumigatus affect individuals with respiratory conditions?

17. Discuss the pharmacological action of diphenhydramine and its common uses.

18. Explain the significance of Tropomyosin as an allergen in shellfish.

19. Describe the health effects of tobacco smoke on fetal development.

20. What is PCP, and what are the potential risks associated with its use?

Long Answer Type Questions (Subjective)

1. Discuss the classification, mechanism of action, and effects of hallucinogens on the human brain, with a focus on LSD and psilocybin.

2. Explain the concept of teratogens, providing detailed examples of pharmaceutical, environmental, and substance abuse-related teratogens and their impact on fetal development.

3. Analyze the role of natural allergens in respiratory conditions, including a detailed discussion of common allergens like pollen, mold, and animal dander, and the management of allergic reactions.

4. Discuss the therapeutic uses, risks, and modern regulatory controls associated with thalidomide, considering its historical context as a teratogen.

5. Explain the pharmacological effects of dissociative hallucinogens like PCP and ketamine, focusing on their mechanism of action, therapeutic uses, and potential for abuse.

6. Describe the various allergic reactions caused by food allergens such as peanuts and shellfish, their underlying immunological mechanisms, and approaches to diagnosis and treatment.

7. Discuss the effects of fetal alcohol syndrome on child development, including the underlying mechanisms, prevention strategies, and long-term outcomes for affected individuals.

8. Explain the pharmacological actions of nicotine in tobacco products, its effects on human health, and the associated risks of tobacco use during pregnancy.

9. Analyze the use of valproic acid in epilepsy and bipolar disorder treatment, focusing on its mechanism of action, side effects, and teratogenic risks during pregnancy.

10. Describe the role of molds like Aspergillus and Penicillium in allergic reactions and respiratory conditions, with a focus on their allergenicity, health risks, and treatment options.

Answer Key for MCQs

1. (b) Agonizing serotonin receptors
2. (c) PCP
3. (b) Alcohol
4. (c) Psilocybin
5. (b) Fel d 1
6. (c) Agonism of 5-HT2A receptors
7. (a) Ara h 1
8. (b) Thalidomide
9. (c) Aspergillus fumigatus
10. (c) Developmental and neurological issues
11. (c) Psilocybin
12. (d) Can f 1

13.(b) Thalidomide

14.(b) Tropomyosin

15.(b) Ketamine

16.(b) Antihistamine

17.(b) Nicotine

18.(c) Valproic Acid

19.(b) Aspergillus fumigatus

20.(b) PCP

CHAPTER – 11

CARBOHYDRATES

INTRODUCTION:

1. Overview: Carbohydrates are a diverse and abundant group of organic compounds that serve as a primary source of energy for most organisms. They are composed of carbon (C), hydrogen (H), and oxygen (O), usually in the ratio of 1:2:1, which gives them the general formula $(CH_2O)_n$. Carbohydrates are classified based on their chemical structure and the complexity of their molecules.

2. Classification: Carbohydrates are broadly classified into three major groups based on their size, structure, and complexity:

a. **Monosaccharides:** These are the simplest form of carbohydrates, consisting of a single sugar unit. They are the building blocks of more complex carbohydrates. Common examples include glucose, fructose, and galactose. Monosaccharides can be further classified based on the number of carbon atoms:

   i. **Trioses** (3 carbon atoms): Glyceraldehyde
   ii. **Tetroses** (4 carbon atoms): Erythrose
   iii. **Pentoses** (5 carbon atoms): Ribose, Xylose
   iv. **Hexoses** (6 carbon atoms): Glucose, Fructose
   v. **Heptoses** (7 carbon atoms): Sedoheptulose

b. **Disaccharides:** These are formed by the combination of two monosaccharide units through a glycosidic bond. The bond formation involves the elimination of a water molecule. Common examples include:

   i. **Sucrose** (glucose + fructose)
   ii. **Lactose** (glucose + galactose)
   iii. **Maltose** (glucose + glucose)

c. **Polysaccharides:** These are complex carbohydrates composed of long chains of monosaccharide units linked by glycosidic bonds. They can be linear or branched structures. Polysaccharides serve as energy storage or structural components. Examples include:

  i. **Starch:** A storage form of glucose in plants, composed of amylose (linear) and amylopectin (branched).

  ii. **Glycogen:** A storage form of glucose in animals, highly branched, found in the liver and muscles.

  iii. **Cellulose:** A structural component in the cell walls of plants, composed of β-glucose units.

3. Structure: Carbohydrates have different structures depending on their complexity:

a. **Monosaccharides** have a simple structure with a backbone of carbon atoms linked by single bonds. Each carbon atom, except for one, is bonded to a hydroxyl group (-OH), with the remaining carbon atom involved in a carbonyl group (C=O). The position of the carbonyl group determines if the monosaccharide is an aldose (if it's an aldehyde group) or a ketose (if it's a ketone group).

b. **Disaccharides** have a structure where two monosaccharides are linked by a glycosidic bond. The nature of this bond (α or β) determines the properties of the disaccharide.

c. **Polysaccharides** have complex structures with long chains of monosaccharide units. The branching pattern, bond type, and chain length affect the solubility, digestibility, and function of the polysaccharide.

4. Functions of Carbohydrates: Carbohydrates play several critical roles in biological systems:

a. **Energy Source:** Carbohydrates are a primary source of energy. During cellular respiration, glucose is broken down to release energy in the form of ATP (adenosine triphosphate).

b. **Energy Storage:** Polysaccharides like starch and glycogen store energy in plants and animals, respectively, for later use.

c. **Structural Components:** Cellulose in plants provides structural support, while chitin (a modified carbohydrate) is found in the exoskeleton of insects and the cell walls of fungi.

d. **Cell Signaling and Recognition:** Carbohydrates on the surface of cells are involved in cell recognition, signaling, and immune responses. Glycoproteins and glycolipids, which have carbohydrate groups attached, play key roles in these processes.

5. **Properties:** Carbohydrates exhibit a range of physical and chemical properties:

a. **Solubility:** Simple carbohydrates like monosaccharides and some disaccharides are generally soluble in water due to their polar hydroxyl groups. However, complex carbohydrates like cellulose are insoluble in water.

b. **Sweetness:** Monosaccharides and disaccharides tend to be sweet, with fructose being one of the sweetest naturally occurring sugars.

c. **Reducing Nature:** Some carbohydrates can act as reducing agents due to the presence of a free aldehyde or ketone group. These are known as reducing sugars (e.g., glucose, maltose).

d. **Hydrolysis:** Disaccharides and polysaccharides can be broken down into their monosaccharide components through hydrolysis, which is catalyzed by enzymes or acids.

6. **Tests for Identification:** Several biochemical tests are used to identify and quantify carbohydrates:

a. **Benedict's Test:** Used to detect reducing sugars. A positive result is indicated by a color change from blue to green, yellow, or red, depending on the amount of reducing sugar.

b. **Fehling's Test:** Similar to Benedict's test, it detects reducing sugars. A positive result is shown by the formation of a red precipitate.

c. **Barfoed's Test:** Differentiates between monosaccharides and disaccharides. Monosaccharides react faster, giving a positive result.

d. **Iodine Test:** Used to detect the presence of starch. A positive result is indicated by a blue-black color.

7. Importance in Diet: Carbohydrates are a crucial component of a balanced diet. They provide energy, aid in digestion, and support proper brain function. However, excessive consumption, especially of refined sugars, can lead to health issues like obesity, diabetes, and heart disease.

ACACIA

1. General Introduction: Acacia, commonly known as Gum Arabic, is a natural gum derived from the sap of the Acacia tree, particularly *Acacia senegal* and *Acacia seyal*. It is a complex mixture of glycoproteins and polysaccharides, primarily composed of arabinose and galactose sugars. Gum Arabic has been used for centuries in various industries, including pharmaceuticals, food, and cosmetics, due to its unique properties as an emulsifier, stabilizer, and thickening agent.

2. Detailed Study with Respect to Chemistry:

a. **Chemical Composition:** Gum Arabic is a highly branched polysaccharide consisting of arabinose, galactose, rhamnose, and glucuronic acid. The polysaccharide backbone is mainly composed of β-D-galactopyranose units, with side chains containing L-arabinofuranosyl, L-rhamnopyranosyl, and D-glucopyranosyluronic acid residues.

b. **Structure:** The structure of Gum Arabic is complex, with a combination of carbohydrate chains and protein components. The protein fraction, although small, plays a crucial role in its emulsifying properties. The carbohydrate part is primarily responsible for its viscosity and solubility in water.

c. **Solubility:** Gum Arabic is soluble in water, forming a viscous solution. It is insoluble in ethanol, acetone, and other organic solvents. The solubility and viscosity of Gum Arabic can vary depending on the source and processing methods.

3. Sources:

a. **Botanical Source:** Gum Arabic is harvested from the Acacia tree, particularly *Acacia senegal* and *Acacia seyal*. These trees are native to the Sahelian region of Africa, especially Sudan, where they are extensively cultivated for gum production.

b. **Geographical Distribution:** The major producers of Gum Arabic are Sudan, Chad, and Nigeria. The climate and soil conditions in these regions are favorable for the growth of Acacia trees.

4. Preparation:

a. **Harvesting:** The gum is harvested by making incisions in the bark of the Acacia tree. The sap exudes from the incision and hardens upon exposure to air, forming a brittle, amber-colored resin.

b. **Collection:** The hardened gum is collected manually after it has dried sufficiently on the tree. The collected gum is then sorted, cleaned, and graded based on its size, color, and purity.

c. **Processing:** The raw gum is further processed to remove impurities and standardize its quality. It may be ground into a fine powder or dissolved in water to create a liquid form, depending on its intended use.

5. Evaluation:

a. **Physical Tests:** The quality of Gum Arabic can be evaluated based on its color, odor, and taste. It should be odorless or have a faint characteristic odor, and it should have a bland taste.

b. **Solubility Test:** The solubility of Gum Arabic in water is a key quality parameter. A good quality Gum Arabic should dissolve completely in water to form a clear or slightly opalescent solution.

c. **Viscosity Measurement:** The viscosity of Gum Arabic solutions is measured to ensure consistency in its thickening properties. This is typically done using a viscometer.

d. **Purity Tests:** Gum Arabic is tested for the presence of impurities, such as sand, bark, or other foreign materials. It is also tested for microbial contamination to ensure it is safe for use in pharmaceutical and food products.

6. Preservation and Storage:

a. **Storage Conditions:** Gum Arabic should be stored in a cool, dry place, away from direct sunlight and moisture. Proper storage is essential to prevent microbial growth and maintain its quality.

b. **Shelf Life:** When stored properly, Gum Arabic has a long shelf life, typically several years. However, exposure to moisture can lead to degradation, reducing its effectiveness and quality.

c. **Preservatives:** In some cases, preservatives may be added to prevent microbial growth during storage. However, this is more common in food-grade Gum Arabic rather than pharmaceutical-grade products.

7. Therapeutic Uses:

a. **Pharmaceutical Aids:** Gum Arabic is widely used as an excipient in the pharmaceutical industry. Its primary functions include:

    i. **Emulsifier:** It stabilizes emulsions, ensuring uniform distribution of active ingredients in liquid formulations.

    ii. **Suspending Agent:** Gum Arabic is used to suspend insoluble particles in liquid formulations, preventing them from settling.

    iii. **Tablet Binder:** It acts as a binder in tablet formulations, ensuring that the tablets remain intact until ingestion.

    iv. **Film-Forming Agent:** It is used in coating tablets and capsules to protect them from moisture and enhance their shelf life.

b. **Medicinal Uses:** Although Gum Arabic itself is not an active therapeutic agent, it has been traditionally used in folk medicine for its soothing and protective properties. It is used in treating throat and stomach irritations due to its demulcent action.

8. Commercial Utility:

a. **Food Industry:** Gum Arabic is extensively used in the food industry as a stabilizer, emulsifier, and thickening agent. It is used in the production of soft drinks, candies, and bakery products.

b. **Cosmetics:** In the cosmetics industry, Gum Arabic is used as a stabilizer and thickening agent in lotions, creams, and other personal care products.

c. **Printing and Textile:** Gum Arabic is used in the printing industry as a sizing agent and in textiles for its adhesive properties.

d. **Adhesives:** Gum Arabic is used in the production of adhesives, particularly in the manufacture of postage stamps and envelopes.

AGAR

1. General Introduction: Agar, also known as agar-agar, is a gelatinous substance derived from the cell walls of certain species of red algae, particularly *Gelidium* and *Gracilaria*. It is primarily composed of polysaccharides and is widely used in the food industry, microbiological culture media, and as a pharmaceutical aid. Agar is known for its ability to gel, even at low concentrations, making it a valuable agent in various applications.

2. Detailed Study with Respect to Chemistry:

a. **Chemical Composition:** Agar is a mixture of two main polysaccharides: agarose and agaropectin.

   i. **Agarose** is a linear polymer made up of repeating units of D-galactose and 3,6-anhydro-L-galactopyranose. It is the primary gelling component of agar.

ii. **Agaropectin** is a branched polysaccharide that contains sulfate and pyruvate ester groups in addition to the galactose units. It contributes to the viscosity and elasticity of agar gels.

b. **Structure:** The structure of agar involves alternating residues of D-galactose and L-galactose, with some of the L-galactose units being modified into 3,6-anhydro-L-galactose. Agarose forms the backbone of the gel network, while agaropectin enhances its elasticity.

c. **Gel Formation:** Agar exhibits unique gelation properties. It dissolves in hot water and forms a gel upon cooling, typically solidifying between 32-40°C and remaining stable up to about 85°C. This property is due to the formation of a double-helix structure by agarose molecules, creating a network that traps water.

3. Sources:

a. **Botanical Source:** Agar is primarily obtained from red algae species, including *Gelidium*, *Gracilaria*, and *Pterocladia*. These algae are found in marine environments, especially in coastal regions.

b. **Geographical Distribution:** Major sources of agar-producing algae are found in Japan, Indonesia, Chile, and Morocco. These regions have favorable conditions for the growth of red algae.

4. Preparation:

a. **Harvesting:** The red algae are collected from the sea, washed to remove impurities like sand and salt, and then sun-dried.

b. **Extraction Process:**

i. The dried algae are boiled in water to extract the agar.

ii. The hot solution is then filtered to remove insoluble residues, and the filtrate is cooled to form a gel.

iii. The gel is frozen, thawed, and pressed to remove excess water, which improves the quality of the agar.

c. **Purification:** The agar may be further purified by repeating the freezing and thawing process or by using chemical treatments to remove impurities. The purified agar is then dried and ground into a powder for commercial use.

5. Evaluation:

a. **Physical Tests:** Agar is evaluated based on its gel strength, which is a critical parameter for its application. The gel strength is measured by applying a force to break the gel and is typically expressed in grams per square centimeter (g/cm^2).

b. **Purity Tests:** Agar is tested for impurities, such as residual salts and proteins, which can affect its gelation properties. It should be free from visible contaminants and have a neutral odor and taste.

c. **Chemical Tests:** The sulfate content and the presence of 3,6-anhydrogalactose are assessed to ensure the quality of agar. High sulfate content can reduce gel strength.

d. **Microbial Testing:** As agar is used in microbiological culture media, it is tested for sterility to ensure it does not support unwanted microbial growth.

6. Preservation and Storage:

a. **Storage Conditions:** Agar should be stored in a cool, dry place, away from moisture and direct sunlight. Proper storage prevents degradation and preserves its gelling properties.

b. **Shelf Life:** Agar has a long shelf life when stored properly. However, exposure to moisture can lead to microbial contamination and loss of gelling capacity.

c. **Packaging:** Agar is typically packaged in airtight containers to protect it from moisture and contamination. The packaging should also shield it from light to prevent photodegradation.

7. Therapeutic Uses:

a. **Laxative:** Agar is used as a bulk-forming laxative in the treatment of constipation. It absorbs water in the intestine, increasing stool bulk and promoting bowel movements.

b. **Appetite Suppressant:** Agar expands in the stomach after ingestion, which can create a feeling of fullness and reduce appetite, aiding in weight management.

c. **Demulcent:** Due to its soothing properties, agar is used in some formulations to relieve irritation in the digestive tract.

d. **Pharmaceutical Aids:**

    i. **Suspending Agent:** Agar is used to stabilize suspensions, preventing the sedimentation of insoluble particles.

    ii. **Emulsifier:** It helps stabilize emulsions in various pharmaceutical formulations.

    iii. **Gel Forming Agent:** Agar's gelation properties are utilized in the preparation of gels and jellies, which are used in both food and pharmaceutical products.

    iv. **Culture Media:** Agar is an essential component in microbiological culture media, where it provides a solid surface for the growth of microorganisms.

8. Commercial Utility:

a. **Food Industry:** Agar is widely used as a gelling agent in the food industry, particularly in the production of jellies, puddings, candies, and ice creams. It is valued for being a vegetarian substitute for gelatin.

b. **Microbiology:** Agar is indispensable in the preparation of culture media for microbiological studies. It provides a solid surface for the cultivation and isolation of bacteria, fungi, and other microorganisms.

c. **Cosmetics:** Agar is used in cosmetics as a thickener and stabilizer in lotions, creams, and hair care products.

d. **Biotechnology:** In molecular biology, agarose (a component of agar) is used in gel electrophoresis for the separation of DNA and RNA fragments.

e. **Textile and Paper Industries:** Agar is also used as a sizing agent in the textile industry and as a surface treatment in the paper industry.

TRAGACANTH

1. General Introduction: Tragacanth is a natural gum obtained from the dried sap of several species of *Astragalus*, primarily *Astragalus gummifer*. It is a complex polysaccharide that is used in pharmaceuticals, food products, and cosmetics due to its excellent thickening, emulsifying, and stabilizing properties. Tragacanth is particularly valued for its ability to form viscous gels in water, even at low concentrations.

2. Detailed Study with Respect to Chemistry:

a. **Chemical Composition:** Tragacanth gum consists of two major components: tragacanthin and bassorin.

   i. **Tragacanthin** is a water-soluble polysaccharide, primarily composed of D-galacturonic acid, D-galactose, L-fucose, and D-xylose units. It dissolves in water to form a viscous colloidal solution.

   ii. **Bassorin** is an insoluble but water-swellable polysaccharide, responsible for the gel-forming properties of tragacanth.

b. **Structure:** The polysaccharide structure of tragacanth involves complex chains of sugars that create a three-dimensional network in water, leading to its gel-forming ability. The exact structure of tragacanth is intricate and varies slightly depending on the species of *Astragalus* from which it is derived.

c. **Solubility:** Tragacanth gum is partially soluble in water. The soluble portion (tragacanthin) forms a colloidal solution, while the insoluble fraction (bassorin) swells and forms a gel.

3. Sources:

    a. **Botanical Source:** Tragacanth is harvested from various species of *Astragalus*, particularly *Astragalus gummifer*, *Astragalus adscendens*, and *Astragalus microcephalus*. These shrubs are native to the arid and semi-arid regions of the Middle East.

    b. **Geographical Distribution:** The major producing countries of tragacanth gum are Iran, Turkey, Syria, and Greece. The plants thrive in dry, mountainous regions where they are cultivated for their gum.

4. Preparation:

    a. **Harvesting:** Tragacanth gum is collected by making incisions in the stems and roots of the *Astragalus* plant. The gum exudes from the incisions and hardens upon exposure to air, forming white to yellowish flakes or ribbons.

    b. **Collection:** The hardened gum is manually collected after it has dried sufficiently on the plant. The gum is then sorted based on its color, size, and purity.

    c. **Processing:** The raw tragacanth is often ground into a fine powder for commercial use. It may also undergo further purification to remove impurities, ensuring a higher quality product.

5. Evaluation:

    a. **Physical Tests:** The quality of tragacanth is evaluated based on its appearance (color and shape), viscosity in water, and swelling index. A good quality tragacanth gum should form a highly viscous, uniform gel when mixed with water.

    b. **Purity Tests:** The gum is tested for impurities such as sand, plant debris, and other foreign materials. It is also tested for moisture content, as excessive moisture can affect its quality and shelf life.

c. **Chemical Tests:** The content of soluble and insoluble fractions (tragacanthin and bassorin) is measured. The pH of a 1% solution is also tested to ensure it falls within the acceptable range (typically around 5-6).

d. **Microbial Testing:** Tragacanth is evaluated for microbial contamination to ensure it is safe for use in pharmaceutical and food products.

6. Preservation and Storage:

a. **Storage Conditions:** Tragacanth should be stored in a cool, dry place, away from moisture and direct sunlight. Proper storage prevents microbial growth and preserves its gelling properties.

b. **Shelf Life:** When stored correctly, tragacanth has a long shelf life, typically several years. However, exposure to moisture can lead to degradation and loss of efficacy.

c. **Packaging:** Tragacanth is typically packaged in airtight containers or moisture-resistant bags to protect it from environmental factors that could compromise its quality.

7. Therapeutic Uses:

a. **Demulcent:** Tragacanth is used as a demulcent in cough syrups and lozenges. It forms a protective film over the mucous membranes, soothing irritation and reducing discomfort.

b. **Bulk Laxative:** Tragacanth is employed as a bulk-forming laxative. It absorbs water in the intestine, increasing stool bulk and promoting bowel movements.

c. **Emollient:** In topical applications, tragacanth is used in creams and ointments as an emollient, providing a soothing effect on the skin.

d. **Pharmaceutical Aids:**

    i. **Thickening Agent:** Tragacanth is widely used as a thickening agent in various pharmaceutical formulations, including suspensions, emulsions, and gels.

ii. **Emulsifier:** It stabilizes emulsions by preventing the separation of oil and water phases.

iii. **Suspending Agent:** Tragacanth is effective in suspending insoluble particles in liquid formulations, ensuring uniform distribution and preventing sedimentation.

iv. **Binder:** It is used as a binder in tablet formulations, helping to hold the ingredients together.

8. Commercial Utility:

a. **Food Industry:** Tragacanth is used as a thickening, stabilizing, and emulsifying agent in the food industry. It is commonly found in salad dressings, sauces, and ice creams.

b. **Cosmetics:** In the cosmetics industry, tragacanth is used in lotions, creams, and hair care products for its thickening and stabilizing properties.

c. **Textile Industry:** Tragacanth is used as a sizing agent in the textile industry to stiffen fabrics and prevent the fraying of threads.

d. **Paper Industry:** It is used in the paper industry as a sizing agent to improve the surface properties of paper, making it suitable for printing and writing.

HONEY

1. General Introduction:

Honey is a natural sweet substance produced by honeybees (*Apis* species) from the nectar of flowers or secretions of plants. It is a carbohydrate-rich food product with a history of use dating back thousands of years, valued not only for its sweetness but also for its therapeutic properties. Honey is widely used in food, medicine, and cosmetics due to its nutritional benefits and bioactive compounds.

2. Detailed Study with Respect to Chemistry:

a. **Chemical Composition:** Honey is primarily composed of carbohydrates, mainly fructose (~38%) and glucose (~31%). It also contains small amounts of water (around 17-20%), proteins, amino acids, enzymes, vitamins, minerals, and various phenolic compounds.

b. **Sugars:** The two main sugars, fructose and glucose, are simple monosaccharides that make honey a quick source of energy. Other minor sugars include maltose, sucrose, and various oligosaccharides.

c. **Enzymes:** Honey contains enzymes such as invertase, diastase (amylase), and glucose oxidase, which play a role in its formation and contribute to its antioxidant properties.

d. **Phenolic Compounds:** These are responsible for honey's antioxidant activity and include flavonoids, phenolic acids, and other polyphenols. These compounds contribute to the color, flavor, and therapeutic properties of honey.

e. **Acidity:** Honey is slightly acidic, with a pH range of 3.2 to 4.5, which helps inhibit the growth of many bacteria and microorganisms.

3. Sources:

a. **Botanical Source:** Honey is derived from the nectar of various flowering plants. The exact composition of honey varies depending on the floral source.

b. **Geographical Distribution:** Honey is produced worldwide, with significant production in countries like China, Turkey, the United States, and India. The specific characteristics of honey, such as flavor and color, are influenced by the regional flora where the bees forage.

4. Preparation:

a. **Harvesting:** Honey is collected by beekeepers from honeycombs in beehives. The honeycomb is either removed and the honey extracted by centrifugal force, or it is pressed to release the honey.

b. **Filtration:** After extraction, honey is filtered to remove impurities like wax, dead bees, and other debris.

c. **Processing:** Most commercial honey undergoes minimal processing to retain its natural properties. However, some honey is pasteurized to kill yeast cells and prevent fermentation. Pasteurization also helps to delay crystallization.

d. **Varieties:** Honey can be classified based on its floral source (e.g., clover honey, acacia honey), processing method (raw vs. pasteurized), and geographical origin (e.g., Manuka honey from New Zealand).

5. Evaluation:

a. **Physical Tests:** The quality of honey is evaluated by its color, aroma, flavor, viscosity, and crystallization tendency. The color can range from nearly colorless to dark brown, depending on the floral source.

b. **Chemical Tests:**

   i. **Moisture Content:** Honey's moisture content is typically between 17-20%. Lower moisture content is preferred as it indicates better shelf stability.

   ii. **Hydroxymethylfurfural (HMF) Content:** HMF is a degradation product that increases with heating and storage. High HMF levels indicate poor quality or adulteration.

   iii. **Diastase Activity:** This enzyme activity is an indicator of honey's freshness and quality. Higher diastase activity suggests minimal processing and better quality.

   iv. **Sugar Profile:** The ratio of fructose to glucose is important in determining honey's tendency to crystallize. Honey with higher fructose content tends to remain liquid longer.

6. Preservation and Storage:

a. **Storage Conditions:** Honey should be stored in a cool, dry place, away from direct sunlight and heat. Proper storage helps prevent fermentation and preserves its natural properties.

b. **Crystallization:** Honey can crystallize over time, especially at lower temperatures. This is a natural process and does not indicate spoilage. To liquefy crystallized honey, it can be gently warmed.

c. **Shelf Life:** Honey has an exceptionally long shelf life due to its low water activity and natural acidity, which inhibit microbial growth. Properly stored honey can last indefinitely without spoiling.

d. **Packaging:** Honey is typically packaged in airtight containers made of glass, plastic, or metal to prevent moisture absorption and contamination.

7. Therapeutic Uses:

a. **Wound Healing:** Honey has been used topically to treat wounds, burns, and ulcers due to its antibacterial properties, osmotic effect, and ability to maintain a moist wound environment.

b. **Antibacterial:** The low pH, high sugar content, and production of hydrogen peroxide (via glucose oxidase) give honey natural antibacterial properties, making it effective against a range of pathogens.

c. **Cough Suppressant:** Honey is commonly used in traditional medicine as a remedy for sore throats and coughs. It is often mixed with lemon or herbal teas for symptomatic relief.

d. **Digestive Health:** Honey is used to alleviate digestive issues, such as gastritis and indigestion. It may also promote the growth of beneficial gut bacteria.

e. **Antioxidant:** The phenolic compounds in honey contribute to its antioxidant activity, which can help protect cells from oxidative damage.

f. **Anti-inflammatory:** Honey's anti-inflammatory properties make it useful in reducing swelling and irritation in various conditions, including skin inflammations and sore throats.

8. Commercial Utility:

a. **Food Industry:** Honey is widely used as a natural sweetener in various food products, including baked goods, beverages, cereals, and confectioneries. It is also used in salad dressings, sauces, and marinades.

b. **Pharmaceuticals:** In the pharmaceutical industry, honey is used in cough syrups, lozenges, and topical ointments due to its soothing and antimicrobial properties.

c. **Cosmetics:** Honey is a popular ingredient in cosmetics and personal care products, such as moisturizers, shampoos, and face masks, due to its hydrating and antibacterial effects.

d. **Traditional Medicine:** Honey is used in various traditional medicine systems, including Ayurveda and Traditional Chinese Medicine, for its health benefits and therapeutic properties.

Multiple Choice Questions (Objective)

1. Which of the following is the simplest form of carbohydrates?

    A) Disaccharides

    B) Monosaccharides

    C) Polysaccharides

    D) Oligosaccharides

2. Which of the following monosaccharides is commonly known as fruit sugar?

    A) Glucose

    B) Fructose

    C) Galactose

    D) Ribose

3. Sucrose is composed of which two monosaccharides?

    A) Glucose and Galactose

    B) Glucose and Fructose

C) Fructose and Galactose

D) Glucose and Ribose

4. What is the main storage form of glucose in animals?

    A) Starch

    B) Cellulose

    C) Glycogen

    D) Fructose

5. Which disaccharide is known as milk sugar?

    A) Maltose

    B) Sucrose

    C) Lactose

    D) Raffinose

6. Which carbohydrate is a major component of dietary fiber in plant cell walls?

    A) Glycogen

    B) Starch

    C) Cellulose

    D) Amylose

7. What enzyme is required to digest lactose into glucose and galactose?

    A) Sucrase

    B) Amylase

    C) Lactase

    D) Maltase

8. Which polysaccharide is composed of $\alpha(1\rightarrow4)$ and $\alpha(1\rightarrow6)$ glycosidic bonds and is highly branched?

    A) Starch

    B) Cellulose

    C) Glycogen

    D) Chitin

9. Fructo-oligosaccharides (FOS) primarily function as what type of dietary component?

    A) Sweetener

    B) Energy Source

    C) Prebiotic

    D) Protein

10. Which of the following is not digested by human enzymes and passes into the colon where it is fermented by gut bacteria?

    A) Glucose

    B) Sucrose

    C) Raffinose

    D) Maltose

11. Which carbohydrate serves as the primary structural component of the exoskeletons of arthropods?

    A) Cellulose

    B) Chitin

    C) Glycogen

    D) Starch

12. What is the main sugar component in honey?

    A) Glucose and Galactose

    B) Glucose and Sucrose

    C) Glucose and Fructose

    D) Glucose and Maltose

13. Which of the following tests is used to detect the presence of starch?

    A) Benedict's Test

    B) Iodine Test

    C) Barfoed's Test

    D) Fehling's Test

14. Which polysaccharide is known for its gel-forming ability and is widely used in microbiological culture media?

    A) Glycogen

    B) Starch

    C) Agar

    D) Cellulose

15. What is the main component of Agar that contributes to its gelation properties?

    A) Amylose

    B) Agarose

    C) Galactose

    D) Bassorin

16. Which carbohydrate is a trisaccharide found in beans and is known to cause gastrointestinal discomfort due to its fermentation in the colon?

    A) Sucrose

    B) Lactose

    C) Raffinose

    D) Stachyose

17. Which enzyme breaks down starch into maltose?

    A) Amylase

    B) Sucrase

    C) Lactase

    D) Invertase

18. Chitin is composed of which monomeric unit?

    A) Glucose

    B) Fructose

    C) N-acetylglucosamine

    D) Galactose

19. Which disaccharide is composed of two glucose units linked by an $\alpha(1\rightarrow4)$ glycosidic bond?

    A) Sucrose

    B) Lactose

    C) Maltose

    D) Raffinose

20. Which carbohydrate is used in wound healing due to its osmotic effect and antibacterial properties?

    A) Lactose

    B) Sucrose

    C) Honey

    D) Maltose

Short Answer Type Questions (Subjective)

1. Define monosaccharides and provide examples.

2. Explain the structure and function of glycogen.

3. What is lactose intolerance and what enzyme is involved?

4. Describe the structure of cellulose and its role in the diet.

5. How are disaccharides formed, and what are some examples?

6. What are fructo-oligosaccharides (FOS) and their function in the human gut?

7. Explain the process of starch digestion in the human body.

8. What are the primary components of honey and their nutritional significance?

9. Discuss the role of chitin in the animal kingdom.

10. Describe the properties and uses of Agar in microbiology.

11. What is the difference between amylose and amylopectin?

12. Explain the significance of cellulose in human health.

13. What are prebiotics and how do they benefit the digestive system?

14. Describe the structure of sucrose and its digestion in the human body.

15. What is the role of glucose in cellular respiration?

16. Explain the therapeutic uses of honey in wound healing.

17. What is raffinose and where is it commonly found?

18. Describe the biochemical tests used to identify carbohydrates.

19. What are polysaccharides and their importance in plants?

20. Discuss the metabolic fate of galactose in the human body.

Long Answer Type Questions (Subjective)

1. Discuss in detail the classification of carbohydrates and their biological significance.

2. Explain the structure, digestion, and metabolism of starch, including the roles of amylose and amylopectin.

3. Describe the chemical composition, therapeutic uses, and commercial applications of Agar.

4. Discuss the structure and function of chitin, including its role in the animal kingdom and potential health benefits.

5. Explain the role of carbohydrates in human health, focusing on their functions, dietary sources, and impact on metabolic diseases.

6. Describe the process of carbohydrate digestion, starting from ingestion to absorption in the small intestine.

7. Discuss the prebiotic effects of fructo-oligosaccharides (FOS) and their impact on gut health.

8. Explain the role of cellulose in the diet, its digestion, and its benefits to human health.

9. Analyze the role of honey in traditional and modern medicine, focusing on its chemical composition and therapeutic properties.

10. Discuss the pharmacological effects and potential health benefits of raffinose and stachyose in the diet.

Answer Key for MCQs

1. **B**) Monosaccharides

2. B) Fructose

3. B) Glucose and Fructose

4. C) Glycogen

5. C) Lactose

6. C) Cellulose

7. C) Lactase

8. C) Glycogen

9. C) Prebiotic

10. C) Raffinose

11. B) Chitin

12. C) Glucose and Fructose

13. B) Iodine Test

14. C) Agar

15. B) Agarose

16. C) Raffinose

17. A) Amylase

18. C) N-acetylglucosamine

19. C) Maltose

20. C) Honey

CHAPTER – 12

PROTEINS AND ENZYMES

Proteins

roteins are large, complex molecules composed of amino acids linked together by peptide bonds. They are essential macromolecules for all living organisms, playing a vital role in structural support, catalysis of metabolic reactions (enzymes), signal transduction, immune responses, and cellular communication.

Classification of Proteins

Proteins can be classified based on several criteria:

1. Based on Structure

- **Simple Proteins**: Proteins that are composed only of amino acids and do not contain any prosthetic groups.
  - Example: **Albumin** (found in egg white, blood serum), **Globulin** (found in serum, seeds).
- **Conjugated Proteins**: Proteins that consist of a protein portion and a non-protein component (prosthetic group), such as carbohydrates, lipids, metals, etc.
  - Example: **Glycoproteins** (proteins with a carbohydrate group like in mucin), **Lipoproteins** (proteins combined with lipids, like in cell membranes).
- **Derived Proteins**: These are proteins derived from simple or conjugated proteins through physical or chemical changes.
  - Example: **Peptones** (obtained by the partial hydrolysis of proteins), **Proteoses**.

2. Based on Composition

- **Fibrous Proteins**: These proteins have elongated structures and are insoluble in water, playing structural roles.

- o Example: **Collagen** (found in connective tissues), **Keratin** (found in hair, nails).
- **Globular Proteins**: These proteins have a spherical or globular structure and are soluble in water, typically functioning as enzymes, hormones, or transport molecules.
  - o Example: **Hemoglobin** (oxygen transport in blood), **Enzymes** like **Amylase**.

3. Based on Function

- **Structural Proteins**: Provide support and structure to cells and tissues.
  - o Example: **Collagen** (in skin, tendons), **Elastin** (in connective tissue).
- **Enzymatic Proteins**: Catalyze biochemical reactions.
  - o Example: **Pepsin** (digestive enzyme), **DNA polymerase**.
- **Transport Proteins**: Transport substances within the organism.
  - o Example: **Hemoglobin** (transports oxygen in blood), **Albumin** (transports fatty acids).
- **Defensive Proteins**: Involved in immune responses.
  - o Example: **Antibodies** (immunoglobulins), **Fibrinogen** (blood clotting).
- **Storage Proteins**: Store nutrients or molecules.
  - o Example: **Ferritin** (stores iron in the liver), **Casein** (in milk).

4. Based on Nutritional Value

- **Complete Proteins**: Contain all essential amino acids required by the body.
  - o Example: **Animal Proteins** (meat, eggs, milk).
- **Incomplete Proteins**: Lack one or more essential amino acids.
  - o Example: **Plant Proteins** (rice, wheat).

Chemical Tests for Proteins

1. **Biuret Test:**

- o **Principle**: Peptide bonds in proteins react with copper(II) sulfate in an alkaline solution, forming a violet-colored complex.
  - o **Procedure**: Add a few drops of dilute copper sulfate to the protein solution in an alkaline medium (sodium hydroxide).
  - o **Positive Result**: Violet or purple color.
  - o **Application**: Widely used to detect the presence of proteins in biological samples.

2. **Ninhydrin Test**:
   - o **Principle**: Ninhydrin reacts with free amino acids or proteins, producing a deep blue or purple color (Ruhemann's purple).
   - o **Procedure**: Heat the sample with a few drops of ninhydrin reagent.
   - o **Positive Result**: Blue or purple color.
   - o **Application**: Used for detecting free amino acids and proteins.

3. **Xanthoproteic Test**:
   - o **Principle**: Aromatic amino acids like tyrosine and tryptophan react with concentrated nitric acid, forming yellow nitro derivatives.
   - o **Procedure**: Add concentrated nitric acid to the protein solution, followed by heating.
   - o **Positive Result**: Yellow color.
   - o **Application**: Identifies the presence of aromatic amino acids in proteins.

4. **Millon's Test**:
   - o **Principle**: Phenolic groups of tyrosine react with Millon's reagent (mercury nitrate in nitric acid), producing a red color.
   - o **Procedure**: Add Millon's reagent to the protein solution and heat it.
   - o **Positive Result**: Red precipitate or color.
   - o **Application**: Specifically detects tyrosine-containing proteins.

5. **Sulfhydryl Test**:

- o **Principle**: Proteins with sulfhydryl (-SH) groups react with lead acetate to form a black precipitate of lead sulfide.
- o **Procedure**: Add lead acetate to the protein solution.
- o **Positive Result**: Black precipitate.
- o **Application**: Detects cysteine in proteins.

Applications of Proteins

1. **Nutritional Role**:

Proteins are essential nutrients required for growth, repair, and maintenance of tissues in the body. They are a source of essential amino acids that the body cannot synthesize.

2. **Enzymatic Activity**:

Many enzymes are proteins that catalyze biochemical reactions in the body, such as digestion (e.g., pepsin, trypsin), DNA replication, and metabolic pathways.

3. **Structural Function**:

Proteins like collagen, keratin, and elastin provide structural support to cells, tissues, and organs. They maintain the integrity of skin, bones, and connective tissues.

4. **Transport and Storage**:

Proteins such as hemoglobin and albumin transport vital substances like oxygen, fatty acids, and hormones throughout the body. Storage proteins, like ferritin, store essential minerals such as iron.

5. **Defense Mechanism**:

Proteins play a crucial role in the immune system. Antibodies (immunoglobulins) are proteins that recognize and neutralize foreign invaders like bacteria and viruses.

6. **Hormonal Function**:

Many hormones are protein-based, including insulin and growth hormone, which regulate physiological processes such as metabolism and growth.

7. **Industrial and Biotechnological Applications**:

   Proteins such as enzymes are used in various industrial processes, including food production (amylase in baking, proteases in cheese making), biotechnology (recombinant DNA technology), and pharmaceutical production (therapeutic enzymes and antibodies).

ENZYMES:

Enzymes are biological catalysts that speed up the rate of biochemical reactions in living organisms without being consumed in the process. They are highly specific to the substrates they act upon and operate under mild conditions of temperature and pH.

Classification of Enzymes

Enzymes are classified based on the type of reaction they catalyze. The International Union of Biochemistry and Molecular Biology (IUBMB) has established a system of enzyme classification into six major classes, each with subclasses.

1. Oxidoreductases

- **Function**: Catalyze oxidation-reduction (redox) reactions, where electrons are transferred from one molecule (the reductant) to another (the oxidant).
- **Example**:
  - **Alcohol dehydrogenase**: Converts alcohol to aldehydes.
  - **Cytochrome oxidase**: Involved in cellular respiration.
- **Reaction Type**: Oxidation-reduction.

2. Transferases

- **Function**: Transfer functional groups (like methyl, amino, phosphate groups) from one molecule to another.

- **Example**:
  - **Aminotransferase (Transaminase)**: Transfers amino groups from amino acids to keto acids.
  - **Hexokinase**: Transfers a phosphate group from ATP to glucose in glycolysis.
- **Reaction Type**: Group transfer.

3. Hydrolases

- **Function**: Catalyze the hydrolysis of chemical bonds, often splitting large molecules into smaller ones by adding water.
- **Example**:
  - **Lipase**: Breaks down lipids into fatty acids and glycerol.
  - **Amylase**: Hydrolyzes starch into sugars.
- **Reaction Type**: Hydrolysis.

4. Lyases

- **Function**: Catalyze the addition or removal of groups to form double bonds or to break double bonds by means other than hydrolysis or oxidation.
- **Example**:
  - **Decarboxylase**: Removes a carboxyl group from organic acids.
  - **Aldolase**: Involved in glycolysis, cleaves fructose 1,6-bisphosphate into two three-carbon molecules.
- **Reaction Type**: Addition or removal of groups to form double bonds.

5. Isomerases

- **Function**: Catalyze the rearrangement of atoms within a molecule to form isomers.
- **Example**:
  - **Phosphoglucoisomerase**: Converts glucose-6-phosphate to fructose-6-phosphate in glycolysis.

- o **Racemase**: Converts stereoisomers from one form to another (e.g., L-amino acids to D-amino acids).
- **Reaction Type**: Isomerization.

6. Ligases (Synthetases)

- **Function**: Catalyze the joining of two molecules with the hydrolysis of ATP or another high-energy molecule.
- **Example**:
  - o **DNA ligase**: Joins two strands of DNA together by forming a phosphodiester bond.
  - o **Glutamine synthetase**: Catalyzes the formation of glutamine from glutamate and ammonia.
- **Reaction Type**: Bond formation coupled with ATP hydrolysis.

Chemical Tests for Enzymes

1. **Biuret Test**:
   - o **Principle**: Detects peptide bonds in enzymes, which are proteins. Copper sulfate in an alkaline medium reacts with peptide bonds, resulting in a violet color.
   - o **Procedure**: Add copper sulfate and sodium hydroxide to the enzyme solution.
   - o **Positive Result**: Violet color indicates the presence of protein-based enzymes.

2. **Enzyme Assay**:
   - o **Principle**: Measures enzyme activity by detecting the conversion of substrate to product. The rate of product formation is proportional to enzyme concentration.
   - o **Example**:
     - **Amylase Assay**: Measures the breakdown of starch to maltose. Iodine is used to detect the presence of starch. In

the presence of amylase, the blue-black color of starch disappears.

- o **Application**: Used to quantify enzyme activity.

3. **Sodium Dodecyl Sulfate Polyacrylamide Gel Electrophoresis (SDS-PAGE)**:
   - o **Principle**: Separates enzymes based on their molecular weight. Enzymes are denatured and coated with a negative charge by SDS, and the proteins are then separated through a polyacrylamide gel in an electric field.
   - o **Procedure**: Load enzyme samples onto a polyacrylamide gel and apply an electric current.
   - o **Positive Result**: Proteins appear as bands of different molecular weights.

4. **Zymography**:
   - o **Principle**: A specialized form of gel electrophoresis used to detect enzyme activity. A substrate for the enzyme is embedded in the gel, and areas where the enzyme is active will produce clear bands.
   - o **Example**: Gelatin zymography is used to detect gelatinase enzymes.
   - o **Positive Result**: Clear bands in the gel indicate active enzyme regions.

Applications of Enzymes

1. **Medical Applications**:
   - o **Enzyme Replacement Therapy**: Enzymes are used to treat conditions where specific enzymes are deficient or malfunctioning (e.g., pancreatic enzymes for cystic fibrosis, glucocerebrosidase for Gaucher's disease).
   - o **Diagnostic Enzymes**: Enzymes are used as biomarkers to diagnose diseases (e.g., elevated levels of **aspartate aminotransferase**

(AST) and **alanine aminotransferase** (ALT) indicate liver damage).

2. **Industrial Applications:**
   - **Food Industry**: Enzymes like **amylase, lipase,** and **protease** are used in the production of bread, dairy products, and beverages. They help improve texture, flavor, and shelf life.
   - **Textile Industry**: Enzymes like **cellulase** are used for fabric softening and bio-polishing. Enzymes replace harsh chemicals in textile processing, reducing environmental impact.
   - **Detergent Industry**: Enzymes like **protease** and **lipase** are added to detergents to help break down protein stains (e.g., blood) and fat-based stains (e.g., oils), increasing cleaning efficiency.

3. **Biotechnology:**
   - **Genetic Engineering**: Enzymes like **restriction enzymes** and **DNA ligase** are essential tools for gene cloning, gene editing (e.g., CRISPR), and recombinant DNA technology.
   - **PCR (Polymerase Chain Reaction): Taq DNA polymerase** is a thermostable enzyme used to amplify DNA in molecular biology techniques.

4. **Environmental Applications:**
   - **Bioremediation**: Enzymes like **laccase** and **peroxidase** are used to degrade pollutants and toxins in the environment, helping to clean up oil spills, pesticides, and industrial waste.
   - **Wastewater Treatment**: Enzymes help break down organic material in sewage and industrial effluents, making water safer for release into the environment.

5. **Pharmaceutical Industry:**

- o Enzymes are used to manufacture drugs and as active ingredients in therapeutic products (e.g., **streptokinase** for dissolving blood clots, **lactase** for lactose intolerance).

6. **Agriculture**:

   - o **Pesticide and Herbicide Development**: Enzymes are used in developing biopesticides that target specific pests without harming other organisms or the environment.
   - o **Animal Feed**: Enzymes like **phytase** are added to animal feed to enhance nutrient absorption and reduce environmental pollution caused by undigested phosphates.

Gelatin: General Introduction

Gelatin is a natural, water-soluble protein derived from collagen, a key component of animal connective tissue, bones, and skin. It is used extensively in the pharmaceutical, food, and cosmetic industries. Gelatin forms gels when dissolved in hot water and is widely employed as a pharmaceutical aid, excipient, and in therapeutic applications.

Chemistry of Gelatin

- **Molecular Composition**: Gelatin is composed of amino acids (predominantly glycine, proline, and hydroxyproline) arranged in polypeptide chains. It has a molecular weight ranging from 15,000 to 250,000 Da.
- **Chemical Nature**: Gelatin is obtained by the partial hydrolysis of collagen, which involves breaking down the triple-helical structure of collagen into single chains.
- **Isoelectric Point**: Gelatin has an isoelectric point (pH where the net charge is zero) ranging from 4.8 to 9.4, depending on its type (Type A or B) and the method of production.

Sources of Gelatin

- **Animal Sources**: Gelatin is derived from the collagen found in animal bones, skin, and connective tissues. Common sources include bovine (cows), porcine (pigs), and fish.
- **Types of Gelatin**:
  - **Type A Gelatin**: Produced by acid treatment, commonly from pork skin.
  - **Type B Gelatin**: Produced by alkaline treatment, commonly from bovine hides and bones.

Preparation of Gelatin

1. **Pre-Treatment**:
   - **Acid or Alkaline Treatment**: Raw materials like bones or hides undergo either an acid or alkaline treatment to break down the collagen structure. Acid treatment produces Type A gelatin, and alkaline treatment produces Type B gelatin.

2. **Hydrolysis**:
   - The treated collagen is subjected to hydrolysis (partial breakdown), which transforms the collagen into soluble gelatin. The process involves controlled heating.

3. **Extraction**:
   - The gelatin is extracted through repeated hot water extraction. The extracted solution is filtered and purified.

4. **Concentration and Drying**:
   - The gelatin solution is concentrated and then dried, often in a vacuum dryer, to produce gelatin in powder, granules, or sheet form.

5. **Grinding and Sizing**:
   - Finally, the dried gelatin is ground into different particle sizes depending on the intended use.

Evaluation of Gelatin

1. **Physical Properties**:
   - **Bloom Strength**: Measures the firmness of the gelatin gel. A higher Bloom number indicates stronger gel strength.
   - **Viscosity**: The viscosity of a gelatin solution is crucial for applications where specific consistency is required.
   - **Clarity**: Gelatin solutions should be clear without impurities.
2. **Chemical Properties**:
   - **pH**: Gelatin solutions typically have a pH of 4.5 to 6.0, depending on the type.
   - **Moisture Content**: Gelatin must have controlled moisture content to maintain stability.
   - **Heavy Metal Content**: Low levels of heavy metals are essential for pharmaceutical-grade gelatin.
3. **Microbiological Testing**:
   - Gelatin is tested for microbial contamination, including bacteria, molds, and endotoxins, as it is used in products that must be sterile, such as injectables.

Preservation and Storage of Gelatin

- **Preservation**:

   Gelatin is stable when dry but can degrade in the presence of moisture. It should be protected from humidity, light, and microbial contamination.

- **Storage**:

   Gelatin should be stored in tightly sealed containers, away from direct sunlight, in a cool, dry environment. The ideal storage temperature is below 25°C, and relative humidity should be kept below 50% to prevent clumping or microbial growth.

Therapeutic Uses of Gelatin

1. **Plasma Expanders**:

Gelatin is used as a plasma substitute in the form of **gelatin-based plasma expanders**. It helps maintain blood volume in patients suffering from blood loss or shock.

2. **Wound Healing**:

Gelatin can be used as a wound dressing due to its biocompatibility and hemostatic properties, promoting clot formation and tissue regeneration.

3. **Capsule Production**:

Gelatin is widely used in the manufacture of hard and soft capsules for pharmaceutical and dietary supplement formulations.

4. **Suppositories**:

Gelatin is used as a base for suppositories, particularly in combination with glycerin.

5. **Hemostatic Agents**:

Gelatin is used in surgical procedures as a hemostatic agent (e.g., Gelfoam) to control bleeding by facilitating clotting.

Commercial Utility of Gelatin

1. **Pharmaceutical Applications**:
   - **Encapsulation**: Gelatin is the primary material for producing hard and soft gelatin capsules, which encase medicines and supplements.
   - **Stabilizer**: Gelatin acts as a stabilizer in vaccines and injectables, protecting the active ingredients from degradation.
   - **Tablet Binding**: It is used as a binder in tablet formulations to hold the ingredients together.

2. **Food Industry**:
   - Gelatin is used in the production of jelly, marshmallows, gummy candies, and desserts. It acts as a gelling agent, stabilizer, and thickener.

3. **Cosmetics Industry**:

o Gelatin is used in skincare products, hair care, and face masks due to its ability to provide moisture and support skin elasticity.

4. **Photography**:

    o In photographic films, gelatin is used as a carrier for light-sensitive silver halide crystals.

5. **Nutritional Supplements**:

    o Gelatin is used in the production of collagen supplements, which promote joint health, skin elasticity, and overall wellness.

Casein: General Introduction

Casein is a group of phosphoproteins that are the primary proteins found in milk and cheese. It makes up about 80% of the proteins in cow's milk and about 20-45% of the proteins in human milk. Casein plays a critical role in nutrition, particularly as a slow-digesting protein, and is widely used in the pharmaceutical, food, and cosmetic industries.

Chemistry of Casein

- **Molecular Composition**:

  Casein is composed of amino acids and is rich in proline and glutamic acid. It has a high number of hydrophobic residues, making it relatively insoluble in water. It exists in milk as a suspension of particles called micelles, which are stabilized by calcium and phosphorus.

- **Isoelectric Point**:

  The isoelectric point of casein is around pH 4.6. At this pH, casein precipitates out of solution, which is the principle behind cheese-making.

- **Types of Casein**:

    o **α-casein**: The most abundant, comprising about 40-50% of total casein.

    o **β-casein**: Comprises about 25-35% of total casein.

    o **κ-casein**: Stabilizes micelle formation in milk, important in cheese-making.

Sources of Casein

- **Milk:**

Casein is predominantly obtained from milk, with the largest quantities coming from cow's milk. Other sources include buffalo, goat, and sheep milk. Human milk also contains casein, though in lower proportions.

Preparation of Casein

1. **Acid Precipitation:**
   - **Acidification**: The pH of milk is lowered to 4.6 using lactic acid or hydrochloric acid, causing casein to precipitate out of solution as a curd.
   - **Separation**: The curd is separated from the whey (liquid portion) through filtration or centrifugation.
   - **Washing**: The curd is washed to remove residual lactose and other impurities.
   - **Drying**: The casein curd is dried into a powder or granules, which can be further processed for different applications.

2. **Enzymatic Precipitation:**
   - **Rennet (Chymosin)**: An enzyme obtained from calf stomachs, is added to milk to coagulate casein. This method is primarily used in cheese-making.

3. **Industrial Extraction:**
   - Industrial preparation often involves using both enzymatic and chemical methods for large-scale extraction. After precipitation, the curds are washed, neutralized, and dried for commercial use.

Evaluation of Casein

1. **Physical Properties:**
   - **Solubility**: Casein is insoluble in water but soluble in dilute alkalis or strong acids.

- o **Micelle Structure**: Evaluation of micelle formation is important, as it affects the functionality of casein in different applications, such as food and pharmaceuticals.

2. **Chemical Properties**:
   - o **pH**: Casein has an isoelectric point of around 4.6, and its behavior in different pH conditions is evaluated for various applications.
   - o **Protein Content**: High protein content is essential for its nutritional and pharmaceutical applications.

3. **Purity Tests**:
   - o **Lipid Content**: Casein is tested for the presence of fats and other impurities.
   - o **Moisture Content**: Casein is evaluated for moisture levels to prevent degradation during storage.

4. **Microbiological Testing**:
   - o Casein is tested for microbial contamination, especially when used in pharmaceuticals and food products.

Preservation and Storage of Casein

- **Preservation**:

Casein is generally stable when dry, but moisture can lead to spoilage or microbial contamination. It should be preserved in a moisture-free environment.

- **Storage**:

Casein should be stored in tightly sealed containers in a cool, dry place. Exposure to light and moisture can degrade its quality. Optimal storage temperature is below 25°C, and the relative humidity should be less than 50%.

Therapeutic Uses of Casein

1. **Nutritional Supplements**:

o **Slow-Release Protein**: Casein is used in protein supplements and meal replacements because it provides a slow and sustained release of amino acids into the bloodstream, making it ideal for muscle recovery and growth.

2. **Wound Healing**:

Casein-derived peptides have been shown to promote wound healing and tissue regeneration. It is sometimes used in wound dressings or in topical formulations.

3. **Drug Delivery Systems**:

Casein has been explored as a drug carrier due to its biocompatibility and ability to form nanoparticles, which can improve the solubility and stability of drugs. It is also being researched for targeted drug delivery systems.

4. **Dental**   **Applications**:

Casein phosphopeptides have been incorporated into dental care products to help remineralize enamel and reduce tooth decay.

Commercial Utility of Casein

1. **Pharmaceutical Applications**:

   o **Encapsulation and Coating**: Casein is used as a coating material for tablets and capsules. Its biocompatibility and slow-digesting nature make it an ideal excipient for controlled-release formulations.

   o **Emulsifying Agent**: Casein acts as an emulsifier in various pharmaceutical formulations.

2. **Food Industry**:

   o **Cheese Making**: Casein is the main protein in cheese production. The coagulation of casein forms curds that are processed into cheese.

- o **Protein Supplements**: Casein is widely used in sports nutrition and protein bars due to its high protein content and slow digestion rate.
- o **Food Stabilizer**: It is used as a thickener, emulsifier, and stabilizer in processed foods, such as yogurt, sauces, and ice creams.

3. **Cosmetic Industry**:
   - o **Skin and Hair Care**: Casein is used in creams, lotions, and hair care products due to its moisturizing and nourishing properties.

4. **Industrial Uses**:
   - o **Adhesives**: Casein-based adhesives are used in woodworking, paper products, and textiles due to their strong binding properties.
   - o **Paints and Coatings**: Casein is used as a binder in casein paints, which are water-based and used for eco-friendly interior painting.

Proteolytic Enzymes: General Introduction

Proteolytic enzymes, also known as proteases, are enzymes that break down proteins by hydrolyzing the peptide bonds between amino acids. These enzymes play a critical role in numerous biological processes, including digestion, immune function, and tissue repair. Proteolytic enzymes are widely used in pharmaceuticals, medicine, food processing, and industrial applications.

Chemistry of Proteolytic Enzymes

- **Molecular Composition**:

  Proteolytic enzymes are proteins composed of long chains of amino acids. Their active sites contain amino acids critical for catalyzing the hydrolysis of peptide bonds.

- **Enzyme Specificity**:

  Different proteolytic enzymes exhibit varying specificities for cleaving peptide bonds based on the amino acid sequences in the substrate. Some are endopeptidases (cleaving peptide bonds within a protein), while others are exopeptidases (cleaving peptide bonds at the ends of a protein chain).

Types of Proteolytic Enzymes

1. Papain

- **Source:**

  Derived from the latex of the papaya plant (*Carica papaya*).

- **Chemistry:**

  Papain is a cysteine protease, meaning it contains a cysteine residue at its active site, which plays a key role in its catalytic activity.

- **Preparation:**

  Papain is extracted from the papaya latex by slicing the fruit and collecting the latex, which is then purified and dried to form a powder.

- **Therapeutic Uses:**

  - Wound debridement.

  - Anti-inflammatory agent in treating edema.

  - Digestive aid for breaking down proteins.

- **Commercial Utility:**

  - Used in meat tenderizers, brewing, and pharmaceuticals.

  - Ingredient in topical ointments and enzyme supplements.

2. Bromelain

- **Source:**

  Extracted from the stems and juice of pineapples (*Ananas comosus*).

- **Chemistry:**

  Bromelain is a mixture of proteases, including cysteine proteases, similar to papain.

- **Preparation:**

  The stem of the pineapple plant is crushed, and the juice is extracted and processed to purify bromelain. It is then freeze-dried into powder form.

- **Therapeutic Uses:**

- Anti-inflammatory, especially for musculoskeletal injuries.
  - Promotes digestion by breaking down dietary proteins.
  - Used in sinusitis treatment.
- **Commercial Utility**:
  - Used as a meat tenderizer, in dietary supplements, and in the food industry.
  - Used in enzyme-based wound healing preparations.

3. Serratiopeptidase

- **Source**:

Derived from the bacterium *Serratia marcescens*.

- **Chemistry**:

Serratiopeptidase is a proteolytic enzyme that breaks down protein-based waste and inflammatory substances in the body.

- **Preparation**:

Produced by culturing *Serratia marcescens* bacteria and then isolating and purifying the enzyme through filtration and precipitation methods.

- **Therapeutic Uses**:
  - Anti-inflammatory properties used in treating swelling and pain.
  - Reduces inflammation and improves mucous clearance in respiratory disorders.
- **Commercial Utility**:
  - Used in oral preparations for treating inflammation, post-surgical swelling, and pain.
  - Included in supplements for joint health.

4. Urokinase

- **Source**:

Derived from human urine or cultured kidney cells.

- **Chemistry**:

Urokinase is a serine protease that activates plasminogen to plasmin, which helps dissolve blood clots.

- **Preparation**:

Isolated from human urine or from kidney cells in culture. Purified through filtration and chromatography processes.

- **Therapeutic Uses**:
  - Used as a thrombolytic agent in the treatment of deep vein thrombosis, pulmonary embolism, and myocardial infarction.
- **Commercial Utility**:
  - Administered as an injectable drug for breaking down blood clots in emergency situations.

5. Streptokinase

- **Source**:

Produced by certain strains of *Streptococcus* bacteria.

- **Chemistry**:

Streptokinase is a non-enzymatic protein that activates plasminogen to plasmin, initiating fibrinolysis (breakdown of blood clots).

- **Preparation**:

Streptokinase is produced by culturing *Streptococcus* bacteria, followed by purification through filtration and precipitation methods.

- **Therapeutic Uses**:
  - Used in the treatment of acute myocardial infarction, pulmonary embolism, and other thrombotic conditions.
- **Commercial Utility**:
  - Administered as a thrombolytic agent (clot-buster) in clinical settings.

6. Pepsin

- **Source**:

Derived from the gastric mucosa of pigs or calves.

- **Chemistry**:

Pepsin is an endopeptidase that breaks down proteins into smaller peptides in the stomach. It works optimally at an acidic pH.

- **Preparation**:

Isolated from the stomach lining of animals, then purified and dried into powder form.

- **Therapeutic Uses**:
  - Used as a digestive aid in cases of dyspepsia (indigestion).
- **Commercial Utility**:
  - Used in digestive enzyme supplements.
  - Employed in the food industry for hydrolyzing proteins in food processing.

Evaluation of Proteolytic Enzymes

1. **Activity Assays**:
   - Enzyme activity is measured by assessing the rate of protein hydrolysis. Common substrates like casein or hemoglobin are used, and the products are quantified spectrophotometrically.
2. **Purity Tests**:
   - Purity of proteolytic enzymes is tested using electrophoresis, chromatography, and enzyme kinetics.
3. **Stability Testing**:
   - Proteolytic enzymes are evaluated for their stability in different pH, temperature, and storage conditions.

Preservation and Storage of Proteolytic Enzymes

- **Preservation**:

Proteolytic enzymes should be stored in dry form to prevent degradation.

In liquid formulations, stabilizers like glycerol or mannitol are used to maintain enzyme activity.

- **Storage Conditions**:

These enzymes should be stored at low temperatures (preferably in a refrigerator or freezer) and away from moisture. Proteolytic enzymes are often stored as lyophilized powders to extend their shelf life.

Therapeutic Uses of Proteolytic Enzymes

1. **Digestive Aid**:

Papain, bromelain, and pepsin are used in digestive enzyme supplements to aid in protein digestion for individuals with digestive disorders.

2. **Anti-inflammatory Agents**:

Bromelain and serratiopeptidase are used to reduce inflammation and edema in conditions such as arthritis, sports injuries, and postoperative swelling.

3. **Thrombolytic Agents**:

Urokinase and streptokinase are used as clot-dissolving agents in emergency treatment for thromboembolic conditions, including heart attacks and strokes.

4. **Wound Healing**:

Proteolytic enzymes such as papain are used in topical preparations to debride dead tissue and promote wound healing.

Commercial Utility of Proteolytic Enzymes

1. **Pharmaceutical Industry**:

   - **Digestive Enzymes**: Used in supplements to treat indigestion and other gastrointestinal disorders.
   - **Thrombolytic Drugs**: Urokinase and streptokinase are important in treating thrombotic disorders in hospitals.
   - **Anti-inflammatory Supplements**: Serratiopeptidase and bromelain are included in supplements to reduce inflammation.

2. **Food Industry**:
   - o **Meat Tenderizers**: Papain and bromelain are used to break down proteins in meat, making it more tender.
   - o **Brewing and Baking**: Proteolytic enzymes help in modifying gluten proteins for better dough quality and in improving beer clarity.

3. **Cosmetics Industry**:
   - o Proteolytic enzymes like papain are used in exfoliating creams and anti-aging products for their ability to remove dead skin cells.

Multiple Choice Questions (Objective)

1. What are the building blocks of proteins?

   A) Nucleotides

   B) Fatty acids

   C) Amino acids

   D) Monosaccharides

2. Which level of protein structure is defined by the sequence of amino acids?

   A) Primary

   B) Secondary

   C) Tertiary

   D) Quaternary

3. Which protein function is exemplified by hemoglobin?

   A) Structural support

   B) Transport

   C) Defense

   D) Enzymatic activity

4. What is the role of enzymes in biochemical reactions?

   A) They provide energy for the reaction.

B) They catalyze reactions by lowering activation energy.

C) They increase the reaction's energy requirement.

D) They are consumed in the reaction.

5. Which type of enzyme catalyzes the hydrolysis of chemical bonds?

A) Oxidoreductases

B) Transferases

C) Hydrolases

D) Lyases

6. What is gelatin primarily composed of?

A) Collagen

B) Casein

C) Albumin

D) Keratin

7. Which process is used to extract gelatin from animal tissues?

A) Fermentation

B) Hydrolysis

C) Precipitation

D) Crystallization

8. What is the primary source of casein?

A) Chicken eggs

B) Soybeans

C) Cow's milk

D) Fish scales

9. Which enzyme is derived from papaya and used in wound debridement?

A) Bromelain

B) Serratiopeptidase

C) Papain

D) Pepsin

10.Which of the following is a globular protein found in blood plasma?

A) Casein

B) Gelatin

C) Albumin

D) Collagen

11. Which class of enzymes catalyzes the rearrangement of molecular structures?

A) Isomerases

B) Ligases

C) Lyases

D) Hydrolases

12. What are glycoproteins composed of?

A) Protein and lipids

B) Protein and carbohydrates

C) Protein and nucleic acids

D) Protein and metal ions

13. Which structural protein is primarily found in connective tissues?

A) Albumin

B) Collagen

C) Hemoglobin

D) Myosin

14. What is the main function of lipoproteins?

A) Catalyzing biochemical reactions

B) Transporting lipids in the bloodstream

C) Providing structural support to cells

D) Acting as hormones

15. Which of the following proteins is used as a volume expander in hypovolemia?

A) Hemoglobin

B) Albumin

C) Collagen

D) Casein

16. Which enzyme is commonly used in thrombolytic therapy to dissolve blood clots?

A) Pepsin

B) Papain

C) Streptokinase

D) Bromelain

17. What type of enzyme is urokinase?

A) Hydrolase

B) Oxidoreductase

C) Ligase

D) Serine protease

18. Which protein is used in the food industry as a gelling agent?

A) Albumin

B) Collagen

C) Casein

D) Gelatin

19. What are prolamins primarily found in?

A) Meat

B) Cereal grains

C) Dairy products

D) Fish

20. Which of the following is a metalloprotein involved in oxygen transport?

A) Hemoglobin

B) Albumin

C) Fibrinogen

D) Keratin

Short Answer Type Questions (Subjective)

1. Define proteins and describe their primary structure.
2. What are the main functions of proteins in the human body?
3. Explain the role of enzymes as biological catalysts.
4. Describe the process of enzyme-substrate complex formation.
5. What are the different types of enzyme inhibition?
6. Discuss the sources and preparation of gelatin.
7. How is casein extracted from milk?
8. Describe the therapeutic uses of proteolytic enzymes.
9. What is the role of albumin in maintaining oncotic pressure?
10. Explain the difference between simple and conjugated proteins.
11. What are glycoproteins and why are they important in biological processes?
12. Describe the function of lipoproteins in the body.
13. How are phosphoproteins regulated within the cell?
14. Explain the significance of metalloproteins in enzyme function.
15. What are peptides and how are they synthesized?
16. Discuss the commercial applications of protein hydrolysates.
17. How does collagen contribute to tissue structure?
18. What are the main characteristics of scleroproteins?
19. Describe the importance of enzyme kinetics in understanding enzyme activity.
20. Explain the role of proteases in protein digestion.

Long Answer Type Questions (Subjective)

1. Discuss the structure and function of proteins, detailing the levels of protein structure and their significance.
2. Explain the classification of enzymes, including examples of each class and their specific functions in biochemical reactions.

3. Describe the process of gelatin production, its evaluation, and its various applications in pharmaceuticals and the food industry.

4. Analyze the role of casein in the dairy industry, including its preparation, evaluation, and therapeutic uses.

5. Discuss the significance of proteolytic enzymes in medicine, including the mechanisms and therapeutic applications of papain, bromelain, and serratiopeptidase.

6. Explain the structure, function, and therapeutic uses of albumin, emphasizing its role in maintaining blood volume and pressure.

7. Describe the chemical nature, sources, and functions of glycoproteins, with examples of their roles in health and disease.

8. Analyze the role of metalloproteins in biological systems, including their classification, sources, and therapeutic uses.

9. Discuss the preparation, evaluation, and commercial applications of protein hydrolysates in the food and pharmaceutical industries.

10. Explain the classification and importance of scleroproteins and prolamins, detailing their sources, properties, and uses in various industries.

Answer Key for MCQs

1. C) Amino acids
2. A) Primary
3. B) Transport
4. B) They catalyze reactions by lowering activation energy
5. C) Hydrolases
6. A) Collagen
7. B) Hydrolysis
8. C) Cow's milk
9. C) Papain
10. C) Albumin

11.A) Isomerases

12.B) Protein and carbohydrates

13.B) Collagen

14.B) Transporting lipids in the bloodstream

15.B) Albumin

16.C) Streptokinase

17.D) Serine protease

18.D) Gelatin

19.B) Cereal grains

20.A) Hemoglobin

CHAPTER – 13

LIPIDS (WAXES, FATS, FIXED OILS)

INTRODUCTION:

Lipids are a diverse group of hydrophobic organic compounds that are essential for various biological functions. They are classified into several categories, including waxes, fats, and fixed oils. Here's a detailed introduction to each category:

1. Waxes

Definition: Waxes are long-chain fatty acids esterified with long-chain alcohols. They are generally solid at room temperature.

Structure: Waxes consist of a fatty acid linked to a long-chain alcohol. The ester linkage between the fatty acid and the alcohol creates a structure that is highly hydrophobic.

Properties:

    a. **Hydrophobic:** Waxes repel water and do not dissolve in it.

    b. **Melting Point:** Typically have high melting points compared to other lipids.

    c. **Texture:** They are often solid and can be hard or soft depending on the specific structure.

Functions:

    a. **Protection:** Waxes provide protective coatings in plants and animals. For example, the waxy cuticle on plant leaves helps reduce water loss.

    b. **Insulation:** In animals, waxes can help in insulation and protection of skin and feathers.

Examples:

    a. **Beeswax:** Produced by honeybees and used in various applications including cosmetics and candles.

b. **Carnauba Wax:** Extracted from the leaves of the carnauba palm and used in car polish and cosmetics.

2. Fats

Definition: Fats are esters of glycerol with three fatty acids, commonly known as triglycerides.

Structure: Fats consist of a glycerol backbone esterified with three fatty acid chains. The fatty acids can be saturated or unsaturated.

Properties:

a. **Saturated Fats:** Have no double bonds between carbon atoms, making them solid at room temperature (e.g., butter).

b. **Unsaturated Fats:** Contain one or more double bonds, making them liquid at room temperature (e.g., olive oil).

Functions:

a. **Energy Storage:** Fats serve as a major energy reserve in the body. They provide more energy per gram compared to carbohydrates and proteins.

b. **Insulation and Protection:** Fats provide thermal insulation and cushion for organs.

Examples:

a. **Animal Fats:** Lard (pork fat) and tallow (beef fat).

b. **Vegetable Fats:** Olive oil, canola oil.

3. Fixed Oils

Definition: Fixed oils are triglycerides similar to fats but are usually liquid at room temperature. They are also derived from plants and some animals.

Structure: Like fats, fixed oils are esters of glycerol with fatty acids. The primary difference is their state at room temperature.

Properties:

a. **Liquid at Room Temperature:** Fixed oils remain liquid at room temperature due to the presence of unsaturated fatty acids.

b. **Non-Volatile:** Unlike essential oils, fixed oils do not evaporate easily.

Functions:

   a. **Nutritional:** Fixed oils are a source of essential fatty acids and vitamins in the diet.

   b. **Industrial Uses:** They are used in the production of soaps, paints, and other products.

Examples:

   a. **Vegetable Oils:** Sunflower oil, soybean oil.

   b. **Essential Oils:** Often mistaken for fixed oils, but essential oils are actually volatile and extracted for different uses.

Applications and Importance

   a. **Nutritional:** Both fats and fixed oils are essential in the diet for energy and as carriers of fat-soluble vitamins (A, D, E, and K).

   b. **Industrial:** Waxes and fixed oils have various industrial applications, including lubrication, waterproofing, and as ingredients in personal care products.

   c. **Pharmaceutical:** Some lipids are used in drug formulations and as carriers for drug delivery systems.

CASTOR OIL

Castor oil is a significant fixed oil derived from the seeds of the castor bean plant, *Ricinus communis*. It is rich in various primary metabolites, notably ricinoleic acid, which contributes to its unique properties and uses. Here's a detailed study on the primary metabolites of castor oil, focusing on their chemistry, sources, preparation, evaluation, preservation, storage, therapeutic uses, and commercial utility as pharmaceutical aids and/or medicines.

General Introduction

Castor Oil: Castor oil is a pale yellow, viscous liquid with a distinctive odor. It has been used for centuries for its medicinal and industrial properties. The primary active component in castor oil is ricinoleic acid, which accounts for approximately 90% of its fatty acid content.

Detailed Study

1. Chemistry

    a. **Primary Metabolites**: The key primary metabolite in castor oil is **ricinoleic acid**. It is an 18-carbon fatty acid with a hydroxyl group on the 12th carbon, which is unusual in natural fatty acids.

    b. **Chemical Structure**: Ricinoleic acid (C18H34O3) is a hydroxy fatty acid with a double bond between the 9th and 10th carbons and a hydroxyl group on the 12th carbon.

Chemical Reactions and Properties:

    a. **Hydrolysis**: Castor oil hydrolyzes to form ricinoleic acid and glycerol.

    b. **Saponification**: Castor oil can be saponified to produce soap and glycerol.

    c. **Transesterification**: Castor oil can be transesterified to produce biodiesel and glycerol.

2. Sources

    a. **Plant Source**: Castor oil is extracted from the seeds of *Ricinus communis*, commonly known as the castor bean plant.

    b. **Geographical Distribution**: The plant is grown in tropical and subtropical regions worldwide, including Africa, India, and South America.

3. Preparation

    a. **Extraction**: Castor oil is obtained through cold pressing or solvent extraction of castor seeds. The oil is then refined to remove impurities.

    b. **Refining Process**: Includes degumming, neutralization, bleaching, and deodorization to produce a high-quality oil.

4. Evaluation

    a. **Physical Properties**:

        i. **Appearance**: Pale yellow, viscous liquid.

        ii. **Odor**: Characteristic, slightly nutty.

iii. **Density**: Around 0.961–0.964 g/cm³.

iv. **Viscosity**: High viscosity compared to other vegetable oils.

b. **Chemical Properties**:

i. **Acid Value**: Indicates the amount of free fatty acids; castor oil has a relatively high acid value.

ii. **Saponification Value**: Measures the amount of alkali required to saponify the oil. Castor oil has a high saponification value due to the presence of ricinoleic acid.

iii. **Iodine Value**: Indicates the degree of unsaturation; castor oil has a moderate iodine value.

5. Preservation

a. **Antioxidants**: To prevent oxidation and rancidity, antioxidants such as tocopherols (vitamin E) or BHT (butylated hydroxytoluene) are often added.

b. **Temperature Control**: Store at cool temperatures away from light and air to prevent degradation.

c. **Sealed Containers**: Use airtight containers to minimize exposure to oxygen.

6. Storage

a. **Conditions**: Store in a cool, dark place to maintain stability and prevent oxidation.

b. **Packaging**: Use opaque or dark-colored containers to protect from light, which can accelerate degradation.

7. Therapeutic Uses

a. **Laxative**: Ricinoleic acid in castor oil acts as a powerful stimulant laxative. It stimulates the intestines, promoting bowel movements.

b. **Anti-inflammatory**: Castor oil has anti-inflammatory properties, useful for reducing pain and swelling.

c. **Skin Care**: Used in topical formulations for its moisturizing and emollient properties. It can help in treating dry skin and minor wounds.

8. Commercial Utility

a. **Pharmaceutical Aids**: Castor oil is used as a laxative in over-the-counter medications. It also serves as a solvent in some pharmaceutical formulations.

b. **Cosmetics**: Widely used in cosmetics and personal care products for its moisturizing properties.

c. **Industrial Applications**: Used in the production of biodiesel, lubricants, and as a plasticizer in various industrial processes.

Commercial Products:

a. **Laxatives**: Available as oral solutions or capsules.

b. **Cosmetic Products**: Found in moisturizers, lip balms, and lotions.

c. **Industrial Products**: Used in manufacturing adhesives, coatings, and resins.

CHAULMOOGRA OIL

Chaulmoogra oil, derived from the seeds of the *Hydnocarpus wightiana* or *Hydnocarpus laurifolia* tree, is a fixed oil rich in unique primary metabolites. This oil has historical significance and modern applications in both pharmaceuticals and cosmetics..

General Introduction

Chaulmoogra Oil: This oil is extracted from the seeds of the chaulmoogra tree and is notable for its high content of chaulmoogric acid and other fatty acids. Historically, chaulmoogra oil has been used in traditional medicine for treating various skin diseases and infections.

Detailed Study

1. Chemistry

a. **Primary Metabolites**: The key components of chaulmoogra oil are:

i. **Chaulmoogric Acid**: A unique fatty acid that is a major component of the oil. It has a complex structure with a cyclopentane ring.

ii. **Hydnocarpic Acid**: Another significant fatty acid in the oil, known for its role in various therapeutic applications.

iii. **Other Fatty Acids**: Includes palmitic acid, stearic acid, and oleic acid.

Chemical Structure:

a. **Chaulmoogric Acid**: This is a cyclopentane fatty acid with a complex structure. It contains a cyclopentane ring fused with a long hydrocarbon chain.

b. **Hydnocarpic Acid**: Similar to chaulmoogric acid but without the cyclopentane ring.

Chemical Reactions and Properties:

a. **Saponification**: Chaulmoogra oil can be saponified to produce soap and glycerol.

b. **Hydrolysis**: The oil undergoes hydrolysis to release fatty acids and glycerol.

2. Sources

a. **Plant Source**: Chaulmoogra oil is extracted from the seeds of *Hydnocarpus wightiana* or *Hydnocarpus laurifolia*, trees native to tropical regions of Asia, particularly India and Sri Lanka.

b. **Geographical Distribution**: Found in tropical and subtropical forests, especially in the Indian subcontinent.

3. Preparation

a. **Extraction**: Chaulmoogra oil is extracted from the seeds of the chaulmoogra tree using methods such as cold pressing or solvent extraction.

b. **Refining**: The oil is refined to remove impurities and to improve its quality for pharmaceutical and cosmetic applications.

4. Evaluation

a. **Physical Properties:**

   i. **Appearance**: Typically a yellowish to brownish liquid.

   ii. **Odor**: Characteristic, somewhat pungent odor.

   iii. **Density**: Approximately 0.92–0.94 g/cm^3.

   iv. **Viscosity**: Moderate viscosity.

b. **Chemical Properties:**

   i. **Acid Value**: Measures the amount of free fatty acids; chaulmoogra oil has a relatively high acid value due to its fatty acid content.

   ii. **Saponification Value**: Indicates the amount of alkali needed to saponify the oil, reflecting its fatty acid composition.

   iii. **Iodine Value**: Measures the degree of unsaturation; chaulmoogra oil has a moderate iodine value.

5. Preservation

a. **Antioxidants**: To prevent oxidation and rancidity, antioxidants like vitamin E may be added.

b. **Temperature Control**: Store at cool temperatures to maintain stability.

c. **Sealed Containers**: Use airtight containers to minimize exposure to air.

6. Storage

a. **Conditions**: Keep in a cool, dark place to avoid degradation.

b. **Packaging**: Use opaque or dark-colored containers to protect from light and heat.

7. Therapeutic Uses

a. **Antiseptic and Antimicrobial**: Chaulmoogra oil has been used for its antiseptic and antimicrobial properties, particularly in treating skin infections.

b. **Anti-inflammatory**: The oil is known for its anti-inflammatory effects, useful in treating conditions such as arthritis.

c. **Leprosy Treatment**: Historically, chaulmoogra oil was used in the treatment of leprosy due to its antimicrobial and anti-inflammatory properties.

8. Commercial Utility

a. **Pharmaceutical Aids**: Used in the preparation of topical formulations for skin conditions and as a base in certain medicinal ointments.

b. **Cosmetics**: Incorporated into skin care products for its emollient and therapeutic properties.

c. **Industrial Applications**: Used in the production of soaps and other personal care products due to its fatty acid composition.

Commercial Products:

a. **Medicinal Ointments**: Used in topical applications for treating skin infections and inflammatory conditions.

b. **Cosmetic Products**: Found in lotions, creams, and other skincare products.

WOOL FAT

Wool fat, also known as lanolin, is a complex lipid mixture derived from the wool of sheep. It has various applications in pharmaceuticals, cosmetics, and other industries due to its unique properties. Here's a detailed study of wool fat, focusing on its chemistry, sources, preparation, evaluation, preservation, storage, therapeutic uses, and commercial utility.

General Introduction

Wool Fat (Lanolin): Lanolin is a natural, waxy substance extracted from the sebaceous glands of sheep. It serves as a natural moisturizer and emollient. Lanolin is widely used in skincare products and pharmaceuticals due to its ability to moisturize and protect the skin.

Detailed Study

1. Chemistry

    a. **Primary Metabolites**: Wool fat primarily consists of:

        i. **Cholesterol and Cholesterol Esters**: Lanolin contains significant amounts of cholesterol, which helps in maintaining skin barrier function.

        ii. **Fatty Acids**: Various fatty acids, including oleic acid, linoleic acid, and stearic acid.

        iii. **Wax Esters**: Complex mixtures of long-chain fatty acids esterified with long-chain alcohols.

        iv. **Hydrocarbons**: Various alkanes and alkenes.

Chemical Structure:

    a. **Cholesterol Esters**: Composed of cholesterol esterified with fatty acids.

    b. **Wax Esters**: Contain a long-chain fatty acid and a long-chain alcohol linked by an ester bond.

Chemical Reactions and Properties:

    a. **Hydrolysis**: Lanolin can be hydrolyzed to release fatty acids and cholesterol.

    b. **Saponification**: Lanolin can be saponified to produce soap and glycerol.

    c. **Oxidation**: Lanolin is prone to oxidation, which can affect its stability and efficacy.

2. Sources

    a. **Animal Source**: Wool fat is obtained from the wool of sheep. It is secreted by the sebaceous glands in the sheep's skin and coats the wool fibers.

    b. **Geographical Distribution**: Wool fat is collected from sheep in various regions worldwide, with significant production in Australia, New Zealand, and the UK.

3. Preparation

a. **Extraction**: Wool fat is extracted from raw wool using solvents such as ethyl alcohol or through a process of washing and centrifugation.

b. **Purification**: The extracted lanolin is purified through refining processes to remove impurities and unwanted substances.

c. **Refining Process**: Includes degumming, neutralization, bleaching, and deodorization to ensure high-quality lanolin.

4. Evaluation

a. **Physical Properties:**

   i. **Appearance**: Lanolin is a yellow to light brown, waxy substance.

   ii. **Odor**: Slightly characteristic, but typically deodorized for use in products.

   iii. **Melting Point**: Typically ranges from 36°C to 42°C.

b. **Chemical Properties:**

   i. **Acid Value**: Measures the free fatty acids in lanolin.

   ii. **Saponification Value**: Indicates the amount of alkali required to saponify lanolin, reflecting its ester content.

   iii. **Iodine Value**: Measures the degree of unsaturation; lanolin has a low iodine value due to its high wax ester content.

5. Preservation

a. **Antioxidants**: Antioxidants like tocopherols (vitamin E) may be added to prevent oxidation and rancidity.

b. **Temperature Control**: Store at cool temperatures to prevent degradation.

c. **Sealed Containers**: Use airtight containers to minimize exposure to air and moisture.

6. Storage

a. **Conditions**: Store in a cool, dry place away from light and heat to maintain stability.

b. **Packaging**: Use opaque or dark-colored containers to protect from light and reduce oxidative damage.

7. Therapeutic Uses

a. **Moisturizer**: Lanolin is widely used in skincare products due to its excellent emollient properties. It helps to hydrate and protect the skin.

b. **Wound Healing**: Used in ointments and creams to promote healing of minor wounds and abrasions.

c. **Barrier Protection**: Acts as a protective barrier for the skin, preventing moisture loss and shielding against irritants.

8. Commercial Utility

a. **Pharmaceutical Aids**: Lanolin is used as a base in various topical formulations, including creams, ointments, and lotions. It helps in the delivery of active pharmaceutical ingredients and improves the texture and spreadability of products.

b. **Cosmetics**: Found in a range of cosmetic products such as lip balms, moisturizers, and conditioners due to its moisturizing and emollient properties.

c. **Industrial Applications**: Used in the production of textile lubricants, leather conditioning products, and as a component in some industrial coatings.

Commercial Products:

a. **Topical Ointments**: Used in medicinal ointments for its emollient and healing properties.

b. **Skincare Products**: Incorporated into lotions, creams, and lipsticks.

c. **Industrial Lubricants**: Applied in textile and leather industries.

BEES WAX

Beeswax is a natural wax produced by honeybees and is used extensively in pharmaceuticals, cosmetics, and various industrial applications. It is known for its unique properties, which are largely attributed to its primary metabolites.

Here's a detailed study of beeswax, focusing on its chemistry, sources, preparation, evaluation, preservation, storage, therapeutic uses, and commercial utility.

General Introduction

Beeswax: Beeswax is a complex mixture of fatty acids, alcohols, and esters secreted by honeybees to construct honeycombs. It is a yellow to brown substance that has been used for thousands of years in various applications, from ancient Egyptian mummification to modern cosmetics and pharmaceuticals.

Detailed Study

1. Chemistry

a. **Primary Metabolites**: Beeswax is composed of a variety of chemical components, including:

i. **Fatty Acids**: Mainly long-chain fatty acids such as palmitic acid, oleic acid, and linoleic acid.

ii. **Alcohols**: Long-chain fatty alcohols such as myricyl alcohol and cetyl alcohol.

iii. **Esters**: Wax esters formed by the esterification of fatty acids and fatty alcohols.

iv. **Hydrocarbons**: Long-chain alkanes and alkenes.

Chemical Structure:

a. **Wax Esters**: These are formed from the esterification of fatty acids with long-chain alcohols. Examples include myricyl palmitate and cerotic acid esters.

b. **Fatty Acids and Alcohols**: Long-chain fatty acids and alcohols contribute to the wax's rigidity and melting point.

Chemical Reactions and Properties:

a. **Hydrolysis**: Beeswax can be hydrolyzed to yield fatty acids and fatty alcohols.

b. **Saponification**: Beeswax can be saponified to produce soap and glycerol.

c. **Melting Point**: Beeswax has a melting point range of approximately 62°C to 64°C, which is higher than many other natural waxes.

2. Sources

a. **Biological Source**: Beeswax is produced by honeybees (*Apis mellifera*) in their wax glands. It is secreted as a liquid and solidifies into wax scales.

b. **Geographical Distribution**: Collected from beehives worldwide, with significant production in regions with large honeybee populations, such as the United States, China, and various European countries.

3. Preparation

a. **Extraction**: Beeswax is extracted from the honeycomb of beehives. The honeycomb is melted in hot water, and the wax rises to the surface where it is skimmed off.

b. **Purification**: The raw beeswax is purified through filtering and sometimes bleaching to remove impurities and improve quality.

4. Evaluation

a. **Physical Properties:**

   i. **Appearance**: Typically yellow to brown, with a characteristic odor.

   ii. **Melting Point**: Ranges from 62°C to 64°C.

   iii. **Consistency**: Solid at room temperature but becomes pliable when warmed.

b. **Chemical Properties:**

   i. **Acid Value**: Measures the amount of free fatty acids; beeswax has a low acid value.

   ii. **Saponification Value**: Reflects the amount of alkali required to saponify beeswax, indicating its ester content.

    iii.   **Iodine Value**: Indicates the degree of unsaturation in the wax; beeswax has a low iodine value due to its saturated nature.

5. Preservation

a. **Antioxidants**: Beeswax is relatively stable but may benefit from antioxidants to prevent degradation, especially in high-temperature environments.

b. **Temperature Control**: Store at stable temperatures to avoid melting or solidifying excessively.

c. **Sealed Containers**: Use airtight containers to prevent contamination and moisture absorption.

6. Storage

a. **Conditions**: Keep in a cool, dry place away from direct sunlight and heat.

b. **Packaging**: Use containers that protect from light and air to maintain stability and prevent oxidation.

7. Therapeutic Uses

a. **Skin Care**: Beeswax is used in various topical formulations for its moisturizing and protective properties. It creates a barrier that helps retain moisture in the skin.

b. **Wound Healing**: Applied in ointments to promote healing of minor wounds and abrasions.

c. **Anti-inflammatory**: Has mild anti-inflammatory properties that can help soothe irritated skin.

8. Commercial Utility

a. **Pharmaceutical Aids**: Beeswax is used as a base for ointments, creams, and other topical formulations due to its emulsifying and stabilizing properties.

b. **Cosmetics**: Commonly found in lip balms, lotions, and creams for its emollient properties. It helps in creating a protective barrier and improving the texture of cosmetic products.

c. **Industrial Applications**: Used in the production of candles, polishes, and as a component in various industrial coatings and adhesives.

Commercial Products:

a. **Topical Ointments**: Used in medicinal ointments for its emollient and protective properties.

b. **Cosmetic Products**: Incorporated into skincare products such as lip balms, moisturizers, and conditioners.

c. **Industrial Products**: Found in candles, polishes, and coatings.

CLASSIFICATION:

Lipids, including waxes, fats, and fixed oils, are a diverse group of organic compounds characterized by their hydrophobic nature. They play various roles in biological systems and are utilized in numerous industrial applications. Here's a detailed classification of lipids with examples:

1. Waxes

Definition: Waxes are esters of long-chain fatty acids and long-chain alcohols. They are solid at room temperature and are used for their protective and waterproofing properties.

Examples:

a. **Beeswax**: Extracted from honeycombs of bees (*Apis mellifera*), used in cosmetics and pharmaceuticals.

b. **Carnauba Wax**: Derived from the leaves of the carnauba palm (*Copernicia cerifera*), used in polishes and coatings.

c. **Candelilla Wax**: Obtained from the candelilla plant (*Euphorbia cerifera*), used in cosmetics and as a food additive.

2. Fats

Definition: Fats are triglycerides, which are esters formed from glycerol and three fatty acids. They are typically solid at room temperature and are mainly used for energy storage and insulation in organisms.

Examples:

a. **Animal Fats**:

  i. **Lard**: Rendered fat from pigs, used in cooking and baking.

  ii. **Tallow**: Rendered fat from cattle or sheep, used in soap making and as a lubricant.

b. **Vegetable Fats**:

  i. **Cocoa Butter**: Fat extracted from cocoa beans, used in chocolate and cosmetics.

  ii. **Palm Fat**: Derived from the fruit of the oil palm (*Elaeis guineensis*), used in cooking and processed foods.

3. Fixed Oils

Definition: Fixed oils are liquid triglycerides at room temperature, derived from plants and seeds. They are used in cooking, as carriers in pharmaceuticals, and in cosmetic formulations.

Examples:

a. **Vegetable Oils**:

  i. **Olive Oil**: Extracted from olives (*Olea europaea*), used in cooking and skincare products.

  ii. **Sunflower Oil**: Obtained from sunflower seeds (*Helianthus annuus*), used in cooking and as a base in many products.

b. **Essential Oils**:

  i. **Castor Oil**: Extracted from the seeds of the castor bean plant (*Ricinus communis*), used as a laxative and in industrial applications.

  ii. **Jojoba Oil**: Obtained from the seeds of the jojoba plant (*Simmondsia chinensis*), used in cosmetics for its moisturizing properties.

Multiple Choice Questions (Objective)

1. What is the main type of fatty acid found in cocoa butter?

A) Oleic acid

B) Linoleic acid

C) Stearic acid

D) Palmitic acid

2. Which fatty acid is most prevalent in palm fat?

A) Stearic acid

B) Oleic acid

C) Linoleic acid

D) Palmitic acid

3. What percentage of cocoa butter is composed of oleic acid?

A) 10-15%

B) 20-25%

C) 35-40%

D) 50-55%

4. What is a common therapeutic use of cocoa butter?

A) Sunscreen

B) Scar treatment

C) Antiseptic

D) Anti-inflammatory ointment

5. What is a primary pharmacological property of cocoa butter?

A) Antimicrobial

B) Emollient

C) Anti-inflammatory

D) Analgesic

6. Which of the following is NOT a pharmacological property of cocoa butter?

A) Moisturizing

B) Antioxidant

C) Anti-inflammatory

D) Antiviral

7. Which component in cocoa butter contributes to its antioxidant properties?

A) Vitamin A

B) Vitamin E

C) Linoleic acid

D) Palmitic acid

8. What is a potential risk associated with the use of cocoa butter on the skin?

A) Acne

B) Skin whitening

C) Hair loss

D) Muscle cramps

9. What is the main component of palm fat?

A) Triglycerides

B) Carbohydrates

C) Proteins

D) Phospholipids

10. What is a common use of palm fat in the food industry?

A) Salad dressing

B) Baking

C) Soft drink production

D) Cereal manufacturing

11. Which vitamin found in palm fat contributes to its antioxidant properties?

A) Vitamin C

B) Vitamin D

C) Vitamin E

D) Vitamin K

12. Which of the following is a potential risk of consuming palm fat?

A) Increased HDL cholesterol levels

B) Decreased blood pressure

C) Increased LDL cholesterol levels

D) Reduced risk of stroke

13. What percentage of palm fat is composed of linoleic acid?

    A) 1-2%

    B) 5-6%

    C) 10%

    D) 15-20%

14. Why is palm fat commonly used in industrial applications like soap making?

    A) High carbohydrate content

    B) High triglyceride content

    C) Low melting point

    D) High vitamin content

15. Which fatty acid is found in both cocoa butter and palm fat?

    A) Stearic acid

    B) Linoleic acid

    C) Palmitic acid

    D) Oleic acid

16. What is a benefit of cocoa butter for skin care?

    A) It lightens skin

    B) It moisturizes and softens skin

    C) It removes hair

    D) It treats acne

17. What environmental concern is associated with palm oil production?

    A) Water pollution

    B) Air pollution

    C) Deforestation

    D) Ozone depletion

18. What makes palm fat suitable for frying and high-temperature cooking?

    A) Low smoke point

    B) High carbohydrate content

C) High smoke point

D) Low-fat content

19. Which of the following is a risk associated with the cosmetic use of cocoa butter?

A) Dry skin

B) Acne

C) Hair loss

D) Skin rash

20. Which type of fatty acid is present in the highest concentration in cocoa butter?

A) Saturated fatty acids

B) Monounsaturated fatty acids

C) Polyunsaturated fatty acids

D) Trans fats

Short Answer Type Questions (Subjective)

1. What are the main fatty acids found in cocoa butter?

2. Describe the moisturizing properties of cocoa butter.

3. What are the antioxidant properties of cocoa butter, and how do they benefit the skin?

4. Discuss the therapeutic uses of cocoa butter in skin care.

5. What are the potential risks of using cocoa butter on the skin?

6. Describe the chemical composition of palm fat.

7. What are the primary uses of palm fat in the culinary industry?

8. How does the saturated fat content in palm fat impact cardiovascular health?

9. What are the antioxidant components of palm fat?

10. Discuss the potential health risks associated with the consumption of palm fat.

11. How does palm fat contribute to industrial applications like soap making?

12. Compare the fatty acid composition of cocoa butter and palm fat.

13. What are the pharmacological properties of palm fat?

14. Describe the therapeutic uses of palm fat in cosmetics.

15. What is the significance of vitamin E in cocoa butter and palm fat?

16. How does cocoa butter help in scar treatment?

17. What is the role of linoleic acid in the composition of palm fat?

18. Discuss the environmental concerns related to palm oil production.

19. How can cocoa butter be comedogenic for certain individuals?

20. What makes palm fat stable at high temperatures?

Long Answer Type Questions (Subjective)

1. Discuss the chemical composition of cocoa butter and palm fat, highlighting their similarities and differences in fatty acid content.

2. Explain the pharmacological properties of cocoa butter and how they contribute to its use in dermatological applications.

3. Analyze the potential health benefits and risks associated with the consumption and topical use of cocoa butter.

4. Discuss the various therapeutic uses of palm fat in culinary, cosmetic, and industrial applications, along with its potential health risks.

5. Examine the role of saturated and unsaturated fatty acids in cocoa butter and palm fat in terms of their impact on cardiovascular health.

6. Describe the extraction and refining process of cocoa butter and palm fat, and how these processes affect their final chemical composition and use.

7. Evaluate the environmental impact of palm oil production and suggest sustainable practices that could mitigate these effects.

8. Compare and contrast the antioxidant properties of cocoa butter and palm fat, focusing on their effects on skin health.

9. Discuss the commercial and therapeutic applications of cocoa butter in the skincare industry, including its effectiveness in treating scars and stretch marks.

10. Analyze the risks and benefits of using palm fat in food production, particularly in relation to its saturated fat content and potential health implications.

Answer Key for MCQs

1. C) Stearic acid
2. D) Palmitic acid
3. C) 35-40%
4. B) Scar treatment
5. B) Emollient
6. D) Antiviral
7. B) Vitamin E
8. A) Acne
9. A) Triglycerides
10. B) Baking
11. C) Vitamin E
12. C) Increased LDL cholesterol levels
13. C) 10%
14. B) High triglyceride content
15. C) Palmitic acid.
16. B) It moisturizes and softens skin
17. C) Deforestation
18. C) High smoke point
19. B) Acne
20. A) Saturated fatty acids

CHAPTER – 14

MARINE DRUGS

INTRODUCTION:

Marine drugs are substances derived from marine organisms, including seaweeds, marine invertebrates, and marine microorganisms, that have potential therapeutic uses. The study of marine drugs, also known as marine pharmacology or marine natural products, is a field dedicated to exploring the bioactive compounds found in these organisms and their potential applications in medicine. Here's a detailed introduction:

1. Importance of Marine Drugs

a. **Biodiversity**: The marine environment is one of the richest sources of biodiversity on the planet. Marine organisms produce a vast array of unique chemical compounds, many of which have never been found in terrestrial organisms.

b. **Novelty**: Marine drugs often have novel structures and mechanisms of action, which can lead to new classes of therapeutic agents.

c. **Pharmaceutical Potential**: Marine-derived compounds have shown promise in various therapeutic areas, including cancer, cardiovascular diseases, antiviral, anti-inflammatory, and antimicrobial agents.

2. Sources of Marine Drugs

a. **Marine Microorganisms**:

    i. **Bacteria**: Marine bacteria are prolific producers of bioactive compounds. For example, **Actinobacteria** from marine environments have produced antibiotics like **actinomycin D**.

    ii. **Fungi**: Marine fungi also produce a range of bioactive substances, including anti-cancer agents.

b. **Marine Invertebrates**:

i. **Sponges**: Marine sponges are a rich source of bioactive compounds, such as **cyclic peptides** and **alkaloids**. For instance, **Cytarabine** is derived from the sponge **Cytarabine** and is used in cancer treatment.

ii. **Corals**: Corals produce compounds with potential anti-inflammatory and anti-tumor activities.

c. **Marine Plants**:

i. **Seaweeds**: Seaweeds (macroalgae) are a significant source of bioactive compounds, including **polysaccharides** and **phlorotannins**, which have antioxidant and anti-cancer properties. **Alginate**, **carrageenan**, and **agar** are well-known polysaccharides derived from seaweeds.

d. **Marine Animals**:

i. **Echinoderms**: These include sea stars and sea urchins, which produce compounds with anti-inflammatory and anti-cancer activities.

ii. **Cnidarians**: Jellyfish and sea anemones produce toxins and peptides with potential pharmaceutical applications.

3. Types of Marine Compounds

a. **Alkaloids**: Nitrogen-containing compounds often with potent biological activities. Example: **Palitoxin** from marine sponges.

b. **Peptides**: Short chains of amino acids with various biological activities. Example: **Gramicidin S**, an antibiotic from marine bacteria.

c. **Polyketides**: A diverse group of compounds derived from polyketide synthases. Example: **Erythromycin** from marine bacteria.

d. **Terpenes**: Compounds formed from isoprene units with anti-cancer and anti-inflammatory activities. Example: **Sarcodictyin** from marine fungi.

e. **Steroids**: Lipid-like compounds with diverse biological activities. Example: **Brassinosteroids** from marine algae.

4. Applications in Medicine

   a. **Anticancer Agents**: Marine compounds like **Trabectedin** (from sea squirt) and **Yondelis** have been used in cancer treatment.

   b. **Antibiotics**: Marine-derived antibiotics such as **Erythromycin** and **Vancomycin** have significant clinical uses.

   c. **Anti-inflammatory Agents**: Compounds from marine sources like seaweeds have been studied for their anti-inflammatory properties.

   d. **Antiviral Agents**: Marine-derived compounds are being investigated for their potential against viral infections, including HIV and hepatitis.

5. Challenges and Future Directions

   a. **Sustainability**: The collection and cultivation of marine organisms must be managed to prevent overexploitation and ensure environmental sustainability.

   b. **Bioavailability**: Marine compounds often face challenges related to bioavailability and stability in human systems.

   c. **Regulatory Issues**: Ensuring the safety, efficacy, and quality of marine-derived drugs requires stringent regulatory frameworks.

6. Research and Development

Ongoing research focuses on:

   a. **Exploring new marine sources**: Discovering and characterizing new marine organisms and their compounds.

   b. **Developing synthetic and semi-synthetic analogs**: Enhancing the efficacy and stability of marine drugs through chemical modifications.

   c. **Understanding mechanisms**: Investigating how marine compounds interact with biological targets.

NOVEL MEDICINAL AGENTS FROM MARINE SOURCES

Novel medicinal agents derived from marine sources represent a fascinating area of pharmacology and drug discovery. Marine organisms, due to their unique and diverse chemical environments, produce a variety of bioactive compounds with potential therapeutic applications. Here's a detailed look at some notable novel medicinal agents from marine sources:

1. Cytarabine (Ara-C)

a. **Source**: Marine sponge (*Cytarabine*).

b. **Therapeutic Use**: Cytarabine is used in the treatment of various cancers, particularly hematologic malignancies such as acute myeloid leukemia (AML) and lymphomas.

c. **Mechanism of Action**: It is a nucleoside analog that inhibits DNA synthesis by incorporating into DNA and causing chain termination.

2. Trabectedin (Yondelis)

a. **Source**: Sea squirt (*Ecteinascidia turbinata*).

b. **Therapeutic Use**: Trabectedin is used for treating soft tissue sarcoma and ovarian cancer.

c. **Mechanism of Action**: It binds to the DNA minor groove and forms covalent bonds with the DNA, leading to the inhibition of transcription and induction of DNA breaks.

3. Ziconotide (Prialt)

a. **Source**: Cone snail venom (*Conus magus*).

b. **Therapeutic Use**: Ziconotide is used as an analgesic for severe chronic pain, particularly in patients who are intolerant to or have inadequate responses to other pain medications.

c. **Mechanism of Action**: It is a peptide that blocks N-type calcium channels in the central nervous system, thereby modulating pain signaling.

4. Halichondrin B and Eribulin (Halaven)

a. **Source**: Marine sponge (*Halichondria okadai*).

b. **Therapeutic Use**: Eribulin is used for treating breast cancer and liposarcoma.

c. **Mechanism of Action**: Eribulin is a microtubule inhibitor that prevents microtubule dynamics, leading to cell cycle arrest and apoptosis.

5. Sarcodictyin

a. **Source**: Marine fungus (*Sarcodictyon*).

b. **Therapeutic Use**: Sarcodictyin has shown potential as an anti-cancer agent.

c. **Mechanism of Action**: It inhibits cell growth by interfering with the cell cycle and inducing apoptosis in cancer cells.

6. Bryostatin 1

a. **Source**: Marine bryozoan (*Bryozoa*).

b. **Therapeutic Use**: Under investigation for its potential use in treating cancer and Alzheimer's disease.

c. **Mechanism of Action**: It acts as a protein kinase C (PKC) modulator, influencing various cellular processes, including cell growth and differentiation.

7. Aplidin (plitidepsin)

a. **Source**: Marine sponge (*Aplidium albicans*).

b. **Therapeutic Use**: Aplidin is being studied for its potential in treating multiple myeloma and other cancers.

c. **Mechanism of Action**: It is a cyclic peptide that inhibits protein synthesis by targeting the eukaryotic translation elongation factor 1A (eEF1A).

8. Lasiocarpine

a. **Source**: Marine sponge (*Lasiocarpus*).

b. **Therapeutic Use**: Research is ongoing to explore its potential in treating cancer and neurodegenerative diseases.

c. **Mechanism of Action**: Lasiocarpine exhibits cytotoxicity against cancer cell lines, although its exact mechanism is still under investigation.

9. Kahalalide F

a. **Source**: Marine mollusk (*Elysia*).

b. **Therapeutic Use**: Kahalalide F is being explored for its anti-cancer and anti-viral properties.

c. **Mechanism of Action**: It induces apoptosis in cancer cells and has demonstrated potential antiviral activity.

10. Pseudopterosin

a. **Source**: Marine soft coral (*Pseudopterogorgia elisabethae*).

b. **Therapeutic Use**: It has anti-inflammatory and analgesic properties.

c. **Mechanism of Action**: Pseudopterosin inhibits the production of pro-inflammatory cytokines and enzymes, making it a potential candidate for treating inflammatory conditions.

11. Antarctin

a. **Source**: Marine bacteria from the Antarctic region.

b. **Therapeutic Use**: Research is focused on its potential antimicrobial and anti-cancer activities.

c. **Mechanism of Action**: It shows activity against various pathogens and tumor cell lines, though detailed mechanisms are still being studied.

12. Fascaplysin

a. **Source**: Marine sponge (*Fascaplysinopsis*).

b. **Therapeutic Use**: Investigated for its anti-cancer properties.

c. **Mechanism of Action**: Fascaplysin inhibits cell proliferation and induces apoptosis in cancer cells by targeting specific cellular pathways.

13. Kuhnlein

a. **Source**: Marine algae (*Kuhnle*).

b. **Therapeutic Use**: Studied for its potential in treating metabolic disorders and obesity.

c. **Mechanism of Action**: It affects metabolic pathways and lipid metabolism, showing promise in weight management.

Challenges and Future Directions

a. **Sustainability**: Ensuring the sustainable collection and cultivation of marine organisms to avoid ecological damage.

b. **Bioavailability**: Enhancing the absorption and efficacy of marine-derived compounds through pharmaceutical modifications.

c. **Regulatory Hurdles**: Navigating the regulatory pathways for approval and commercialization of marine drugs.

Multiple Choice Questions (Objective)

1. Which marine organism is the source of the anticancer drug Cytarabine?

    A) Coral

    B) Seaweed

    C) Marine sponge

    D) Jellyfish

2. What is the primary therapeutic use of Ziconotide, derived from cone snail venom?

    A) Antibiotic

    B) Analgesic

    C) Anticancer agent

    D) Antiviral agent

3. Which marine-derived compound is used in the treatment of soft tissue sarcoma?

    A) Cytarabine

    B) Trabectedin

    C) Vancomycin

    D) Halichondrin B

4. What is the mechanism of action of Actinomycin D?

    A) Inhibition of DNA synthesis

B) Inhibition of cell wall synthesis

C) Blockage of N-type calcium channels

D) Activation of ion channels

5. Which marine drug is derived from the sea squirt and used in ovarian cancer treatment?

    A) Cytarabine

    B) Ziconotide

    C) Trabectedin

    D) Discodermolide

6. What type of bioactive compound is Sarcodictyin, derived from marine fungi?

    A) Alkaloid

    B) Peptide

    C) Polyketide

    D) Terpenoid

7. Which marine-derived antibiotic is known for its effectiveness against Methicillin-resistant Staphylococcus aureus (MRSA)?

    A) Vancomycin

    B) Cytarabine

    C) Erythromycin

    D) Gramicidin S

8. From which marine organism is the anticancer drug Halichondrin B derived?

    A) Marine algae

    B) Sea anemone

    C) Marine sponge

    D) Jellyfish

9. Which marine-derived drug acts by inhibiting microtubule dynamics, leading to cell cycle arrest?

    A) Trabectedin

B) Ziconotide

C) Halichondrin B

D) Actinomycin D

10. What is the main function of alginates derived from brown seaweeds?

A) Anticancer agent

B) Gelling agent

C) Antibiotic

D) Antiviral agent

11. Which marine-derived compound is currently under investigation for its potential in treating Alzheimer's disease?

A) Cytarabine

B) Bryostatin 1

C) Vancomycin

D) Palitoxin

12. Which of the following is an adverse effect commonly associated with Cytarabine?

A) Myelosuppression

B) Nephrotoxicity

C) Hepatotoxicity

D) Neurotoxicity

13. What type of compound is Palitoxin, known for its extreme toxicity?

A) Steroid

B) Alkaloid

C) Peptide

D) Terpenoid

14. Which marine drug is used primarily as an analgesic for severe chronic pain?

A) Trabectedin

B) Cytarabine

C) Ziconotide

D) Actinomycin D

15. Which of the following is a challenge in the development of marine drugs?

   A) High bioavailability

   B) Easy regulatory approval

   C) Sustainability of sources

   D) Abundant terrestrial alternatives

16. Which marine compound is used in wound dressings due to its ability to absorb exudate and maintain a moist environment?

   A) Carrageenan

   B) Agarose

   C) Alginates

   D) Cytarabine

17. What is the source of the compound Trabectedin?

   A) Marine algae

   B) Sea sponge

   C) Sea squirt

   D) Coral

18. Which of the following is a marine-derived terpenoid with anti-cancer properties?

   A) Cytarabine

   B) Halichondrin B

   C) Sarcodictyin

   D) Gramicidin S

19. What is the primary action of the marine-derived compound Discodermolide?

   A) DNA synthesis inhibition

   B) Protein synthesis inhibition

   C) Microtubule stabilization

   D) Ion channel modulation

20.Which marine compound is used as a thickener and stabilizer in food and pharmaceutical products?

    A) Alginates

    B) Carrageenan

    C) Agarose

    D) Fucodian

Short Answer Type Questions (Subjective)

1. Explain the significance of marine drugs in modern pharmacology.
2. Describe the therapeutic uses of Cytarabine.
3. What are the sources of marine drugs and their classifications?
4. How does Trabectedin exert its anticancer effects?
5. Discuss the challenges faced in the development and sustainability of marine-derived drugs.
6. Explain the mechanism of action of Ziconotide.
7. What are the pharmacological effects of Halichondrin B?
8. How is Actinomycin D used in cancer treatment, and what is its mechanism of action?
9. Describe the applications of alginates in medicine.
10.What are the adverse effects associated with Vancomycin?
11.Discuss the role of marine fungi in producing bioactive compounds.
12.What are the potential therapeutic applications of Sarcodictyin?
13.Explain the significance of marine-derived peptides in drug development.
14.How is Discodermolide used in cancer therapy?
15.What are the common sources of marine-derived alkaloids?
16.Discuss the pharmacokinetics of Cytarabine.
17.What are the mechanisms of resistance against marine-derived antibiotics like Vancomycin?
18.Explain the importance of sustainability in the collection of marine drugs.

19. Describe the potential uses of Cnidarian venom peptides in medicine.

20. What are the challenges in the bioavailability of marine-derived compounds?

Long Answer Type Questions (Subjective)

1. Discuss in detail the various sources of marine drugs and their potential therapeutic applications.

2. Explain the mechanism of action, pharmacokinetics, and clinical uses of Cytarabine in the treatment of hematologic malignancies.

3. Describe the pharmacological properties and clinical applications of Trabectedin, including its mechanism of action and adverse effects.

4. Analyze the challenges and future directions in the development of marine-derived drugs, focusing on sustainability, bioavailability, and regulatory hurdles.

5. Explain the significance of marine-derived peptides, such as Ziconotide, in pain management, including their mechanism of action and therapeutic uses.

6. Discuss the classification and pharmacological activities of marine-derived terpenoids, providing examples of their therapeutic applications.

7. Describe the role of marine microorganisms in the production of antibiotics, including a detailed discussion on Vancomycin and its clinical significance.

8. Explain the process of drug development from marine sources, from discovery to clinical application, with examples of successful marine-derived drugs.

9. Discuss the role of marine natural products in cancer therapy, focusing on compounds like Halichondrin B and Discodermolide.

10. Analyze the regulatory challenges in the approval of marine-derived drugs, including the specific requirements for safety, efficacy, and quality control.

Answer Key for MCQs

1. C) Marine sponge

2. B) Analgesic

3. B) Trabectedin

4. A) Inhibition of DNA synthesis

5. C) Trabectedin

6. D) Terpenoid

7. A) Vancomycin

8. C) Marine sponge

9. C) Halichondrin B

10. B) Gelling agent

11. B) Bryostatin 1

12. A) Myelosuppression

13. B) Alkaloid

14. C) Ziconotide

15. C) Sustainability of sources

16. C) Alginates

17. C) Sea squirt

18. C) Sarcodictyin

19. C) Microtubule stabilization

20. B) Carrageenan